TRANSFORMING
COMPARATIVE EDUCATION

TRANSFORMING COMPARATIVE EDUCATION

FIFTY YEARS OF THEORY BUILDING AT STANFORD

Martin Carnoy

STANFORD UNIVERSITY PRESS
Stanford, California

Stanford University Press

Stanford, California

©2019 by the Board of Trustees of the Leland Stanford Junior
University. All rights reserved.

Printed in the United States of America on acid-free,
archival-quality paper

Library of Congress Cataloging-in-Publication Data
available upon request.

ISBN 9781503608429 (cloth)

ISBN 9781503608818 (paper)

ISBN 9781503608825 (electronic)

Cover design: Cadence Design Studio

For Jean, Juliet, David, Jonathan, Lisa, Natalie, William, Catherine, and Andrew

Contents

Acknowledgments

MANY THANKS TO MY BRILLIANT FELLOW faculty at Stanford who helped me in this project: Hans Weiler, John Meyer, Francisco Ramirez, Karen Mundy (who moved back to her beloved Toronto), Joel Samoff, Prashant Loyalka, Christine Min Wotipka, and Patricia Bromley; to my former colleague and great friend Henry Levin, who left these hallowed halls for Teachers College Columbia; to David H. Smith, whom I cold-called in Florida and who sent me detailed, insightful notes about the making of *Becoming Modern*; to the former SIDEC students whom I interviewed about the early days—Richard Sack, Robert Arnove, Doug Foley—and to all my wonderful Stanford students who made being at Stanford worthwhile and worth writing about; to those who read the manuscript and gave me great feedback—David Post, David Plank, Rebecca Tarlau, Erwin Epstein and Ruth Hayhoe—to my editor Marcela Cristina Maxfield, who had a profound impact on the way I wrote this book; and, of course, to my fantastic family, Jean, Juliet, David, Jon, Lisa, and my grandchildren, none of whom ever reads my writings but each of whom is a constant source of love and support—nothing works without that.

CHAPTER I

The Strands of Comparative and International Education
A Brief History

THIS IS A BOOK about fifty years of new theoretical approaches to comparative and international education and how those approaches transformed that academic field. There are already several excellent comparative and international education readers available (see, e.g., Altbach and Kelly, 1986; Arnove et al., 1992; Crossley et al., 2007; Arnove et al., 2013), as well as comparative education textbooks (Kubow and Fossum, 2007; Phillips and Schweisfurth, 2007). This book differs from those because it focuses on the ideas that have changed the way we conceptualize and do comparative and international education. It also differs in another way. It is partly an institutional memoir. Because comparative and international education research has been shaped by "collectives" of researchers and students coming together at various times, influencing one another in institutional settings, it is important to recognize these institutional histories. Every intellectual history refers to such collectives, and the field of comparative and international education is no different (see, e.g., Noah and Eckstein, 1969).

In the pages that follow, I take this institutional approach. Stanford is the "collective" where I have spent most of my academic career, and because it played such an important role in developing innovative theoretical approaches to comparative and international education over such a long period of time, I use the research done at Stanford to frame the discussion of what I consider the major theoretical contributions to comparative and international education of the past fifty years. I hope that you, the reader, can kindly forgive this institutional chauvinism.[1]

Consistent with this approach, I devote a chapter to how Stanford University's international and comparative education program "survived" the ups and downs of comparative education in this period. After considerable reflection, I decided that the story of the comparative and international education program in the Stanford School of Education (now the

Stanford Graduate School of Education) is an important one to tell. The institutional trajectories of comparative and international education research (and training), whether in universities or in international agencies such as the World Bank, have been fraught with difficulties. Comparative education faculties at different universities have tried different strategies to survive, and some did not survive. The Stanford program was in similarly hot water throughout its five decades, and its faculty had to scramble politically many times to make it to the next round. All that is an integral part of the theoretical contributions that form the core of this book. In some cases, the intellectual work contributed to the program's difficulties, and in other cases, it gave the university reason to protect the program from its foes inside and outside the School of Education.

The book tries to provide the reader with each of the author's intellectual history in his or her own voice, focusing on how they came to develop their theories and the research featured in each chapter, and why each one thinks her or his theoretical approach is important to the field of comparative and international education. The theoretical contribution chapters are placed in approximately chronological order. This is to reflect that each of the works emerged in the context of a specific period, and that comparative education as an intellectual activity is strongly influenced by the economic and political environment of the time.

Reading through the research as it moves from decade to decade gives us an important insight into this field. Comparative and international education, after all, studies the world. It compares how nations educate their populations, and it develops theories of education and educational change based on those comparisons. In the five decades covered by this book, the world has become increasingly "smaller," increasingly interdependent, and increasingly networked and connected. With that process of globalization, not only has comparative and international education become much more important as a source of knowledge about education; globalization has itself become more central to the theories underlying the comparisons. Because education is so fundamental to the politics and economics of nation-states, the field of comparative education is a prism through which we can begin to understand how social science and epistemology confront economic and cultural globalization. In a sense, the story of this book is a chronicle of episodes in the dramatic globaliza-tion of the period—of how intellectuals interpreted the changing world as it was changing.

THE TRANSFORMATION OF COMPARATIVE
EDUCATION IN THE 1950S AND 1960S

The roots of the ideas I present here can be found in the profound changes in comparative education ideas in the immediate post–World War II pe-riod. Reconstruction in Europe and Asia and the advent of the Cold War between the United States and the Soviet Union contributed to a spike in foreign assistance and a growing interest in economic development. Influ-encing "hearts and minds" and a new focus on education as a potentially important factor for higher economic productivity and social mobility put comparative and international education research front and center in influencing the political and economic course of nations. In turn, as the role played by the field grew in ideological importance through the 1950s and 1960s, an intense discussion developed around comparative educa-tion methodology and the direction the field should take.

This discussion and the interaction of academic interests with gov-ernment and foundation funding in comparative and international edu-cation produced three different yet overlapping strands of research and teaching. By the late 1960s, the three strands had been largely defined. Amazingly, all three continue to dominate the field to this day, in much the same structural forms as in the 1960s. The main challenge to these strands dominating international educational comparisons have come from the development of competing theories in the 1970s and early 1980s, mainly antifunctionalist institutionalist theories and "critical" economic-political theories.[2] This is where Stanford made and continues to make its most important contribution to the field.

The first strand of the postwar period had already begun in the 1930s and 1940s with the work of I. L. Kandel at Teachers College, but it ac-celerated in the 1950s at meetings initiated by UNESCO. The strand was organized around introducing social scientific methods into compara-tive education. This was a major departure from the traditional version of comparative education, which was, according to Columbia's Harold

Noah (1973), essentially descriptive of different educational systems, usually as case studies.[3]

The second strand emerged from US government and United Nations efforts in the immediate postwar period to promote democracy, modernization, and economic growth in developing countries. Paul Hanna at Stanford, Adam Curle at Harvard, Freeman Butts at Teachers College, and Philip Coombs at UNESCO were major players in what became known as "international development education." This strand focused on applying academic research to educational and development activism.

The third strand was motivated by the need for more data to compare educational systems and was the project mainly of educational psychometricians, particularly those with a strong policy focus, such as Sweden's Torsten Husén, the University of Hamburg's Welsh-born and Swedish-trained Neville Postlethwaite, and Columbia University's Richard Wolfe. This strand focused on educational system comparison through measurement of student achievement and other "outcomes" of schooling. It gave birth to international testing and, in the early 1960s, to the formation of the International Association for the Evaluation of Educational Achievement (IEA).

Comparative Education and the Social Sciences

Much of the early work in comparative education was in comparing national systems of education

in terms of their potentialities either for countering parochialism or ethnocentrism, or for assisting in the improvement of education at home. Basically, researchers and writers were asking such questions as: What is characteristically French about the French secondary school curriculum? or, What is happening in German schools that we might profit from? (Noah, 1973, p. 109)

By the 1930s and 1940s, however, writers such as I. L. Kandel, Nicholas Hans, and Friedrich Schneider defined comparative education as the study of both the practices of education in various countries and the factors and forces that influenced national systems to take on their current characteristics. These comparativists' attempts to analyze such factors and forces, based on rather limited data, laid the groundwork for the social science approach to comparative education that emerged two decades later (Noah and Eckstein, 1969, chap. 5).

It is notable that in the very first issue of the *Comparative Education Review*, in 1957, George Bereday, professor at Teachers College Columbia and one of the most influential writers in comparative education in the 1950s and 1960s, was already insisting that mere descriptions of single countries was insufficient to qualify as "comparative education": "No method is comparative unless it is preceded by a formulation of an abstract theme which serves as a guiding hypothesis for the collection and presentation of comparative data" (Bereday, 1957, p. 13).

The main locus for the social science methods approach to comparative education in the late 1950s and early 1960s was the Comparative Education Center at the University of Chicago, headed by C. Arnold Anderson. The faculty at Chicago in those years was interdisciplinary (economics, sociology, history, and psychology) and focused on research and the training of PhD students (Anderson, 1966). Anderson and his colleagues promoted an empirical, social scientific approach to educational issues without rejecting the idea that researchers also had to know a lot about the educational systems they were analyzing. As important, Anderson argued for a research agenda that challenged existing ideas about the relation between education and society:

It is only candor to admit that one outcome of this particular academic climate— facilitated no doubt by the personalities of the Center's staff—is a critical view on many of the most widely discussed topics in comparative education. We try to examine important topics, especially those that are used to undergird public policy, from a fresh point of view. . . . This has meant . . . that in taking up the questions of educational planning, we have been more impressed with the defects than with the positive features of that technique. Again, in looking at the recruitment function of schools, it has seemed to us that formal education does not itself play a major part in the restructuring of the social system. On the economics of education, it has seemed prudent to warn against premature or exaggerated conclusions from what is a quite new line of research. (Anderson, 1966, p. 83)

The faculty at Chicago's Comparative Education Center produced several classic articles in the early 1960s that challenged traditional views in education using empirical social science and the comparative method. These ranged from Anderson's (1961a) work on education's role in social mobility, Philip Foster's (1965) "vocational education fallacy," Remi Clignet and Foster's (1964) analyses of French and British colonial education in Africa, and Mary Jean Bowman's (1964) review of the human capital contribution to economic growth.

The Ford Foundation was an important source of funding for the center at Chicago, as part of the foundation's commitment after World War II to bring social scientific methods to studying social problems (Gordon, 2015). Ford also funded other programs in international and comparative education, including the one at Stanford, where it provided significant seed money for faculty billets in the mid-1960s and early 1970s. Three of those were in Stanford's international education program. In the 1970s and 1980s, Ford also funded many fellowships for students from Latin America, Southeast Asia, and Africa. These major resources from the foundation not only helped international education gain a foothold in elite US universities but also transformed their training and research toward the social sciences. The interest in this period of private foundations, such as Ford and Rockefeller, in social science approaches to education and health, and their special interest in international comparative work in both fields, obviously had an important impact on research, as did funding from the US Agency for International Development and, after it was founded in 1965, the US Department of Education.

By the mid-1960s, other researchers joined this push for the new approach. Harold Noah, who was initially trained in economics, and Max Eckstein, a sociologist, became major advocates for the social scientific method in comparative education. The two had met as graduate students at Teachers College, and both took teaching jobs in New York in the mid-1960s, Noah at Teachers College and Eckstein, at Queens College, City University of New York. The Teachers College program was permeated with progressive education and a reaction to the economic depression exemplified in George Counts's (1932) *Dare the School Build a New Social Order?*, as well as John Dewey's writings in the 1930s. Noah and Eckstein inherited that "progressive view" of using the school to change society, but they wanted to use social science methods and data to estimate how to do that. In reflecting on his and Eckstein's contribution to comparative education in this period, Noah stated: "We wanted to draw on methods used in political science, economics, sociology. Not that we wanted to throw out history or philosophy—by no means. We were accused of that, however. We never persuaded our colleagues that we were not hostile to the humanistic approach" (Teachers College, n.d.).

In his contribution to a 1971 new comparative methods conference organized by the UNESCO Institute of Education in Hamburg, Noah wrote: "The theme of recent work may perhaps be seen as a progressive transfer of attention from *country characteristics* to *problems,* and from *problems* to the *specification of relationships* and the formulation and testing of *theories*" (Noah, 1973, p. 109). In 1969, Noah and Eckstein published their challenge to the comparative education field to use social science quantitative methods to test hypotheses about (differing) relations in educational systems rather than simply identifying and describing differences. Their book, *Toward a Science of Comparative Education*, while hailed as a "shot across the bow" of more traditional approaches in the field, was largely a repetition of the much earlier insights developed by Anderson in 1961:

One of the foremost tasks of comparative education is to identify what education contributes, after partialing out other factors, to various traits of societies. Before imputing to schools an effect on economic productivity we must disentangle education from physical capital investment or extra school socialization. We find it difficult to estimate the income yield from different amounts of schooling since much of the income education correlation reflects the association of both with parental status or native ability. . . . Indispensable in any attack on problems of this kind are data with regard to critical elements in the cause-effect interaction patterns, and use of techniques of analysis of co-variation. But problems of measurement and statistical techniques aside, the first and most basic element in analysis is necessarily the formulation of the hypotheses to be tested. . . . Formulating of effective research plans therefore requires specification of models or typologies that include hypotheses concerning interaction processes and their causal web or nexus. (Anderson, 1961b, pp. 10–11)

This shift in comparative education came at a time when more data were becoming available, including from the national censuses (income, age, and education), from longitudinal surveys of individuals, such as the Malmö study in Sweden (Husén, 1968), and from the first data on student achievement related to student socio-economic background and school variables (Coleman, 1966). As I discuss here, the call for more data and a more "empirical" comparative education also led to large international student testing projects and attempts to relate student achievement comparatively to student and school characteristics (Husén, 1967).

Noah and Eckstein (1969, chap. 9) attempted to formulate the "fit" of comparative education in the social science framework, partly by laying out how comparative education analysis should test hypotheses that emerged from theoretical constructs, derived either deductively from larger theories of society or theories of learning or inductively by constructing "a 'map' of relations between education and society. Such maps, or theories, need not have any direct instrumental uses. However, empirical methods in comparative education can also be regarded as the equivalent of route-marking on maps, for they have very special practical uses . . . [such as] guiding change" (pp. 108–109). For Noah and Eckstein, it is the second, or inductive, construction of theory, which was clearly preferable. Much of the rest of their book focuses on using data to construct explanations in comparative education—to construct "maps" by using comparative data and then test hypotheses using those maps.

It is difficult to say how much Noah and Eckstein's broader call for the formulation and testing of theories influenced comparative education in the late 1960s and early 1970s. There is no doubt that the early 1970s was a period of intense development of and debate over theories of the relation between education and society. Most of the discussion was indeed accompanied by empirical "testing" of hypotheses. Yet one reason Noah and Eckstein's approach may not have been crucial to the 1970s debates was that it was less concerned with using comparative analysis to question the role of education in society or the shaping of education by society than to focus on bringing comparative education out of the "age of description" into the "age of social science methodology," and perhaps, as important, from the "age of careful observation" into the "age of empirical testing of hypotheses." Less central to their concerns was examining the validity of the theories that underlay the models that they were "testing" with empirical data.

These models were set in the context of highly functionalist theories, such as human capital and educational production functions, that were already flourishing as a method of comparative education analysis by the time Noah and Eckstein wrote their book. They seemed to accept such functionalist theories at face value. Human capital had introduced a controversial economic view of the relation between education and society (as an investment in higher income and better jobs and as a form of consumption) that was rooted in neoclassical economic theory. In comparative education analysis, the concept of human capital assumed that markets behaved similarly in capitalist economies worldwide and that human beings were similarly rational economic actors in every society, from developed to low income (Tax, 1953). The main argument of economists in this period, therefore, was that human capital theory was a valuable tool for explaining a similar relation between education and the economy in all countries, because humans behaved similarly as economic actors across societies, and the educational system was an institution that functioned to serve an important goal of society, namely to contribute to economic growth. The concept of human capital thus helped fill the gap in economists' ability to account for economic growth when only traditional physical capital and labor measures were included as inputs (Schultz, 1961).

In addition, sociologists and economists had already borrowed the notion from the economic theory of the firm of a production function in education to describe the relation between school outputs and inputs, including students' family characteristics and school resources, particularly teacher characteristics (Coleman, 1966). Production function analysis was partially rooted in a neoclassical economic theory of the firm and—for sociologists—rooted in a functionalist approach made popular by an influential economist turned sociologist, Talcott Parsons (Parsons and Shils, 1951). Parsons theorized that individual action was conditioned by cultural values and social structures that shaped their choices and determined their decisions. Thus, students' outcomes in school were in part a function of their family's socioeconomic background and the social structure of the community and the school as well as the cultural values of the society in which they were situated.

The underlying theoretical bases for these models, such as human capital theory and the educational production function (the functional role of schooling to improve student learning), were beginning to be questioned in the 1960s, but this questioning was not discussed in Hamburg or Chicago or New York's Teachers College. It did not enter the comparative education debate until the early 1970s.

International Development Education

World War II, postwar German and Japanese reconstruction, the Cold War with the Soviet Union, and the establishment of the United Nations and its educational organization, UNESCO, framed the role of many academics interested in comparative and international education after 1945. The US government had already set the stage for the role of education in the postwar period when it established Nelson Rockefeller's Office of International Affairs during the war. That office used education to counter fascism and to promote US-style democracy in the Western Hemisphere by bringing individuals from Latin America to US universities and developing pro-US materials for local schools and the local media in Latin American countries. After the war, many US education experts participated in reconstructing the German and Japanese education systems with new social studies and history curricula and teacher training—all focused on replacing prewar ideology.

The Cold War brought this same emphasis on education as a mechanism to promote Western-style democracy and free-market capitalism to low-income countries. Educational expansion and reform policies were particularly applicable in countries considered susceptible to communist ideology. The educational issue in low-income countries, however, extended beyond shaping social studies curricula and teacher training. Many of these countries lacked the capacity to provide basic education, and by the 1950s, education was considered an important factor in economic development and social and political modernization.

Both the US Agency for International Development and the United Nations, through its education agency, UNESCO, began to expand their efforts in the 1950s to influence developing countries' educational systems. US universities' education and social science faculties were prime recipients of research and consulting contracts from USAID and UNESCO aimed specifically to promote educational expansion in developing countries and to shape the curriculum and other aspects of their educational systems.

Just as one strand of comparative education was gaining traction academically by testing interesting hypotheses about the relation between education and society and between social class, educational resources, and student academic performance, a new strand emerged called international development education. This strand focused on applying educational and social science methods to shape educational systems into the service of a specific economic and social development model.

Given the historical context and the deeply held view among educators (e.g., John Dewey, George Counts, I. L. Kandel) that schooling could play a significant role in influencing children's attitudes, it was logical that the World War II generation of educators—flush from a near-apocalyptical struggle against fascism—should want to be involved in promoting democratic ideals worldwide. The concept emerging in the 1950s of education as important to economic development also made the international development education project attractive to the new group of social science–based comparative educators. For both groups, large amounts of government funding available for studies in developing countries stimulated the expansion of international comparative education research in this direction.

Teachers College's George Bereday, writing in the mid-1960s, saw this as reflecting a methodological direction of the field, even though it had much less to do with methodology than with the close relationship that had developed between government and universities during and after World War II and with the political struggles of the Cold War:

In answer to the interest of economists and manpower studies and hence in education there has arisen a field concerned with the dynamics of modernization, particularly in the newer nations. Economists, planners, and politicians have come to regard expenditure on education not as a service and consequently a marginal budget expenditure, but as an investment and hence the primary budget item. . . . This new interest coincided with the renaming of the UNESCO-sponsored fundamental education movement as development education. Henceforth, the concerns with the manpower flow through schools, with planning for and financing of educational expansion, and with the relationship of education to the political power structure and political decision-making, have among others, become part of development education. (Bereday, 1967, pp. 180–181)

It was in this historical context that Paul Hanna founded the Stanford International Development Education Center (SIDEC) in 1964. Hanna had come to Stanford from Teachers College in the mid-1930s and had established himself as a major figure in social studies curriculum. He was not, by training, a comparativist, but he realized through his experiences in the early 1940s, that the social studies curriculum and the textbooks he wrote for US students were also fundamental to infusing democratic citizenship values in young people through education outside the United States. As an educator, he also reached the conclusion, on trips to South and Central America in 1940–1941, that expanding access to education was crucial to fighting authoritarian ideologies in poor countries (Stallones, 2002, chap. 4). Once the US entered the war in December of that year, Hanna's interest and work shifted increasingly to international education, mainly in terms of combatting Fascism and spreading US democratic values to other countries through curricular reforms:

Hanna's approach to development education was far-reaching. It encompassed the development in students of habits and attitudes of democratic participation as a national and international basis, as well as the specific skills needed to create modern economies and social systems. Many reasons account for that expansion of his interests. . . . First, Hanna realized the potential for development education during and immediately after the war. . . . He recognized that study of the school's role in political social and economic development held great potential both in terms of its immediate application on behalf of American foreign policy and in the abstract is a subject of scholarship. (Stallones, 2002, pp. 249–250)

As Hanna wrote in 1945, the main purpose of international education in his view was the "dissemination of information . . . and promotion of international cultural relations" (Stallones, 2002, p. 113). He thought that "American educational ideals and methods with their emphasis on democracy and quality of opportunity" could be important in reshaping citizenship values in the Pacific region in the post-war period (Stallones, 2002, p. 113). He viewed his role as spreading those ideals though his ideas on education for democratic citizenship.

International development education was largely a phenomenon of the post–World War II US effort to combat totalitarian ideologies world-wide—to eliminate the vestiges of fascism in Germany and militaristic authoritarianism in Japan, and to build stable, democratic capitalist societies in the Third World after the war, especially in the Pacific and Latin America. The idea was to combine research and technical expertise in US universities with government funding. Yet this was not just a US concept. UNESCO, the education wing of the newly founded United Nations, played a leading role in defining and leading international development education. The preamble to the constitution of UNESCO declares, "Since wars begin in the minds of men, it is in the minds of men that the defenses of peace must be constructed."

International development education programs also provided a good academic structure for bringing government funding for international education projects into schools of education. In Stanford's case, well before creating SIDEC, Hanna used his government contacts from his time raising money for Stanford during the war and his work for the government in the immediate postwar period as an educational consultant to the US Office of the Military Government in Germany and to the US Army in the Panama Canal Zone to help establish UNESCO, to get a series of contracts to rebuild and reform the Philippine educational system, and to promote international education more generally:

Under the aegis of the Agency for International Development [USAID], Hanna administered multimillion-dollar contracts spanning the years 1951 through 1966. . . . Stanford resources were devoted to helping the Philippine government rebuild the University of the Philippines' Colleges of Engineering, Business

Administration, Education, and other institutions. Hanna made frequent trips to the Philippines and other regions of East Asia during this period, often staying for weeks or months. The overhead payments alone from these contracts amounted to more than two million dollars for Stanford. (Stallones, 2002, p. 114)

He also raised additional money from the Ford Foundation, which was promoting the study of education as early as the 1950s, to help fund student fellowships for a comparative education program at Stanford (based largely on his curriculum work) that he had started in 1954. Because of all his experiences in Asia, however, by the early 1960s, Hanna's thinking had evolved. He realized that the role of education in development required studying the "complex relationship between education and economic development and social and political change" (Stallones, 2002, p. 114). Therefore, the SIDEC program needed to be built on the University of Chicago–style model of bringing together social scientists from different disciplines and training students with a specialty in one discipline but ensuring they had the knowledge to approach problems with an interdisciplinary perspective. The program at Stanford also focused on combining academic research with "development practice," using education as a tool for improving peoples' economic lives and building a stronger civil society. These hands-on objectives were consistent with the traditional role of education faculties in developing curriculum, administrative plans, and teaching methods working with states and school districts in the US context.

In the activist culture of the 1960s, which included the Peace Corps, SIDEC quickly attracted many idealistic students who had worked in low-income countries or were from low-income countries and wanted to contribute to this process—indeed, this was a prerequisite for admission into the program. In the mid- and late 1960s, there were more than twenty PhD students in the SIDEC program. Hanna succeeded in obtaining faculty billets to hire an anthropologist, then a political scientist, and, by the end of the decade, an economist. He was also able to use his fundraising skills with the Office of Education and foundations, such as Ford, to finance this large group of students, including their doctoral research.

Given the large financial incentives available through US government research funding, other universities also established international development education programs, including Harvard, which, according to George Bereday, "abandoned courses in comparative education after the retirement of Robert Ulich [in 1960] . . . and established instead a Center for the Study of Education and Development" (Bereday, 1967, p. 181), founded by Adam Curle, a British social psychologist, and staffed by Russell Davis, a specialist in educational planning, and Noel McGinn, concerned with the politics of educational planning. The latter two were heavily involved in development work with USAID, and they produced many studies on the practice of implementing education in developing countries. Even Bereday's own institution, Teachers College, had its own important international development education figure in R. Freeman Butts, who wrote many years later, in 1999: "We used to joke that Paul [Hanna] at Stanford was reeducating the new nations of Pacific East Asia and I at Teachers College was trying to do the same for Africa and South Asia. Between us, the world" (Butts, qtd. in Stallones, 2002, p. 273).

The Comparative Education Center at the University of Chicago and the Bereday/Noah part of the Comparative Education Program at Teachers College did not move in this direction. Anderson insisted that although individual faculty members did engage in international consulting and that this was useful in gathering data and studying education in other countries, the center at Chicago consciously did not take on international education development projects at an institutional level (Anderson, 1966). Indeed, in the mid-1960s, in a letter to Philip Coombs, then director of UNESCO's International Institute of Educational Planning in Paris, Hanna listed comparative education programs at twelve universities other than Stanford, and only Harvard and the program headed by Butts at Columbia were considered international development education programs.

Yet it could be argued that the dissertation research produced by Stanford's international development education students in this period was not significantly less "academic" than the research being done at Chicago and Teachers College.

"Comparative and international education" and "international development education" programs have continued until the present, with differences in their missions narrowing. The transformation of the Stanford program occurred quickly without a change in name, whereas programs such as Harvard's continued to maintain their "development" mission much longer, and new programs, such as those at UC Berkeley, Vanderbilt, and Florida State University (not included on Hanna's list for Coombs) moved actively into development education through government contracts.

The most important change in this direction occurred outside of universities: the role of the World Bank in international development education research increased rapidly in the 1970s, 1980s, and well into the 1990s, when the bank became the largest funder of such research. The number of bank personnel who were directly involved in education data collection and analysis increased markedly. By the 1980s and 1990s, it could be said that Bank researchers dominated the empirical discussion about education and development.

International Testing

Beginning in the mid-1950s, the UNESCO Institute of Education, established as part of the United Nations and UNESCO's commitment of postwar Germany, held the first of its annual conferences (1955), bringing together the directors of a dozen research institutes from a corresponding number of countries. Although the topic of the 1955 conference was adult education, probably the most important discussion at the conference was about the lack of student educational outcome data and the difficulties this caused in comparing national school systems. It took several years to launch a project to measure student outcomes, but by the end of the decade, a group was able to pilot a test, and by the middle of the 1960s, the first international achievement study:

To pursue such studies, we needed to produce internationally acceptable and applicable tools, such as standardized achievement tests and interest in attitude tests. We decided in 1958 to carry out a pilot study, in which 12 countries participated. The sampling was done on the basis of judgment rather than strict representativity. . . . The aim of this exploratory study was to ascertain whether it was possible to test the level of knowledge of pupils in a number of countries on a uniform basis and to perform computerized data processing and statistical analysis in one place in accordance with uniform standards. This study was carried out in 1959–61 and published the following year. We found that it was possible to evaluate the results of education in various subjects within institutions which have the resources and the staff qualified to gather data in accordance with agreed procedures. (Husén, 1983, pp. 83–84)

On the basis of the success of the pilot, the group decided to do a full-scale field study, focusing on mathematics, and got funding from the US Office of Education. The twelve country participants also reconstituted themselves in 1961 as the International Association for the Evaluation of Education Achievement (IEA). Thorsten Husén, a Swedish academic who had had experience developing and analyzing the Swedish armed services test and survey of prospective soldiers and had long been involved analyzing Swedish education, became its chair. The results of the First International Mathematics Survey (FIMS) were published in 1967. The IEA was then formally incorporated in Belgium in 1967, and it has been regularly carrying out large-scale international tests and accompanying surveys ever since, mostly in mathematics and science, yet also in reading, with its PIRLS test.

The early effort to test students internationally was consistent with the social science approach to comparative education being promoted at the University of Chicago and others, such as Noah and Eckstein. All were interested in the use of data to analyze the relation between education and society and, in the case of student achievement data, to test hypotheses about the relation between education policies and educational outcomes. All thought that comparisons between countries would provide a particularly interesting and useful prism through which to analyze this relationship:

The idea of a multinational questionnaire survey of education extends deep into the history of comparative education. . . . Today the motivation to carry out such multinational surveys is, in part, the same. Such surveys can enable educators and educational decision-makers "to benefit from the educational experiences of other countries" . . . , often with very different educational systems. Also, they can 'help in the identification and assessment of the relative importance of such factors as school organization of curriculum . . ." on education. Thus, behind the IEA surveys lie the twin motivations—the utilitarian "educational borrowing" and the analytical "social science explanation"—which historically have had important influences on the development of comparative education. (Noonan, 1973, p. 199, citations omitted)

And:

Comparative research on education . . . increases the range of experience necessary to improve the measurement of educational achievement; it enhances confidence in the generalizability of studies that explain the factors important in educational achievement; it increases the probability of dissemination of new ideas to improve the design or management of schools and classrooms; and it increases the research capacity of the United States as well as that of other countries. Finally, it provides an opportunity to chronicle practices and policies worthy of note in their own right. (Bradbum and Gilford, 1990, p. 4, qtd. in Medrich and Griffith, 1992, p. 2)

Thus, from their inception, the IEA evaluations were intended to "identify factors associated with differences in student achievement" (Medrich and Griffith, 1992, p. 12). Even the First International Mathematics Survey was large, applied in twelve countries to more than 130,000 students in two schooling levels (middle and high school) in each country, and to more than 18,000 teachers and 5,400 school directors. This made it possible to do comparative empirical analyses on a much greater scale and to try to gain insights into *why* students in some educational systems achieved at higher levels in mathematics and science than in others.

There is little doubt that the construction of the test instruments and their application to thousands of students across different countries taught test constructors and psychometricians a great deal about the prospects and problems of such undertakings. Given the many technical difficulties with test applications in each country, those closest to the testing, at least in the IEA's first two decades, tried hard to dissuade policy makers from using them to rank the quality of educational systems (Medrich and Griffith, 1992). They have been largely unsuccessful in this effort—if anything, international test results have become even more viewed as a "horse race" among countries' education systems than in the 1970s and 1980s.[4]

International testing has generated much more interest in comparative and international education. It has allowed educators and policy makers to benefit from the educational experiences of other countries with quite different educational systems, as Thorsten Husén had hoped. However, the social science movement in comparative education's high expectations in the 1960s that the vast amounts of data generated by the IEA would provide startling new insights into why some educational systems are more "effective" than others was largely unrealized:

Although a number of hypotheses have been offered, international surveys have been far less successful at explaining why particular groups of students achieve as they do in comparison with students of the same age or comparable grade level from other countries. These studies have not led to consistent conclusions as to why students from other countries perform better academically than their American counterparts, and there are few powerful correlates associated with the overall pattern of achievement across the populations participating in the international surveys. (Medrich and Griffith, 1992, p. 29)

Even so, there were a few important findings to come out of the first five IEA studies in the 1960s, 1970s, and 1980s. One was that "the more content students are taught, the more they learn, and the better they perform on the achievement tests" (Medrich and Griffith, 1992, p. 30). This was confirmed in a series of analyses of the Third International Mathematics and Science Survey (TIMSS) in 1995 (Schmidt et al., 2001). To the outsider, it may seem that "discovering" this link between content and outcome should not have required millions of dollars and some of the best testing and statistical minds in the world. Further, when the US had tried to change the mathematics curriculum (the "new math") in the 1960s to a more European-style curriculum, it was a spectacular failure.

A second finding was that across the developed countries participating in the study, students' family background variables were important explainers of student achievement, and it was very difficult to untangle students' home background and school input effects, as brought out by James Coleman's 1966 study of racial segregation in US schools. Other findings on the effects of tracking and higher rates of inclusion in a specific level of schooling on academic achievement were even more ambiguous (Postlethwaite, 1967)

Thus, although disappointing in a number of ways, the analyses of the data generated by the IEA studies were sufficient not only to expand the IEA's testing program to a degree unimagined by even the most optimistic of its founders but also to produce competitors such as the OECD and its Programme for International Student Assessment (PISA), and additional UNESCO-associated evaluation efforts in Latin America—the Laboratorio Latinoamericano de la Calidad de la Educación (LLECE)—and Africa (Southern and Eastern Africa Consortium for Monitoring Educational Quality, or SACMEQ, and Programme d'Analyse des Systèmes Éducatifs de la Confemen, or PASEC). Together, these have provided many different measures for ranking educational systems and for rating their progress over time. They have also provided masses of data for comparative education analyses, and many across-country analyses that give some insights into how various factors influence student achievement and attitudes about schooling. Nonetheless, beyond the earlier finding on content differences, all the data collected by these large-scale surveys still fail to explain much about why students with similar social background perform better in some educational systems than in others (e.g., Carnoy et al., 2015).

One reason for the modest contribution of the IEA and subsequent projects may be that the implicit theory of learning or of the relation between education and society underlying such international tests was "incorrect" or inadequate for understanding differences in how much students learn in different educational systems. There was an attempt in the IEA surveys to define learning as both cognitive and affective, in keeping with Benjamin Bloom's taxonomy of learning (Bloom, 1956), but the results involving affective outcomes were not particularly illuminating (e.g., students who like math more do better on math tests; boys like math better than girls). Further, because theories of education and society were never at the center of the early UNESCO meetings, it is not surprising that the IEA surveys focused largely on individual student and teacher characteristics and students' and teachers' reported attitudes and reported teacher practices, not on where or how different societies derive their allocation of resources to education or form their educational practices.

And despite its modest contribution to "mapping" relations (in Noah and Eckstein's words) within the educational systems or relations in education and society, this well-intentioned effort in the 1960s by a group of academics to gather data across countries on student performance and teacher and school inputs turned instead into a major international testing industry that mainly lives off ranking nations' educational systems by their students' average scores. How and why the tail came to wag the dog is now as important a question for comparative educators as the original issues addressed in those early meetings in Hamburg.

THE CRITICAL AND INSTITUTIONALIST REACTION

The call for greater use of social science methodologies in comparative and international education was realized both through the direct influence of the research at the Comparative Education Center at the University of Chicago in the 1960s and 1970s and the spread of the economic concepts introduced by human capital theory during that same period. Economics and sociology began to dominate comparative and international education even in programs that stressed international development education. However, it should be remembered that much of the effort in these social science approaches was to gather data that could test *existing* theories of the relation between education and socioeconomic outcomes or between socioeconomic contexts or educational inputs and educational outcomes in schools. The major push described in the third strand to undertake large-scale assessments and data collection on students and teachers was both the result of this effort and had an enormous influence on the kind of research being done in comparative education. The more surveys were available, the more comparative educators focused on using the data rather than rethinking the underlying theories that drove how issues in comparative education were formulated.

Our discussion of the great social science and data "revolutions" in comparative and international education research in the 1950s and 1960s shows that they resulted in important changes in the field, including—for the first time—the systematic, and ultimately pervasive, use of theories from the social science disciplines as the basis for studying education comparatively. Human capital "theory" was an application to analyzing education of the neoclassical economic theory of growth, labor markets, and the production of services. It became a staple of comparative education research. Sociologists began to study education as process that started in families and was subject to the constraints of broader economic and social relations outside school and family (Coleman, 1966). Coleman's theoretical considerations, in turn, were reflected in the survey questionnaires that accompanied the IEA tests and the comparative research that emerged from the data provided by those surveys. These socioeconomic studies of schooling also became ubiquitous in comparative education, especially as international testing—with the help of international organizations—became a global industry.

Despite the groundbreaking nature of applying social scientific theories to education, those who were among the biggest proponents of social science methods in comparative education research, such as Noah and Eckstein, did not bother to challenge the underlying theories themselves. Indeed, until the late 1960s and early 1970s, there was little critical response to the way neoclassical economics, functionalist sociology, and functionalist-pluralist political science defined the economic, social, and political relations on which these comparative education studies were based. However, those challenges did ultimately appear, first in the form of a variety of critical theorists who brought economic and political power relations into theories being used to study education (Wallerstein, 1973; Carnoy, 1972b, 1974; Baudelot and Establet, 1976; Raskin, 1971; Bowles and Gintis, 1975), then in the form of institutionalist sociologists such as John Meyer, Michael Hannon, and Francisco Ramirez (Meyer et al., 1977; Meyer and Hannan, 1979), who rejected the functionalist theories that linked educational expansion and educational outcomes to changes in economic institutions, notably industrialization and the factory system. By the late 1970s and 1980s, the challenges centered on state theory and its application to comparative education. These theoretical discussions are the focus of much of what preoccupied the field in those two decades. They also had a lot to do with how different theories were interpreting the changing world at that time. In later chapters, as I follow new contributions into the 1990s and into the current century, globalization itself and the changes it is wreaking become a focus of analysis, and global institutions as they begin to play a central role in shaping the nature of comparisons and epistemology in the field.

THE ORGANIZATION OF THE BOOK

As promised, this book is about important ideas in comparative and international education research over the past fifty years. Before turning to how various theories came to define approaches to comparative and international education during this period, I describe in greater detail the trajectory of comparative and international education in one of these programs, the international and comparative education program at Stanford University. Research by faculty and students at Stanford was of course greatly influenced by all three of the strands I have discussed. But these faculty and students seemed to be able to find the space to challenge underlying ideas and introduce new ones. They also went through many of the academic political trials and tribulations of other comparative and international education programs. In the next chapter, I show how that program evolved; managed to survive through several attempts to shut it down despite its success; and, throughout these ups and downs, continued to redefine underlying conceptions of comparative research in education.

The ten chapters (Chapters 3–12) that follow this brief history of the program at Stanford go into detail on key contributions to theories in comparative and international education from researchers at Stanford, mainly from the standpoint of those who personally participated in them. I organize the contributions in chronological order, not only because this allows me to weave later contributions into those that preceded, but also because making them chronological allows me to help explain how and why they happened by placing them in their historical context. I firmly believe that intellectual thought, especially social scientific educational thought, is considerably shaped by its economic, social, and political environment. As I mentioned earlier, the chronological approach also provides an important insight into how intellectual work in a field that, from the start, was entwined with the politics and economics of the world, and was itself shaped over time by the changes in that world as its institutions and networks became more globalized.

Chapter 3 opens with a short discussion of human capital theory, which burst onto the education scene in the late 1950s, developing a comprehensive framework for understanding the relation between education and the economy. Human capital theory was "located" at the University of Chicago, but Stanford's School of Education moved early among Schools of Education into the economics of education in the late 1960s when it hired Henry Levin and then me. But with us they also bought a critical and questioning approach to human capital. This is the main focus of Chapter 3.

In the early 1970s, Alex Inkeles arrived at Stanford, bringing with him an important work in progress that focused on the institutional settings in which workers acquired affective skills. Inkeles and his coauthor David Smith called these skills "modernity." Chapter 4 discusses the concept of modernity and its impact on comparative education. It focuses on the major contributions of the book by Inkeles and Smith, *Becoming Modern* (1974).

Also in the late 1960s and early 1970s, in the context of the political upheavals of that time, a new literature emerged that raised important questions about the prevalent ideology of education as a source of upward mobility and social equalization. Chapter 5 is about the challenges raised to the underlying premises of international and comparative education in the period of the 1970s. In particular, I critically discuss my book, *Education as Cultural Imperialism* (1974).

Chapter 6 introduces world society or world culture theory, developed in the 1970s by John Meyer and Francisco Ramirez (and other Stanford sociologists). It is one of the most influential concepts used in comparative education, even to this day. The chapter discusses world society (or world culture theory) in detail, drawing primarily on two articles by Francisco Ramirez and John Meyer.

By the 1980s, various forms of state theory began to be applied to explain educational development, in part as a reaction to earlier world culture theory and neocolonialist theories of international and comparative education. The main innovation in international and comparative education research in this period was the application of state theory to educational system analysis. Chapter 7 presents a discussion of Hans Weiler's concept of compensatory legitimation and its shaping of education policies and systems. The chapter focuses on Weiler's article of the same name, and his article on the relation between knowledge and power as a key to analyzing the politics of higher education.

Chapter 8 continues with a discussion of two versions of another formulation of state theory applied to education and how they came to be written. Like world society theory, these two formulations continue to influence research in international and comparative education to the present day. The first version is exemplified by my and Levin's *Schooling and Work in the Democratic State*, and the second version, by my and Samoff's *Education and Social Transformation in the Third World*.

A decade later, globalization and the information revolution became the new realities of the world economy, and their influence on international and comparative education demanded new frameworks for researchers writing about educational change. In Chapter 9, I discuss how Karen Mundy and I and others came to understand the issues raised by globalization and addressed them. The chapter discusses Mundy's and my articles that have had considerable influence on recasting comparative education analysis under the new conditions of globalization.

Chapters 10 and 11 move into contemporary trends in international and comparative education research—trends in search of new theories or reformulations of earlier conceptualizations, such as world society theory and state theory, in a new context dominated by global institutions and an "efficiency" approach economic and educational ideology, and a "return" to functionalist theories of education. In Chapter 10, I analyze impact evaluation and its possible implications for comparative education with Prashant Loyalka, who does experiments and nonexperimental causal analysis in education, mainly in China but also in Russia. The chapter includes a discussion of some of his recent work on impact evaluation, which contrasts the effectiveness of vocational versus academic secondary education and the role of teacher professional development and wage incentives in China.

Chapter 11 discusses the increasingly influential use of international test data in comparative education analysis and its limitations and pitfalls. Like the future uses of impact evaluation for drawing lessons for education comparatively, the direction that comparative education will be led by the masses of international test data is yet to be determined. There is a considerable disagreement over this direction, as our analysis in Chapter 11 shows.

In Chapter 12, I attempt to foresee new theories in international and comparative education, how they might develop, and the political and economic changes that might inspire them. I discuss the possible influence of feminist theory, organizational theory, and new directions in impact evaluation, world society theory, and state theory on comparative work in the future.

How One Comparative Education Program Managed to Survive and Make Its Mark on the Field

IN THE HALF CENTURY between 1965 and 2015, the Stanford International and Comparative Education Program, part of Stanford's Graduate School of Education, struggled to maintain itself in a sometimes nurturing, but more often highly resource competitive, environment. Despite its continuously precarious position, the program made a series of important contributions to the rapidly growing field of comparative and international education. The Stanford faculty produced several major theoretical advances during this period that greatly influenced researchers elsewhere. Equally important, as part of its research orientation and social science–based interdisciplinary program, modeled largely on the University of Chicago's Comparative Education Center, Stanford produced many graduates who went on to staff university and assistance agency comparative programs and to do innovative research of their own.

Stanford was not the first comparative and international education program to make its mark on the field, and programs at Teachers College Columbia, Harvard, Indiana, Penn State, UCLA, Florida State, Claremont, and others have survived to affect how we think about education comparatively and internationally. It would be worth understanding how they navigated their changing university environments over the decades to accomplish their contributions to the field. Perhaps the story of the program at Stanford can serve as a model for doing that. The key feature of that story is that during these many turbulent decades, Stanford's program managed to sustain influence by continuously innovating in research while maintaining rather traditional, research-driven interdisciplinary PhD and MA programs. This was not an easy task. The survival of international, comparative education programs in schools of education faced several challenges. First, international and comparative programs were (and are) not focused on US education, which puts them at the margins of main intellectual and policy discussions in US education schools. Second, most comparative programs came to be staffed by social scientists—again, not the core type of faculty in education schools. Third, beginning in the 1980s, schools of education themselves came under attack as ineffective and of lower intellectual quality than other parts of the university.

Stanford's international and comparative program was no different in its marginalization from the mainstream of its School of Education and in the periodic threats to its continued existence as a program. Yet somehow it not only survived but also continuously reinvented itself and managed to innovate even as it went through turbulent times. There is no clear explanation for how and why this was the case, although it is possible to identify some clues to an explanation.

Most important, a synergy of three core components always characterized the program. First, Stanford implicitly adopted the University of Chicago model in comparative and international education to become the second program to train its students using an interdisciplinary social science approach to educational issues. Stanford's faculty members were an economist, a political scientist, eventually a sociologist, and, for many years, an anthropologist. The program also required all its PhD students to earn a master's degree in a social science.

Second, using this interdisciplinary approach, the program placed a major emphasis on training students in critically and innovatively applying methods from the social sciences to study education. To put that in context, faculty in many other universities' so-called international development education programs became enmeshed in international consulting as a primary activity. Students were trained in these programs, but the training was less research oriented and more focused on acquiring tools to implement educational planning and policy. Research problems in such programs were often defined by the client organization rather than by faculty and students. This was almost never the case at Stanford. Over these fifty years, Stanford's program graduated more than 225 PhDs and about a thousand master's students. As I shall show, the students of the program took classes taught by many other professors in the school, and these professors came to appreciate the program through interacting with the students. Many of the PhD graduates also went on to teach in other universities. Stanford became the single most important source of faculty staffing in other US comparative education programs, as well as programs in Latin America, Asia, and Africa. Not surprisingly, most major comparative education programs began to look like Stanford's.

Third, the program became a leader in the field through new theoretical approaches to comparative education developed by Stanford faculty. These new approaches had worldwide influence on comparative and international education research and the training of students. The approaches' immediate influence was on the PhD and master's students in the Stanford program. These new theories shaped Stanford PhD dissertations and MA theses. Stanford graduates who went out to teach in other universities developed and extended their research in the context of what they had done at Stanford. Of course, Stanford's was not the first, or the only, program influencing theoretical approaches to comparative education research, but it is notable how broad and continuous Stanford's contribution to theory has been.

It is worth mentioning how Stanford's program, built on the Chicago model, differs from an alternative integration-infusion approach described in John (Jack) Schwille's (2017) compelling account of Michigan State University's efforts to internationalize its School of Education. The considerable number of faculty at MSU engaged in comparative and international education research (some trained in Stanford's program) makes MSU, as Schwille suggests, an important contributor to scholarship in this field. Another upside to the MSU model—which becomes more evident when reading the trials and tribulations of Stanford's program—is that MSU faculty doing comparative and international research were and continue to be situated in subdepartments of the school that have their own "domestic" raison d'être, avoiding exposure as a separate program outside the main domestic education mission of the school.

Yet the most critical output of any university graduate program is, after all, its graduates. In Stanford's case, the program's graduates have reproduced the interdisciplinary training model of its comparative and international program at other universities and have become the new generation of leading researchers in the field. For MSU, this has been a much lower priority. Thus, as compelling as is Schwille's account of MSU's success, there are reasons as compelling, or even more so, to fight for coherent degree programs in comparative and international education—as I hope the Stanford story will show.

THE STANFORD INTERNATIONAL
DEVELOPMENT EDUCATION CENTER

Although the School of Education at Stanford in the 1960s was not central to the discussions of social science methodology or international data collection and their potential contributions to international comparisons, social sciences came to play an important role in the Stanford program. However, rather than in the intellectual reaction to earlier comparative work, social sciences came to comparative education at Stanford from the rapidly growing "hands-on" involvement of the United States in economic and social development after World War II.

Paul Hanna taught comparative education at Stanford beginning in the 1950s, and the course was inspired by his interest in democratic citizenship as an international issue in the context of postwar reconstruction in Europe and Asia. At the same time, Hanna's notion of preparing young people for democratic citizenship was based on developing "the child's ability actually to live more effectively and richly as a member of a social group" (Hanna, qtd. in Stallones, 2002, p. 169). Thus, Hanna as an educator was in tune with the importance of social sciences in understanding how to make education effective. Hanna was very much a "progressive" educator in the John Dewey tradition. He hypothesized that a social education curriculum rooted in social sciences could make a difference in children's affective skills. His travel experiences in the 1940s also convinced him that expanding education in low-income countries was an important factor in promoting economic and social development.

Hanna developed a close relationship with UNESCO in these years—with its hands-on activities in developing countries rather than with the methodological debates at the UNESCO Institute of Education in Hamburg. This relationship with UNESCO lasted well after Hanna's retirement, and it continued to influence his thinking about how to plan and shape educational improvements in developing countries. Hanna's strength was in his incredibly broad network in the US government, international institutions, and US foundations, and his ability to work his contacts.

He traveled extensively, including regularly to Washington and Paris to attend key meetings on international education.

When Hanna formed the Stanford International Development Education Center (SIDEC) in 1964, it was, in the words of his biographer, to expand "his work in international education beyond Southeast Asia" (Stallones, 2002, p. 114). It was also to train "scholar-doers," a term used regularly to describe SIDEC's mission in the 1960s and early 1970s. As noted earlier, from the very beginning Hanna conceived of the SIDEC program as an interdisciplinary social science approach to education and development and its graduates as prepared to bring this interdisciplinary approach to the tackling of complex problems of education in developing countries as "agents of change."

Hanna's first recruit to SIDEC was Robert Textor, an anthropologist with expertise in Southeast Asia, especially in Thailand. Textor's dissertation was titled "An Inventory of Non-Buddhist Supernatural Objects in a Central Thai village," and he had just published *A Cross-Polity Survey* (MIT Press) with Arthur Banks. That large volume classified 115 countries using a set of political variables. The Banks and Textor book fit very much into Hanna's view of development in terms of a society's internalization of democratic values. Textor quickly took leadership of the SIDEC program, implementing Hanna's vision of using research and training to make SIDEC graduates into change agents for educational development. Textor organized a student seminar based on a social science interdisciplinary approach, and over the next several years, he helped Hanna begin to staff the program to be able to deliver that approach.

By 1965–1966, Hanna succeeded in attracting a young German political scientist, Hans Weiler, who studied the development of civic institutions in Africa. As Hanna lobbied to obtain additional tenure-track faculty positions, he temporarily brought in an economist, Eugene Staley, and an economic planner, William Platt, who were both at the nearby Stanford Research Institute (no affiliation with Stanford University). Staley had received his PhD from the University of Chicago almost forty years earlier, had written several books on economic development, and had considerable experience working in developing countries, most recently at the time in South Vietnam.[1]

Hanna retired in 1967, a year after a new dean, Henry Thomas ("Tom") James, took the helm of Stanford's School of Education. James had been a captain in the navy during World War II and a teacher and school district superintendent in the 1950s. After he received his PhD from the University of Chicago, he came to Stanford to teach educational finance in 1958 and was named dean in 1966. James quickly began to transform the school by hiring young social scientists. He supported Hanna's vision of an interdisciplinary social science approach to international education and agreed to a tenure-track economics billet in international development education.

However, the two apparently did not agree on the future course of SIDEC. James wanted to raise the scholarly academic level of international development education at Stanford as part of the larger changes he was introducing in the School of Education. That meant shifting the research and training emphasis more to the University of Chicago model. Hanna almost certainly saw these moves as threatening his vision of a SIDEC program that produced hands on education specialists for development agencies. More SIDEC students were already writing critical scholarly dissertations, often working with faculty outside SIDEC in social science departments. In addition, Tom James had just recruited me to Stanford to be the economist of education in SIDEC. Although I had good "field experience" doing research in Latin America, I had never worked for a development agency or been in the Peace Corps, the kind of practical experience that Hanna valued. My published articles on human capital and empirical research related to Latin American trade were traditionally academic and deeply rooted in economic theory. Thus, my profile and research interests fit more into James's vision than Hanna's on where international education research should head at Stanford. More important, the job talks and interviews I had given at Stanford made clear my politics. At the time of those interviews (May 1968), I was working for the Robert Kennedy campaign in Los Angeles and had been an anti–Vietnam War activist in DC for more than two years. Although I had done my research on human capital in Mexico, I was already entering my "critical" period, in which I had begun to view education as mainly a reproducer of unequal relations in society rather than as a source of social mobility and innovative thinking.

In early 1967, shortly after Hanna's retirement, James asked him to help prepare a US Office of Education grant extension for SIDEC. Hanna did not outright refuse but was clearly upset that James was moving the program in a direction Hanna opposed:

As you have so clearly communicated by word and action, you believe your philosophy in mind with respect to the roles of SIDEC, its program focus, and its management, are somewhat at variance. I would not presume to try to interfere with your efforts to shape SIDEC's future. For me to continue to represent SUSE in the coming negotiations would only mislead the donor as to your expectations and could be a major deterrent to moving the research in the direction you desire. (Hanna, qtd. in Stallones, 2002, p. 13)

A memo written by Hanna in January 1967 eventually served as the outline for the grant extension. It lists twenty-six studies completed or under way by SIDEC students in Asia, Africa, and Latin America, covering a broad range of topics. In Hanna's (1967) words, "We have examined education as it influences economic development; we have looked into the anthropological determinants of education; we have explored the qualitative dimensions of curriculum and modernization; we have investigated problems relating to occupation education and training for development" (p. 1). Yet it is telling that after listing all these different studies, Hanna concluded the memo by defining a direction for SIDEC that went back to Hanna's main interest, curriculum content and instructional methods, not consistent with James's vision of SIDEC's future:

While there is a paramount need for a global scanning of the wide range of problems associated with human resources development and institution and nation building, SIDEC is becoming increasingly interested in limiting research topics for special attention. One major research effort in the next several years will focus on the nature of the curriculum content and instructional methods that are most appropriate for modernization under different stages of a nation's development. By examining in-depth several contrasting national efforts at modernization through curriculum and instructional innovations, we should, by interdisciplinary and comparative methodology, be able to extract general-izations and action principles that may lie unobserved or untested at present. With these generalizations and principles in hand we might construct sets of strategies that would help us in our own problems of educational policy and implementations at home, help us as we attempt to consultant foreign aid pro-grams, and help others who seek educational answers in strengthening human resources. (Hanna, 1967, p. 1)

The proposal for the grant extension was successful, and it is possi-ble that Hanna never intended that SIDEC research focus on curriculum content. In any case, the students funded by this proposal, and SIDEC research more generally, largely moved in the more academic social sci-ence direction envisaged by James.

There was another issue of great concern to Hanna. With the anti–Vietnam War movement gearing up in 1966–1967, some SIDEC students were participating in antiwar protests and signing petitions. According to interviews with students who had been in the program at that time, Hanna was worried that this activity threatened the generous US gov-ernment funding he had been able to secure for student fellowships. His concern may have stemmed from an incident ten years earlier, in 1957, when Hanna's USAID funding was suspended because a government administrator confused him with a leftist writer of the same name. In a letter to USAID, Hanna cleared up the name confusion and wrote, "We on campus would do anything reasonable and honorable to help fight the cold war against communism even though we had to endure rearguard obstruction" (Hanna, qtd. in Stallones, 2002, p. 270).

In retrospect, it is easy to understand Hanna's frustrations at what was happening to "his" program—and more broadly to the underlying foundations of international development education. Hanna had helped combat fascism and believed, with good reason, that communism and the radical actions being taken by students and some faculty in the anti–Vietnam War movement at universities was a similar threat to people's well-being. As was Franklin Roosevelt, Hanna was for dismantling Euro-pean colonialism in developing countries. He wanted to replace colonial institutions, including colonial education, with more progressive, "localized" American-style civil society and schools because he believed in American democracy and that American democratic values would make the world a better place. In the 1960s, the civil rights movement and the anti–Vietnam War movement questioned the underlying premises of these values. Was American society truly that democratic, and was the movement to spread American institutions just a new, softer form of imperialism and colonization? Well-meaning, New Deal–liberal Cold Warriors such as Hanna who had been assailed from the Right in the McCarthy era found themselves criticized by the Left. Sadly for them, the debate on the US role in the world and the role of education in development had moved beyond their post–World War II idealism into the ideologically uncomfortable territory of whether that idealism had become a new form of imperialism, one in which two major empires, the United States and the Soviet Union, were competing for ideological territory in place of traditional colonialism, which had competed for control of physical territory and sources of raw materials.

The changes in SIDEC continued to cause conflict, even after Paul Hanna began to disengage from the program and Tom James left for the calmer waters of the newly formed Spencer Foundation, replaced as dean by Arthur Coladarci. The university itself was going through mass demonstrations over Vietnam, and the whole notion of international development education was under fire, especially given the shift in sentiment about US efforts to "intervene" in Southeast Asia and Latin America with development assistance programs. Staley and Platt, "placeholders" for the economics and planning billet, were no longer faculty members, so the program became less controversial from the antiwar movement's point of view. In 1969, two more politically "neutral" (temporary) hires, Frank Moore, a seasoned foreign assistance specialist retired from US-AID, and George Parkyn, an experienced New Zealand educator active in UNESCO work, were brought in to help with the large number of students. Moore and Parkyn remained at SIDEC until the end of the 1970–1971 academic year.[2] However, as Staley and Platt's economic billet replacement, I was also controversial, certainly raising the hackles of more "conservative" faculty members and even some who were more moderately opposed to the war.

The good news was that in the midst of this political turbulence, SIDEC was becoming an intellectually interesting comparative and international program with increasing national and international visibility. Two years after my appointment to the faculty, Alex Inkeles, an eminent Harvard psychosociologist, joined SIDEC in January 1971, giving the program a full complement of social scientists. Henry Levin, an economist already in the School of Education working on educational finance issues, developed an interest in Latin America and became a regular participant in international research and advising.

More good news for SIDEC was that it received a large grant from the Ford Foundation in late 1969 for scholarships for Latin American students who had the potential to become educational leaders in their home country. In the early 1970s, fifteen to twenty Latin Americans were receiving MA degrees annually from the program. A year after the initial grant, in 1971, Ford funded a similar scholarship program for students from Southeast Asia, with similar results—by 1973, SIDEC was graduating more than twenty Southeast Asian students annually. In a memo to the faculty in early 1973, Hans Weiler reported that in the period 1965–1973, forty-five SIDEC students had earned PhDs and five had earned EdDs, and sixteen PhD students had been admitted to SIDEC in 1971–1972, with another nineteen in 1972–1973. SIDEC faculty taught about 1,500 student units in 1971–1972 (Weiler, 1973).

Some of these Latin American and Southeast Asian MA students also went on to get PhDs. By the end of the 1970s, through its many graduates, SIDEC had become intellectually very influential in both regions. Graduates were not ideologically homogeneous, but they did bring a new kind of analytical thinking into education in their countries. Some worked in government agencies, and many taught in universities. Mexico, Brazil, and the Philippines had so many SIDEC graduates in the 1970s and 1980s that they were considered a new "mafia" in each of these countries' education circles.

The bad news was that the idea of anything "international" was losing credibility in universities. At Stanford, international work came under more fire inside the School of Education than, for example, area studies in the wider university, but all were vulnerable. As an already "marginal" program in the school, SIDEC faced increasing problems in maintaining legitimacy. Some of these were its own doing. Hanna had wanted SIDEC to be a distinct, stand-alone center, and, indeed, the program was housed in Stanford's Quadrangle, in the old law school, several hundred meters from the School of Education. In a time of questioning the role of international programs, such separation did not serve the program well politically. In 1971, the program moved into the basement of the School of Education with refurbished but windowless offices—formally it was in the same building as other programs, but it still chose to be as physically separated as possible.

More bad news for SIDEC was that once Tom James left, the old guard educational "practitioners" in the School of Education reacted to James's hiring of so many social scientists, and SIDEC—totally staffed by social scientists—was part of the backlash. Opposition in the school played into the broader backlash that was simultaneously sweeping the university, this coming from a university administration bent on eliminating the so-called radical threat to the institution's foundational values. Students were expelled, and faculty without tenure who had been active in the antiwar movement were systematically denied tenure and forced to leave Stanford. In my case, the university's strategy was somewhat different. In 1971, my tenure decision was three years in the future, and in my regular three-year review, Dean Coladarci proposed, and the faculty approved, that I be moved off the tenure track, promoted to associate professor without tenure, and my appointment be made coterminous with the Ford Foundation grant, scheduled to end in June 1975.

That faculty action explicitly deleted the economics billet from the SIDEC program (and the school), reflecting SIDEC's and the economics of education's precarious positions in a School of Education, whose faculty still consisted mainly of psychologists and educators specializing in teaching, curriculum, and school administration. Thus, despite SIDEC being at the top of its game in the early 1970s—rich in talented faculty and students, and awash in scholarship and research funding—university politics, with support from the school's faculty, were threatening the program's continued existence. To make things even more complex, Hans Weiler had been on leave in 1971–1972 teaching at Indiana University and

Stanford in Germany,[3] and in 1974, he accepted the prestigious position of director of the International Institute of Educational Planning (IIEP), founded by UNESCO just twelve years before, with Phillip Coombs as its first head. Weiler's appointment linked SIDEC directly into the larger world of comparative and international education, including the IEA and other UNESCO institutions, and renewed the connections established by Paul Hanna with UNESCO in the 1950s. John Bock, one of Weiler's former students, who was also director of the SIDEC's Ford fellowship program for Southeast Asia, filled in for Weiler.

In a report to the faculty in mid-1973, Dean Coladarci expressed support for the international development education program in the School of Education but maintained that additional billets were unlikely to be forthcoming, and that the school had to consider how to fill my and John Bock's positions using soft money. He was not hopeful. The Coladarci report was one reason Weiler was convinced to take the IIEP directorship.

Troubled as these years were for SIDEC's standing in the school, they were also marked by a wave of exciting and influential ideas produced by faculty and students. The theoretical questioning that marked other fields in the early and mid-1970s was reaching into education, and SIDEC was a leader both in challenging comparative and international education and conceptions of education's role in society more generally. These new conceptions went far beyond the discussions in Hamburg or the important research at the University of Chicago's Comparative Education Center in the early 1960s. For example, it was during this period that I published *Education and Cultural Imperialism* (1974), and Alex Inkeles and David Smith published *Becoming Modern* (1974). Both raised important issues about the effects of education on economic outcomes and how to compare the role of education between countries. Even Hanna was upbeat about the program. In letters to Frank Moore in 1973, he reassured Moore that he had met with incoming students and was very pleased with their quality and SIDEC's overall health.

The high quality of SIDEC's students, the winding down of the Vietnam War, and the end of antiwar protests ultimately had a large influence in saving the program. SIDEC students took classes with many other faculty members and impressed them greatly. There were many SIDEC students in the school thanks to the Ford grants, and they gradually built support for the program among faculty. Thinking about education internationally thus became more "legitimate" and acceptable to the school's faculty.

In the 1975–1976 academic year, after much discussion behind the university's closed doors, the political obstacles to restoring the economics billet in SIDEC were removed, and the dean began a search for an tenured professor of economics of education. This effectively ensured that international and comparative education at Stanford would continue well into the future and would preserve its full complement of interdisciplinary strength. With widespread support among economists of education internationally (but still controversial inside the school), I was selected by the search committee to fill the economics billet as a tenured professor. Shifts in personnel continued in the 1970s, yet the fundamental structure of the program remained intact. The program also continued to produce stellar PhD and MA graduates, and they won faculty positions at other universities and started to plant the seeds of the SIDEC program there. The Ford Foundation funded Southeast Asia grant ended in 1975, and the Latin American grant, in 1977 (it had received a two-year extension, which in turn, had helped convince the university to restore the economics billet in SIDEC). Yet in that same year, 1977, Ford awarded Stanford a large fellowship grant, to be run by Hans Weiler (returned from IIEP in 1978), in order to train a new generation of sub-Saharan African PhDs in education. Like the previous two grants, the African grant totally exceeded expectations in terms of both graduates and the leadership positions the graduates took in academia, government, and regional institutions such as the African Development Bank.

Again, despite all these accomplishments, the school's administration again tried to dismantle SIDEC and proposed to assign its (tenured) faculty to other programs. The idea of a separate international development education program in the School of Education was irritating many faculty members. They and Dean Coladarci (who had his own interests in doing more international work) argued that SIDEC tended to close itself off to incorporating other faculty into a broader international and comparative education "community" in the school. The counterargument we made at SIDEC was that dissolving a program distinctly identified as comparative and international, producing MA and PhD graduates in that specialty, would greatly reduce the clear "comparative" identity our students felt, and they would be unlikely to consider themselves part of the comparative education field. We also argued that Stanford's brand identification as a leader in comparative and international education would suffer, and so would our fund-raising capacity. This time, university administration stepped in and stopped the threat to the program, which the university's upper echelons recognized as contributing significantly to Stanford's growing reputation around the world.

The 1980s in the United States saw politics shift in a drastically different direction, as a result of the Reagan presidency. That new political environment seemed to stimulate Stanford's innovations in the theoretical foundations of comparative and international education even more. Carnoy, Levin, Joel Samoff (a political scientist with expertise in Africa, hired on a non-tenure-track contract to expand SIDEC's strength in that region of the world), and Weiler all did foundational work in applying state theory to understanding educational change. Francisco Ramirez, a sociologist who had received his PhD from Stanford thirteen years earlier, joined SIDEC in 1987 and continued collaborating with his mentor, Stanford sociologist John Meyer, on their world society theory, which paralleled Inkeles's forays into modernity and the convergence of social structures worldwide.[4] Meyer and Ramirez used world society theory to explain the convergence of social institutions such as educational systems, and, along with their students, to human rights, girls' education, and the importance of science, technology, engineering, and mathematics (STEM) education, among others.

There were two other notable trends in comparative and international education research in the1980s. The first was that the World Bank became an important locus of empirical research in comparative education. With its considerable funds, it could compete with university-based research in defining the theoretical direction that such research should take. This trend was in part the result of the World Bank devoting increased resources to educational research—mainly based on data collected with its own financing. The World Bank funded household surveys in a number of countries, using them for rate-of-return studies, collected data on students in private and public schools (vocational and academic education), applied achievement tests, and conducted effective school studies. The bank's view of comparative and international education was rooted in the economics of education, specifically human capital theory. George Psacharopoulos, a World Bank staffer, edited the first *International Encyclopedia of the Economics of Education*, and about 20 percent of the encyclopedia's articles were written by World Bank researchers—eleven by Psacharopoulos himself. The second international meeting of the economics of education in Dijon, France, in 1986, also had an inordinate number of presentations by World Bank staff. Eventually, in the 1990s, the bank turned to studies of schooling itself, collecting data on student performance, school costs, and vocational education. The research carried out by bank staffers also pushed the idea that privately run education was more efficient than public.

The increased influence of the World Bank on educational research reflected a new external reality: the Cold War, which, in the 1960s and 1970s, had shaped unidirectional US, European, and Japanese conceptions of "Third World" economic development and had largely defined the debate over international comparisons, had, by the 1980s, morphed into a globalized world economy. Globalization and global institutions played an increasing role in mediating the meanings of "national," "international," and "comparative." Educational research did not escape this shift into the important global sources of development financing and policy analysis, such as the World Bank, that spilled over into comparative and international development education.

The second trend was that USAID initiated a series of major contracts—each on the order of US$10 million for ten years—with university schools of education to study various aspects of education in developing countries. This was a post-Vietnam effort by USAID to reinvent international development education. On the one hand, universities received large amounts of funding to undertake research projects and to provide for student assistantships. On the other hand, USAID had the right under these contracts to call on faculty to participate in education missions to developing countries as consultants on USAID projects.

Both trends affected comparative education research at universities. Faculty in many comparative and international programs engaged in research with the World Bank to get access to its data, even if they had to engage as part of a World Bank project. Stanford faculty had worked on World Bank research projects since the late 1960s and continued until the early 2000s. This included Stanford students, some of whom went on to work for the bank, and bank staffers who came to Stanford for training. Other researchers, including some at Stanford, engaged in responding to bank influence over the direction of comparative education. Debates with World Bank researchers at the annual Comparative and International Education Society (CIES) meeting became a ritual, usually attracting the largest crowds at the conference. The debates were essentially about underlying theories and methodologies, although these were rarely spelled out. More often than not, they turned into clashes of worldviews.

Large USAID projects also affected comparative education research but almost entirely and directly at universities. SIDEC applied for one of these contracts in the late 1980s. The project was for a major, multiyear operation of a "center of excellence" at SIDEC, and we made an enormous effort to win the competition but were not successful. Other universities—for example, Harvard (the Bridges project) and the University of California at Berkeley—won multimillion-dollar USAID contracts. The effect in the short run at both universities was an increase in research activity (mostly in the form of papers that emerged from USAID projects) and in more graduate students funded to work on these USAID projects. In the longer run, the effects were mixed. Faculty and students were increasingly called up to staff USAID missions, and with the end of USAID funding, the international and comparative program at Berkeley was "worn out." Although Berkeley continued to have excellent individual faculty members doing international education research, the coherence of the program never recovered. In contrast, the end of the Bridges program at Harvard reduced international research activity, but Harvard managed to preserve its comparative and international program, mainly by greatly expanding the number of MA students.

Had SIDEC won the contract, it may not have affected us in the same way as it did UC Berkeley, but in retrospect, faculty in the SIDEC program felt they had inadvertently dodged a bullet. SIDEC certainly would have been forced to shift from its focus on developing new ways of thinking about comparative and international education. As Arnold Anderson (1966) noted in the 1960s in commenting on consultancies, working in other countries as a consultant provides opportunities to observe new situations, gather new data, and develop new insights. However, committing a program to a large consultancy contract becomes the elephant in the room, driving research in the program and eliminating the time available to think about and use the insights gained to develop new ideas. It also shapes dissertation research into areas defined by an outside agency rather than by interesting new issues that arise in working with innovative approaches.

SIDEC flourished in this period. It was capped off at the end of the 1980s by three important collaborations. The first was with the International Institute of Education in Stockholm that produced several articles on educational policy research (e.g., Eliason et al., 1987; Chinapah et al., 1989) and a book on education in socialist countries in Latin America, Africa, and Asia (Carnoy and Samoff, 1989). The second and third collaborations were in developing and delivering executive training programs for key policy and research personnel in the Malaysian Ministry of Education and for World Bank education staff. Over an eight-year period, Stanford faculty trained about two hundred Malaysian policy planners and administrators and, in a separate summer program over three years, about one hundred World Bank staff.

Despite the program's worldwide prestige, it never seemed to get out of the woods at home. By the early 1990s, forces both outside and inside universities were threatening education departments more generally, with major implications for SIDEC. Yale and Johns Hopkins had closed their education departments earlier, but the move that precipitated the new crisis for Stanford's School of Education was the closure of Chicago's Graduate School of Education in the early 1980s, and the University of Chicago's subsequent complete absorption of a greatly reduced education department into its Social Science Division. By 1997, the university decided to close even that small department because administrators felt that the quality of the department's research was not up to social science standards. Thus was the ignominious end of what had once been the leading School of Education in the country and the end of a great tradition in comparative and international education:

Until the 1970s, the University of Chicago had a strong commitment to education. In addition to the department, there was a Graduate School of Education devoted to teacher training, with strong links to the laboratory school both for teacher instruction and research projects. . . . Increasingly, insiders and outsiders are contending that the decline started in the late '70s, when Chicago's education department stopped its day-to-day involvement with teacher training and schools, devoting itself more purely to theory. . . . The focus on education shifted away from schools, and research money dried up . . .the department found itself increasingly unable to get money for new appointments since education research often appeared to lack rigor in the eyes of the university administrators who controlled the money. (Bronner, 1997, p. A27)

The argument that the quality of research in departments of education was low entered the discussion at Stanford. In 1992, when the university was in the throes of a turbulent change of presidents, the idea of phasing out the School of Education—based on the Chicago example—gained traction. This ultimately became a problem for SIDEC, even though talk about closing the school dissipated. SIDEC's situation remained problematic—first, because it had entered a turbulent transition itself in 1992–1993, and second, because the school, faced by questions regarding its viability, reorganized itself into three larger "departments," one of which incorporated social science and humanities programs. That department included international education. SIDEC was therefore merged into a larger administrative unit.

SIDEC's turbulent transition, as is the case in most academic changes, centered on changes in personnel. Robert Textor had moved in the mid-1980s to the anthropology department, and then had taken early retirement in 1990. Hans Weiler, after serving in administrative positions in the school, also retired in 1993 to become rector of the Europa-Universität Viadrina in Frankfurt (Oder)—a reorganized university on the Polish border of a newly unified Germany. Textor's faculty billet was used to hire Thomas Rohlen, an anthropologist who had studied the culture of Japanese high schools. Half of his position was in the Institute of International Studies (IIS),[5] founded in 1987 as Stanford's version of the Harvard Institute for International Development (now the Center for

International Development at Harvard). After a few years in the school, Rohlen moved full time into research at the IIS. The SIDEC program also had to fight to preserve Weiler's billet. Thus, at a high point in its international standing—possibly as the world's leading program in international and comparative education—SIDEC again faced a struggle to maintain itself as an identifiable program.

SIDEC was partly threatened internally in this period by the recent hiring of faculty such as Ramirez and Rohlen, who had little invested in the SIDEC "tradition" as a separate program. Ironically, SIDEC was also partly threatened by its own success and by increased globalization. Many more noncomparative Stanford education faculty were traveling to lecture in other countries, interested in comparative education, and engaged in projects abroad, but they were only loosely connected with SIDEC.

The question, then, was whether SIDEC would be incorporated into the new subdepartment of the school as an international program with its traditional identity of well-defined degree program, or whether it would become the "dispersed" comparative and international education program proposed by then outgoing Dean Coladarci in the late 1970s. That dispersed concept—or as Jack Schwille (2017) characterizes it, "integration-infusion"—is one that still characterizes international education at Michigan State. This resurrection of the Coladarci proposal envisaged eliminating the comparative and international degree-granting program and replacing it with a loosely knit group of faculty (and students) that would do comparative and international research in education and form an "interest" group within Stanford School of Education's new social science and humanities "subdepartment."

In the end, the school was reorganized and the new social sciences and humanities subdepartment established, along with two other subdepartments. Comparative and international education remained intact as a degree-granting program with essentially the same interdisciplinary, social science–based required curriculum. SIDEC's name was changed to satisfy certain faculty who wanted to break the program's connection to the two faculty members who had retired and to SIDEC's identity as "international education and development." In 1994, the program adopted its new brand as International and Comparative Education (ICE).

ICE became a subprogram of the larger, aggregated department Social Sciences, Policy, and Educational Practice (SSPEP), but beyond the name, nothing else changed. As already noted, the curriculum, which had been around in some form for the previous forty years, remained identical. Hans Weiler's billet was preserved, albeit at a junior level, which allowed ICE to continue with three full-time faculty members and Rohlen as half-time in the school and half-time in the Institute of International Studies.

There were important gains for the newly named ICE program from this new arrangement, but there were also important losses. After years of being viewed as a "marginal" program within the School of Education and having to develop allies in the school one at a time, ICE had become part of a large "subdepartment" that represented about 40 percent of all faculty in the school. The monthly "subdepartment" meeting put ICE faculty in close contact with other social science and humanities faculty in the school, eliminating SIDEC's "separateness." This larger subdepartment's faculty were now natural supporters of an international program. This was not just a theoretical change—in practice during the following years, the international and comparative program had a secure political position in the School of Education for the first time in its history.

The administrative changes had two major downsides. The first was the program's name change, made as a political compromise to avoid undermining the cohesiveness of the program's curricular structure and organization. Because the name change from SIDEC to ICE coincided with the absorption of ICE into the new SSPEP subdepartment, the larger Comparative and International Education Society community (with certain satisfaction) inferred that the program at Stanford was dead, despite SIDEC (now ICE) continuously graduating students and accepting new ones into an international degree-granting program. In business parlance, the "brand" certainly suffered. It took more than five years for it to recover and for the world comparative and international education community to recognize ICE and accord it a stature equal to that of SIDEC.

The second downside, with more internal effects, was that once absorbed into SSPEP, ICE faculty no longer met regularly to review student progress and intellectual and administrative issues. PhD students were monitored as part of the larger pool of students in SSPEP. Individual ICE faculty members were involved in advising both PhD and MA students, but ICE faculty rarely met as a group, although they often talked and coordinated strategy for presentations at SSPEP meetings.

Once the reform was completed, ICE kept Hans Weiler's position, with the support of SSPEP faculty, and hired Karen Mundy from the University of Toronto to fill it. A new era began, although the fundamentals of the program remained the same—high-quality students at both MA and PhD levels, and an interdisciplinary social science curriculum that adapted over the years to changing ideas. Mundy focused on a new set of challenges: the role of international institutions such as the World Bank, UNESCO, and the Organization for Economic Cooperation and Development (OECD) in defining the comparative education agenda and methodologies in a globalized economy. She developed this research over six years and eventually took it to the Ontario Institute of Studies in Education (OISE) in 2005.

Given the intensification of globalization in the 1990s, it is not surprising that ICE faculty and students (and former students) turned to comparative analyses of how globalization was impacting education internationally. Besides Karen Mundy's research, Ramirez and his students developed many empirical studies of their institutional version of globalization in which norms and institutions converge over time. In collaboration with Manuel Castells at Berkeley, I wrote about the new economy and its impact on labor markets and the family.

It was in the mid-1990s and early 2000s that ICE's MA program became a permanent part of the School of Education's offerings, not dependent on outside funding. As part of a several self-examinations over the years, the school (and the Ford Foundation, in the early 1970s) evaluated the master's programs, and the ICE program was rated the highest among all the MA offerings. There were good reasons for this. ICE's eleven-month MA program required (and still requires) a thesis or research paper. The paper not only helps MA students develop analytical skills that carry over to future work or continued graduate study but also motivates frequent contact with each student's faculty adviser. That contact allows faculty advisers to get to know the student, which in turn helps the adviser write detailed and knowledgeable recommendation letters for the student. The evaluation conducted by the school showed that ICE's MA students had a higher level of satisfaction with their program and with their postgraduation placement than did students in the school's other MA degree programs. Consequently, ICE's MA program received continued funding for an MA director, who, for about eight years, was a recent ICE PhD with lecturer status and a two-year appointment. Beginning in 2001, however, the title was changed to acting assistant professor (Christine Min Wotipka, 2001–2003). In 2005, Min Wotipka returned to Stanford in a regular nontenured appointment, which she has held since. The relatively small MA program, regularly taking twenty to twenty-four students, now has its own research seminar, organized to work through the students' research papers, and a permanent director, in addition to an assigned faculty adviser to each student.[6]

In 2005, Stanford hosted the Comparative and International Education Society's annual meeting for the second time. This meeting was particularly significant because the society's membership and attendance at annual meetings had fluctuated over the previous ten years, but without observable growth. Furthermore, CIES had lost money on several of its recent meetings and was facing a financial crisis. The 2005 meeting began with a reunion of SIDEC and ICE graduates from around the world, including a taped greeting from Alejandro Toledo, then president of Peru, who had been a SIDEC MA and PhD student in the 1970s. The 2005 CIES meeting drew more than 1,200 people (and made a substantial profit—the first of a string of meetings that greatly improved the financial position of the society).

The success of the Stanford CIES meeting and the rapid growth of attendance at subsequent meetings—the meetings from 2015 to 2017 drew about 2,500–3,000 members, and the 2018 meeting in Mexico City drew about 3,400 members—marked a new trend. Interest in education more broadly as a field of study had increased dramatically, and with that increase, researchers from outside the traditional disciplinary bases of psychology, education, and history studying educational issues had multiplied to include economists, sociologists, political scientists, and, more recently, computer scientists, biologists, and neuroscientists. Comparative and international education were not spared this onslaught of new theoretical approaches and new ways to analyze educational systems and educational change.

In addition, the 2000s have witnessed another phenomenon. The amount of information about education and the context in which educational systems operate is increasing enormously, as has the capacity to process it. This has led to an explosion of data and of empirical studies comparing various aspects of education across countries and across regions within countries. Many of these data have come from international tests, which began in the 1960s, and have increased massively in the twenty-first century. More recently, new data sources have been generated in various countries by state and national governments, and by increased spending by researchers on data collection for well-defined experiments and longitudinal studies. All these data are leading to a new emphasis on causal analysis and large-scale international comparisons. Essentially, Harold Noah and Max Eckstein's dreams have come true.

How has ICE successfully reacted to these new trends? First, recognizing the importance of Chinese education as a subject of study, ICE hired Jennifer Adams, a Harvard graduate and an expert on China, in 2006. Although Adams moved to Drexel for personal reasons in 2013, she left a legacy of the ICE program's deepening interest in China and the sense that ICE research capacity should expand to another large Asian country, India.

The program also realized that the whole area of impact evaluation was taking on new importance in international development education and that we needed to cover policy research more adequately from a political and organizational perspective. In 2015, Prashant Loyalka, an expert in China and India and in impact evaluation, and Patricia Bromley, an organizational sociologist, joined the ICE faculty. They represent the continuation of previous research lines in ICE but take completely new approaches to them. Bromley's work on organizational theory promises to bring yet another wave of innovation from Stanford to comparative education research.

The work in impact evaluation is an outgrowth of much more funding for large-scale experimental data collection and longitudinal surveys in countries such as China and India to test hypotheses about the effectiveness of educational interventions to improve student outcomes. It is also a return in different form to Hanna's hands-on approaches to comparative education in the 1960s. Employing causal analysis, impact evaluators have as their objective to convince policy makers in developed and developing countries to take seriously certain interventions with good results for students or to reject other policies that have low or negative impacts. Some of these studies test specific theories of how education should work, but, as in the past, most are simply based on the idea that policy makers will respond to evidence and that the role of the academic is to show evidence to policy makers. Again, it is a return to the functionalism of the 1960s, with little basis for why or why not policy makers are interested in such evidence.

In 2011, ICE also got a major gift from the Lemann Foundation in Brazil to establish a center to train Brazilian education policy analysts in ICE's MA and PhD programs, and to do policy research in Brazil. The center also involved the School of Education's learning sciences and design technology program and its efforts to develop new, sophisticated science teaching using maker technologies and to evaluate the effectiveness of those innovative processes. The Lemann Center is already contributing to new ways of approaching comparative education through exploiting rich data sets in Brazil. It is also contributing to the impact evaluation literature using large-scale Brazilian longitudinal data, and it is in the pilot stages of a major project to transform the preparation of mathematics and science teachers in Brazil.

Thus, SIDEC survived from crisis to crisis from the early 1970s to the early 1990s, and emerged into the twenty-first century intact and continuously innovative and productive. What are the institutional lessons of this survival? I think the main ones are that the program managed to remain at the forefront of comparative and international education research and that it always focused heavily on training PhD and master's students with an interdisciplinary social science approach. Like most of its counterparts in other universities, the Stanford international program has been relatively small, but it has been consistently coherent and creative. The quality of SIDEC's, and now ICE's, MA and PhD students, year after year, has been the main reason for the brand's high standing both inside Stanford and in the outside world. This should not be forgotten—comparative education programs are as good as their graduates.

Eventually, other factors helped ICE survive. The increased "internationalization" of the university over the past forty years, the ability to attract funding that stressed independent research rather than consulting contracts, and the quality of the research and class work in courses across the School of Education and the university done by SIDEC and ICE students have all contributed. In addition, the great increase in interest in social science approaches to education and the increased pressure to reward high-quality research in education have also played a role in the greatly improved position of the program's new brand, ICE, in the past decade. Of course, money for research and student support was key to sustaining the program. During its most difficult years, the program (like programs in other universities) received support from the Ford Foundation for faculty billets and for research and fellowships, won other grant applications, and, by the 1990s, got direct help from the School of Education to fund fellowships for PhD students. All this allowed the SIDEC and ICE programs to avoid the pressure of raising money through consulting or large-scale consulting contracts.

Throughout this period, SIDEC and the newer ICE have maintained close relations with UNESCO, the World Bank, the OECD, and the International Labor Organization, and to a much lesser degree with USAID. It has also had close relations with US foundations and institutions in other countries studying education, including comparative education programs in other universities, many of them staffed by Stanford graduates. These relationships have tied Stanford's program into the broader world of the comparative and international education community. Institutional interactions have not been as intense as in the 1960s and 1970s, when Paul Hanna and Hans Weiler played such a major role in continuously networking with UNESCO and other international organizations, or in the 1980s and 1990s, when there were more educational research projects at the World Bank that involved SIDEC faculty and students. But the direct links with many national research centers are now much stronger than in the past. This makes sense: for better or worse, the main activities in ICE are centered even more on educational research and less on pushing certain education policies through international organizations.

CHAPTER 3

The 1960s and 1970s

Human Capital

BY THE LATE 1960s and early 1970s, the shift to social science techniques in comparative and international education, led by the Comparative
Education Center at the University of Chicago, had permeated the leading
comparative programs. This social science approach modeled the relation
between education and society as a functional one—that is, the models
assumed that schools are functional to society because they improve social
outcomes and help maintain social equilibrium by giving students' skills
that make them better off. At the same time, the increasing amount of
available empirical data collected in the field enabled comparative education researchers to question some of the principal ideas of what this functional relation was, such as the notions that expanding educational systems
greatly increased mobility (Anderson, 1961a), that vocational education
was a fundamentally different version of education from academic education (Foster, 1965), and that more investment in education was typically
necessary to achieve higher rates of economic growth (Denison, 1967).

The most important new theoretical influence on the social science approach to international research on education was human capital. Theodore Schultz's presidential speech at the American Economic Association
meetings in 1961 launched this major break with economists' traditional
definition of capital, but it was quickly accepted by most social scientists
because of its power in understanding the sources of economic growth
and explaining many aspects of how students and families behaved in
taking schooling.[1] It also put the costs of education, including the earnings and activities that young people and their families gave up when
they went to school, front and center in the study of education. Costs
had been notoriously absent from educational policy discussions before
the 1960s, even though they certainly had a very important role in most
educational decisions. To educators, however, the idea that education was
an investment in future income—that economic costs and returns were

driving forces in shaping why and how people approached learning—seemed to be a vulgarization of the value of educational activities, and it caused great dismay:

What is the value of schooling? A babel of voices will respond to this query. It is moral, refines taste, and gives people real satisfactions. It is vocational, develops skills, increases earnings, and is an investment in man. Our task is to treat these and still other values of schooling in a framework of economic analysis. But the moment it is suggested that the economic value of schooling is under consideration, there are many who protest, for they believe that placing a "price" on education is to debase it. "Whatever you do in studying education, do not apply an economic yardstick to its worth," expresses a deep-seated apprehension. This apprehension is groundless analytically. Although it is, of course, true that particular bits of economic knowledge are sometimes misused by those who have an axe to grind in shaping policy, there are no reasons for believing that education is more vulnerable in this respect than are other areas of endeavor. (Schultz, 1963, pp. 6–7)

Despite such qualms, many comparative educators found human capital theory to be an important tool for analyzing education internationally. Human capital theory assumed that humans' economic behavior was similar across different societies, even though Schultz himself seemed to be open to the notion that this was not necessarily true: "How people earn their living is in general an integral part of their culture" (1963, p. 7). Does this mean that universal rules of economic behavior play an important role in unifying all cultures? Or do important cultural differences among societies influence the economic behavior in that culture? Human capital theory never dealt with this issue. But whatever side analysts concerned with the economics of education came down on in the culture-economic behavior debate, most eventually accepted that the relation between education and labor markets could be considered an informative way of describing differences in the role that education played in different countries. It has provided important insights into the nature of education systems themselves, and it could provide insights into understanding the way that economic behavior interacts with culture, because the educational system is such a strong expression of cultural norms. As it turned out, the notion of human capital also became, and still is, an important argument for more spending on education, and for those who may have been wary of economists commodifying education, more money for education was a welcome result. Economists in government agencies, in turn, gradually came to see education budgets as more than just a form of social spending that fulfilled purely political goals.

Stanford hired me in the late 1960s to fill a position in the international development education program mainly because of my University of Chicago economics dissertation research and the resulting publications on human capital in Mexico. My economist colleague at the Brookings Institution, Henry Levin, had already accepted a position at Stanford as its first economist and as part of Thomas James's transformation of the School of Education. SIDEC also needed an economist who studied education, and, in addition, it was interested in bringing on Latin America expertise.

At Chicago, I had been Theodore Schultz's student, and he wanted me to be the first to focus on human capital formation in a developing country. As it turned out, I did something even more novel in my dissertation, at least for an economics graduate student. First, I spent three months in the archives of the Ministry of Education and in the Association of American Universities collecting cost data on schooling and university education in Mexico. I constructed cost data for multiple levels of education going back twenty years. The costs of education were understudied everywhere, and one of Schultz's most important contributions was to estimate the growth of human capital in the United States by quantifying the costs of education—including income foregone by students when they attended school—from 1900 to 1957. He argued that the "educational capital per member of the labor force rose from \$2,236 to \$7,555 in 1956 dollars between 1900 and 1957" (1963, p. 49). I did the same type of estimate for Mexico for the period 1940 to 1962, and I found a massive increase during that twenty-two-year period in the amount that Mexico invested in human capital.

Second, because I was unable to access Mexican census microdata as promised to me by the Mexican government, I was forced to conduct my own, nonrandom but representative labor force survey using a short, nine-question questionnaire to collect the data for my rate-of-return study. I interviewed more than four thousand workers at their places of work in factories and offices in four cities, asking them about their age, education, earnings, and father's education and occupation. I also interviewed farm workers in agriculture areas. It was a remarkable experience. I spoke to workers in a variety of work environments—several textile factories, a brewery, a cottonseed oil processing plant, a bank, the government's electrical power company, and many others—almost seventy enterprises in all. Observing workers at work and recording the variety of learning trajectories that got them to those jobs helped me dig down much deeper into the meaning of human capital than just using census data would have ever allowed me to do.

To estimate income foregone in primary schooling, I interviewed children of primary school age who carried packages for supermarket shoppers to earn tips or worked as shoeshine boys or sold chewing gum and candy on the street. Conducting the interviews myself, I had an intimate knowledge of the possible biases in my data. To gain a better understanding of how education and social class related to an individual's future economic outcomes at the lowest and highest ends of the income spectrum, I also did "side" explorations, such as interviewing *ejidatarios* (collective farmers) on a large *ejido* in northern Mexico and interviewing the entire third-year class in medicine at the Universidad Nacional Autónoma de México (UNAM).

My dissertation work made an indelible impression on me as an economist and a scholar. When I presented my findings at a department workshop six months later, some faculty and students mocked the fact that I had collected the data myself, but it turns out that I had great advantages over researchers who were using secondary data. First, I had a much better sense of my data than did students using secondary-source surveys. Second, I had been able to collect information that was not available to others—in my case, on individuals' socioeconomic background. At that time, no one had done a study that related earnings to education and age and controlled for variables of social class. Third, observing my interviewees in their work context allowed me to get a "feel" for the meaning of human capital represented by the data I collected. All this convinced me that directly observing the reality that social scientists study was essential to doing good economics and good data analyses.

For example, I observed young factory workers next to much older workers in textile mills at large power-driven looms. The young workers had completed primary school and had relatively little factory experience. The older workers had barely attended school and had learned about weaving cloth by working on hand looms in their homes in an earlier era and had been hired into the textile factories at a time when the average level of education was much lower. The younger workers had more schooling but did the same job as the older workers (and earned about the same wage)—there were many younger workers in Mexico with completed primary schooling by the time I was interviewing, and this was considered a good job for someone with that level of schooling. I called this "downward substitution"—the substitution of more educated for less educated workers in the same jobs as the educational system expanded. Observing this phenomenon in many of the factories and offices I visited made me realize that the value of the same level of education as an investment changed as the educational system expanded and that those who attained any level later in the expansion probably benefited less than those who got in earlier.

Several years later, in 1968, just before I came to Stanford and while working at the Brookings Institution in the area of Latin American trade patterns and industrial development, I was asked by the World Bank to construct cost data and to reproduce my Mexico survey in Kenya, a country that had been independent for only a few years and had experienced the bloody, anticolonial Mau Mau Rebellion in the early 1960s. It was incredibly exciting for me to travel to sub-Saharan Africa for the first time. I went there with a young German World Bank researcher, Hans Thias. Although we had to overcome some resistance from the Kenyan authorities, who believed in manpower planning rather than rate-of-return analysis,[2] we successfully drew a random sample of work establishments in three cities and interviewed four thousand Kenyans working in them. In 1972, on the basis of that survey and other analyses we had done while in Kenya, Thias and I published *Cost-Benefit Analysis: A Case Study of Kenya.*

In the Mexico study, I was one of the first to estimate earnings functions using regression analysis, and my results showed that the rate to investment in primary schooling was higher than to investment in secondary schooling and university education. This was the expected result because, according to neoclassical economic theory, marginal returns to investment in capital declined as investment increased. Following the concept of declining returns to capital investment, human capital economists argued that investment in higher levels of schooling would yield lower rates of return than to lower levels of schooling. The assumption was that for individuals and society, investment in secondary and higher education investment represented investment in greater amounts of human capital, and hence was subject to declining payoffs. I accepted this prediction before I went to Kenya because my Mexico study had confirmed that such a pattern of rates of return prevailed.

However, the rates of return we estimated for education in Kenya adjusted for socioeconomic background and a measure of ability were somewhat lower for investment in primary schooling than for investment in secondary education and about the same as the rates to higher education. This was a surprise, but it was rather easily explained if we abandoned simplistic notions of equivalence between schooling as a capital investment good and physical capital markets—specifically that different levels of schooling represent one continuous and equally accessible set of investments. Kenya, unlike Mexico, had had a great expansion in access to primary education in the four years between independence (1963) and the time of our survey (January 1968) but had maintained very limited access to secondary and higher education. At the same time, Kenya had relatively little industry or other formal employment possibilities for primary school graduates. The payoff to completing primary schooling was therefore not any higher than to higher levels of schooling. Because access to secondary and higher education in the mid-1960s was very restricted, and employment opportunities in a growing postindependence government bureaucracy—particularly with the replacement of British civil servants by Kenyan nationals—were relatively abundant, the payoffs to secondary and higher education were as high or higher than to primary education.

The Kenyan results helped me understand a rather obvious educational reality: the supply of places in education is dependent mainly on government's, and somewhat on private investors', willingness and financial capacity to expand successive levels of schooling, and this is often independent of the labor market's capacity to employ graduates from successively higher levels of schooling. Yes, an individual's investment in secondary education required a previous investment in primary, but for families and students to make that investment in the next level of schooling required the availability of schools and teachers. Such availability was largely out of the control of individual family or student investors. Even were a market for private schooling to develop, which it eventually did in Kenya, the quality of most schooling in that market remained abysmally low for decades because of the lack of trained teachers and the low incomes of the families demanding that schooling for their children. Meanwhile, as the primary level of schooling expanded, driving down the payoff to graduates, the average income foregone for students attending the next-highest level fell, thus increasing political demands on government to expand it. It took some time for government to respond to those demands, but expand secondary school it did, and then, ultimately, postsecondary education.

A fundamental assumption of human capital theory is that individuals choose to take more schooling on the basis of how much they perceive they can increase their earnings from investing in more education. This perception is often grounded in an approximate reality of what those in the labor force with higher levels of schooling are actually earning at the time. According to the theory, individuals also decide to stay in school or not stay in school based on other, "consumption" considerations, such as whether they like going to school or whether they think that more schooling will help them get more out of life, exposure to art or literature, or maybe more interesting friends. In human capital theory, every individual has similar "choices," although less able individuals might realize lower returns on the time and money they put into education, and so might be less likely to go further in school than more able individuals.

The Kenya study made me realize that there was another player in this "choice" equation—the state. The state (the political-economic system) has the power to determine how rapidly schooling expands. The state can also decide in which parts of the country or region it expands as well as where the good and not-so-good teachers are placed in schools, and it can regulate how pupils are sorted in the system. I observed that the elites that had an inordinate share of power in places such as Mexico and Kenya organized the educational system largely for their purposes. They responded to pressures from the nonelites for more schooling, but they could exert enough control over this process of expansion to ensure that their children would end up getting higher benefits from schooling than would the children of nonelites.

Armed with this insight, when Thomas LaBelle, then at UCLA, asked me in 1971 to contribute a chapter to a book he was editing on Latin America, I wrote a piece analyzing how rates of return would behave over time as societies expanded successive levels of schooling. I argued that, rather than the pattern of declining rates from primary to higher education maintaining over time—as claimed later by neoclassical economists (Psacharopoulos, 1973, 1981, 1985)—the returns (and rate of return) to primary education would decline first, simultaneously contributing (with the decline in earnings foregone of continuing on to secondary education) to an increase in rates of return to secondary education and hence increasing demand for expanding secondary enrollment. Then, as students graduated in larger numbers from high school, that rate would decline, pushing up the rate of return to investment in university, which, in turn, would eventually decline as enrollment greatly expanded in higher education.

My argument, as suggested earlier, was that the provision of different levels of schooling was not equally available to all students at a given point in time, so the underlying assumption was flawed that students and their families made decisions about investing in different levels of schooling solely based on their estimates of the payoff to them of that investment or other nonpecuniary benefits. Rather, the most usual case was that access to higher levels of schooling was relatively restricted until lower levels of schooling had sufficiently expanded to put increased political pressure on the public sector to expand the next level. In political economy terms, the market for schooling was highly imperfect—serious barriers to entry existed in the overall education system, and these were not academic barriers expected by the workings of the market (lower rates of return to taking more for lower academically able students). Nevertheless, for political as well as rate-of-return reasons, these barriers gradually fell away as lower levels of education became more universal. I wrote:

Schooling is touted as an important allocator of socio-economic roles in such economies, and the ruling group becomes subjected to great pressures from non-elites to provide education for everyone (social demand). Since education is held up by the elite as the legitimator of their rule and as the means to gain economic advantage and social status, access to education becomes a crucial political issue. The more modern (sociologically) the society, the more members of the non-elite pass through the educational system to attain elite or near-elite status. If the educational system does not permit at least some individuals from the non-elite to pass through, education would no longer be accepted by non-elites as a means of attainment status.

A dilemma for the elite is how to satisfy the social demand for more and more schooling without giving away economic and policy-making power. The current structure of the schools solves this dilemma by restricting the high return (in terms of higher income) component of formal education to schooling levels accessible almost exclusively to the elite. Within levels of schooling, the curriculum, teachers, and other inputs are more efficient producers of achievement and modernization for those who enter school with an already higher level of these outputs. The high return component of education is distributed to those with elite characteristics rather than to non-elites. This leaves most of those who believe in education as a road to economic success with more education but little absolute increase in income or political power. Potential disillusionment creates a second dilemma: if the elite provides education without economic (or at least other intangible) benefits, they may be promoting their own overthrow. The elite can deal with this problem by becoming more hierarchical (dictatorial), by attempting to expand the opportunities for employment, or by both means. Again, however, the first line of defense is the education system itself. Schooling socializes the individual to believe that if he fails, it is his fault, not the system's. The system is fair, he is taught; he, the failure, has not met its needs or requirements. If the individual is convinced of this, even lack of employment will not seem unreasonable to him.

Social scientists have long recognized this elite bias in the education system, but they have chosen to ignore that a system with this bias forms its strategy of skill production primarily on political grounds—on income and status distribution considerations—and only secondarily on considerations of maximizing economic growth or the potential social contribution of all members of the society. Economists assume, tacitly, that all students (parents) can choose the amount and nature of skill production desired. They do not recognize that the institutions themselves determine students' future roles through tracking, the system of financing education, and the nature of school social relationships. (Carnoy, 1972a, pp. 179–180)

In the chapter, I argued and tried to show empirically that the organization of the education system is not based on some "neutral" operation of the market that simply seeks to optimize output either in the school system (in terms of bringing the potentially most productive students to the highest levels of schooling) or in the economy (by allocating resources to education in a way that produces the highest payoff to society). Rather, I claim that the elites have multiple goals, but these are all couched in the imperative of reproducing their economic, social, and political power. I did not reject the notion of human capital. Human capital, I agreed, was a fundamental concept contributing to the theory of economic growth and to our understanding of the role of the education system in modern society. Theodore Schultz's estimates of the value of the investment in human beings in the first half of the twentieth century was an invaluable contribution to our understanding of capital and of economic growth. His insights into education as an investment and consumption good redefined how we thought about families' and individuals' decision-making vis-à-vis schooling. That said, my main point was that important parts of the underlying theory of the formation of human capital and how human capital markets worked were deeply flawed. I claimed that, like all markets, the market for human capital was imperfect and especially susceptible to political forces because education and investment in education were so important to the underlying legitimacy of the state and to the distribution of earnings and status in modern society.

Indeed, in my analysis, I used a key idea in the neoclassical economics version of human capital theory, which I had learned so well at the University of Chicago: the rate of return to education represented a measure of the economic value of education and drove how and why individuals invest in education and how and why educational systems expand. I turned the rate of return on its head, claiming that it was driven by not just demand for schooling—by forces in the economy—but also by the supply of schooling, which could be manipulated by state policy, and state policy was heavily influenced by the political power structure in the state. Rates of return could therefore be manipulated by state education policies to affect how different groups in society benefited economically from the pattern of educational expansion:

The model outlined here describes changes in the function of schooling as the percentage of the age cohort attending school increases relative to the growth of the economy. Different levels of schooling assume different roles as the expansion of enrollment occurs. The corollary of the relationship between rates of return and the period of educational-economic development shown in Figure 1 is the possibility of predicting the pattern of rates of return to investment in various levels of schooling and of predicting the function of each level by observing a country's gross national product per capita, the rate of economic growth, enrollment rates at the different levels and socioeconomic background differences between students at different levels of schooling. Two or three of these variables may be sufficiently good predictors. In terms of studying schooling as a distributor of skills, the model distinguishes between the primary outputs of schooling (achievement versus socialization) in the different periods of development. The model also indicates that the contribution of schooling to different groups in the society varies according to their political power or their ability to gain control of resources associated with elite-oriented education. (Carnoy, 1972a, p. 186)

Figure 1 mentioned in that article (reproduced here as Figure 3.1) shows that in an "early" period of economic development and educational expansion, the rates to primary education rise and then begin to fall as the supply of graduates expands. As gross domestic product rises and jobs begin getting harder to find, secondary school rates rise and the secondary level of schooling expands, resulting in a corresponding decline in rates of return to investing in secondary education. Ultimately, the same cyclical pattern reaches the university level:

While Figure 1 depicts a hypothetical pattern of the economic return to schooling over time in a developing country, it can be argued that the paths of both economic growth (industrialization) and the growth of the educational system are fairly universal and that these universal paths generate universal patterns of skill production and concomitant effects of such patterns. The rise in the rate of return to investment in each level is generally caused by an increase in demand for labor with that level of skills in the economy. The supply of primary school graduates lags behind demand in period I, the supply of secondary lags behind demand in period II, and the supply of university graduates lags behind demand in period III.

The rise in wages of primary-school-trained labor in period I raises the income foregone during school of those who attend secondary school and therefore tends to hold down the rise in rates of return to secondary expenditures. As the supply of primary schooling graduates increases relative to demand, it becomes increasingly difficult for those with no schooling to find jobs. Labor force participation to employment rates of unschooled labor tends to fall, especially among young people, during the end of period I and the beginning of period IL This causes income foregone of attending primary school to fall, and private rates of return to primary schooling to rise. However, the increase in primary school graduates also reduces the unemployment adjusted wages of these graduates. Private rates of return rise, but because there is an important public expenditures component of primary schooling cost unaffected by labor force participation, social rates rise less than private rates and eventually fall with increased unemployment.

As labor force participation employment rates (and unemployment corrected wages) of primary school graduates fall, the effect is particularly important among young graduates. The income foregone of secondary school students falls correspondingly, and the private rate of return to secondary school rises rapidly. The social rate may also rise, but less than the private rate.

As the output of secondary schools increases relative to demand, the labor force participation rate of those with secondary schooling falls, and their mean adjusted income also falls, driving the social rate down. The private rate, however, continues to rise, since income foregone falls even further (young primary school graduates find it even more difficult to get work) and its weight in the private rate is much greater than in the social rate. Ultimately, the same sequence of events occurs at the university level. (Carnoy, 1972a, pp. 182–183)

In the empirical part of the article, I tried to bring all the data available at that time—rates of return for twenty-seven countries (Psacharopoulos and Hinchliffe, 1970) and my own work on Mexico, Kenya, and Puerto Rico (Carnoy, 1972c)—to support, in an admittedly approximate way, the dynamic movements of rates of return predicted by my model. I cannot claim that it was entirely convincing, but the results lent some credence to my argument and at least did not contradict it. Further, the most important part of my case was that this dynamic movement of rates of return was crucial to understanding the earnings distributional consequences of how schooling expanded and which groups got access to higher levels of schooling first:

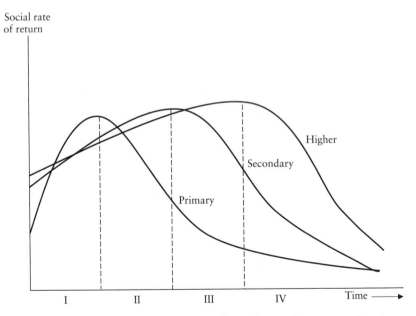

FIGURE 3.1 *Hypothesized dynamic of social rate of return to education over time. Lines show the social rates of return to education over time by level of education.*

Source: Carnoy, 1972a.

On the up side of the rate-of-return curve, the economic value of additional schooling is increasing and the variance of the rate of increase among the students in school tends to be low. On the down side, the economic value of schooling falls, despite possible increases in the quality of teachers (replacement of primary-school-educated teachers teaching primary school by secondary-school-educated teachers, for example). In addition, the variance of the rate of decrease increases as the mean declines, in part because the system of education discriminates between elite and non-elite groups. As large numbers of students begin to enter primary school, the purpose and nature of primary school changes. In the period I phase, primary school prepares students to assume roles as skilled or white-collar, versus unskilled workers. The students have a sense of elitism: if they learn to read and write if they graduate from primary school, they are virtually assured of a job in what is, in period I, a status position. They are being trained as a sub-elite. The move to universal primary schooling, at least in part a public response to the rising rates to investment in primary schooling, turns the primary school into a firm which socializes individuals to become good citizens, and to select particularly successful students for professional training in secondary school. In period II, elite formation, which had taken place at all three levels in period I, shifts out of primary school. There are not enough industrial or high-status service jobs to go around for the rapidly increasing numbers of primary school graduates, and this interacts with the educational process to change the function of primary schooling. . . . Neither teachers nor students see primary schooling as an end in itself.

At the same time, however, there is an increased demand for secondary school-trained teachers due to the expansion of primary schooling. The demand for secondary-school-trained people generated by the replacement of foreign technicians, the growth of service industries and the growth of the government sector also increases. Secondary schools usually expand slowly at first relative to demand, and the rate of return to investment in secondary schooling increases. In period III, secondary school enrollment expands rapidly. The purpose of secondary schooling changes from elite formation to socialization and selection for elite formation in the university. In most countries, this is a gradual process, first moving into the lower years of the secondary cycle and ultimately to the entire cycle. The secondary level ceases to become an exclusive club for already highly socialized students and the screening process for elite status moves upward from the primary level. . . . Secondary teachers, accustomed to teaching rather articulate elite-to-be, become custodians for many who are simply out of the labor force for a year or two, or who are to be channeled into vocational training. . . . At the same time, secondary schooling clearly differentiates between those who are to go on to universities and those who are not. The former group receives elite education which permits access to a university. As in primary schooling during an earlier period (II), the variance in returns to secondary school expenditures is much higher in period III than in period II.

The expansion of secondary schooling (period III) requires more university-trained teachers. Government in most countries expands, becomes more bureaucratically complex, and demands more university graduates. As in the primary-secondary relationship, the relative decrease in secondary wages tends to slow the increase in salaries for university types, but other factors, such as government job requirements, tend to offset this trend in period III.

In period IV, the supply of university-trained labor increases much more rapidly than demand. University training gradually changes from a form of elite professional training to a means of further socializing students to accept sub-elite roles in society and to try to keep them out of the labor force for an additional four or more years. Even when university training ceases to be a path to elite roles for the average student, there will always be some institutions-either certain universities in the country or certain foreign universities-which take on (or continue) the function of elite formation. The secondary schools then screen in several ways: those who will not continue beyond secondary education, those who will go to the run-of-the-mill university, and those who will be in the elite. However, the students who go to the run-of-the-mill university can get a second chance to enter the elite by attending graduate or professional school in one of the elite formation institutions.

At both secondary and university levels, the transformation of the level as a whole from an elite to a socialization-selection orientation still leaves a number of institutions in an elite-formation position. In Mexico, a number of private high schools retain their elite-formation status; in Kenya, the seven national secondary schools; in the United States, the academic track of a number of suburban high schools, the private preparatory schools, and the New York City entrance exam public schools (Bronx Science, Music and Art, etc.); and in Great

Britain, the public schools. At the university level, the same division occurs in those countries which have many universities.

The model outlined here describes changes in the function of schooling as the percentage of the age cohort attending school increases relative to the growth of the economy. Different levels of schooling assume different roles as the expansion of enrollment occurs. The corollary of the relationship between rates of return and the period of educational-economic development shown in Figure 1 [this chapter's Figure 3.1] is the possibility of predicting the pattern of rates of return to investment in various levels of schooling and of predicting the function of each level by observing a country's gross national product per capita, the rate of economic growth, enrollment rates at the different levels and socioeconomic background differences between students at different levels of schooling. (Carnoy, 1972a, pp. 185–186)

I went on to focus on the educational system itself and how it inherently worked to "sort" students in ways that helps higher social class students get to higher levels of schooling. This was an important part of my argument—the allocation of resources by the state to the educational system was key to the impact it had not only on which children got access to schooling but to the "quality" of the schooling received by those pupils in school. I touched here on the inherent social class "sorting" function of schools but would only get to the detail of that part of the equation in other works (see Chapter 4):

Given the present production functions for schools, a very large increase in funds would be necessary to overcome the difference in examination scores between lower-level and middle-level socioeconomic groups. But the production functions can only tell us how to allocate resources more efficiently within a level (or grade) of school, given the values and goals of the school system as they now stand. We can discuss increasing the percentage of poor children who do not drop out of primary (secondary) school or who get into secondary school (university), but in the context of the present school [system], I am discussing poor children who must become more middle class (or urban) and must function in a middle-class child's society. The production function estimates show that under such conditions it is highly likely that even if the poor child finishes a certain grade, he will not be at the same level of competence as the middle-class child. Gearing the school to maximize output in terms of elite group values guarantees that children of elite or sub-elite groups will come out ahead of non-elite children even if the resources devoted to instructing the latter are the same (or somewhat greater) than for children of the elite. In practice of course, resources per pupil are less for the poor, the rural, and blacks, so the production function and the quantity of resources minimize the probability of equal outcomes. (Carnoy, 1972a, pp. 203–204)

Twenty-five years later, some of these ideas worked their way into the empirical social mobility literature. Sociologists such as Adrian Raftery and Michael Hout (1993) and Samuel Lucas (2001) made similar arguments in more sophisticated ways concerning the role of education in the relationship between individuals' educational attainment and their social class and academic ability. Another appealing aspect for me about this 1972 chapter, hidden away in an impressive but practically invisible compendium about education and development in Latin America, was that in the 1990s, when educational systems around the world had expanded sufficiently to test my model, it proved empirically correct (Carnoy, 1995a).[3] It could easily be argued that my attempts to "prove" my thesis regarding the behavior of rates of return over time were crude, but I had implicitly applied Noah and Eckstein's (1969) idea that observation and data would lead to a new theory or at least to a challenge of a prevailing theory. Having estimated rates of return in Kenya that did not fit the predicted declining marginal returns to education and observed downward substitution in Mexico, I was inspired to develop an alternative explanation for the contradictory evidence coming from Mexico and Kenya.

Indeed, the implications for what I found about education systems from comparing the two country's results were much greater than just raising questions about patterns of rates of return over time. I called the 1972 article in Thomas LaBelle's compendium "The Political Economy of Education" for good reason: rates of return reflected educational policies and politics as much as labor-market conditions. Thus, it was very important to use different countries' patterns of rates of return as a starting point to delve into what explained these policies and politics. This realization profoundly affected my later work, particularly on theories of the state and education. A hint of what was to come in that later work appeared in my analysis in the last section on "educational planning," which is the functionalist approach taken by the international agencies then and to this day that still forms an important part of the "development education" strand of comparative education:

The large expansion of education promoted by the social-demand approach tends to be rhetorically acceptable to everyone, especially when applied to the primary level. State capitalist elites are willing to increase the average level of education continuously as long as the education system guarantees their children a better chance of attaining the high-level bureaucracy or technocracy [jobs] than the children of non-functionaries. In a private enterprise economy, the real friends of the social-demand approach are "progressive" industrialists who benefit from their ownership of physical capital when there is a large increase in the educated labor force. The approach rationalizes the expansion of schooling even with low rates of return to investment in schooling on the grounds of significant external economies accruing to a greater stock of education in the labor force. It is implied that the externalities accrue to those taking education through better networks of communication or the teaching capabilities of more efficient co-workers. In most countries, however, these possible externalities are overshadowed by the direct nonpecuniary costs of disillusionment of the unemployed educated. The "externalities" referred to by the social-demand approach probably mean the direct increase in the return to owners of physical capital from a more educated labor force. (Carnoy, 1972a, p. 209)

SOME BRIEF REFLECTIONS ON
RATE-OF-RETURN ANALYSIS

There is another important point to make here. Beginning in the 1980s, some scholars challenged the empirical accuracy of most rate-of-return analyses (Bennell, 1996a, 1996b); others argued that human capital theory's underlying assumptions about labor and education markets are inherently biased toward justifying "neoliberal" social policies (Klees, 2008). More recently, Klees (2016) wrote a longer and more detailed analysis questioning human capital theory and rates of return in the same vein. I believe that these critiques are largely valid. However, contrary to the conclusion reached by the strongest critics of rates of return, such as Klees, that the methodology is analytically unsound and prejudiced, and so should be totally rejected, I believed back in the 1970s, and still do, that we need to separate critiques of the underlying dominant neoclassical theory of human capital, as expressed in most writings on the subject and used in "development education" by international agencies, from the concept of human capital as an important form of capital that contributes to economic growth and helps explain how educational systems function across societies with different political economic systems.

In that same vein, rates of return are simply measures of the economic value of education that can reflect very different economic theories of the relation of schooling and training to labor markets, and different views of how labor market function, including views on their imperfections. Reasonably careful rate-of-return studies over time in a country combined with other information about education (e.g., enrollment and graduation rates over time) can be useful. Their utility is not as the prescriptive tool for educational investment used in World Bank policy papers or as a predictor of economic growth. Rather, their value is as one of a series of measures that describe patterns of change in school systems and labor markets and to help us understand what is driving those patterns of change. Rates of return provide a descriptor of how those with different levels of schooling and training and those of different gender, race, and social class with different levels of schooling are paid in a society and what the incentives are for those different groups to invest in different levels of schooling.

In 2015, at the annual meeting of the Comparative and International Education Society, Najeeb Shafiq, an economics of education professor at the University of Pittsburgh, organized a panel in which I and George Psacharopoulos, the undisputed champion of neoliberal rate-of-return analysis, would debate the pros and cons of rate-of-return analysis. The debate was entertaining, but to the surprise, perhaps, of those present, I did not focus on disputing the value of rate of return as an analytical tool in comparative education. Rather, I argued—persuasively, I think—that "in the right critical hands" estimating national rates of return over time and comparing such estimates between nations could provide a wealth of information about those countries' broader educational and labor market phenomena.

Thus, I continue to use rates of return as such a tool, and almost every time I do so, I learn something new.[4] Yet to learn this new thing, the rates need to be seen more as a way to look into market imperfections and to assess implicit government economic and social distributional policies than as a way to show how individuals and governments should allocate educational resources on the basis of such estimates. The other takeaway—and here I completely agree with the many critics of the dominant neoclassical theory of human capital—is that the theory is very flawed, especially in assuming that the value of education is neutrally determined in a free market and that educational decisions are the product of individuals making free choices in an educational system that serves all groups in society fairly and equally. This would be just as true if the operation of the system were highly privatized, as the Chilean system shows. It is no accident that Chile remains one of the most unequal societies in the world, and its educational system one of the world's most socially stratified.

SUMMING UP

Human capital theory had a great impact on international comparative education over the past six decades. Perhaps the most important effect was that it brought economists and economic analysis into the economics of education and into comparative education as a permanent fixture—even, it could be argued, as a dominant force. For better or worse, education as an investment and as a factor in economic growth is now ingrained into the way we think about education comparatively and internationally. As far as the critical views some economists developed of human capital theory and of related market theories of educational production and choice, these were certainly very influential in the comparative education community but hardly touched the comparative work done by international agencies. Despite considerable empirical evidence to the contrary, these agencies continued to assume that state educational and financial bureaucracies are neutral, technocratic arbiters of public decision making. In later chapters, the role of international agencies in defining the shape of educational reform are front and center in our discussion of more recent contributions to comparative and international education theory.

I have drawn heavily on my article in Thomas LaBelle's 1972 book *Education and Development in Latin America and the Caribbean*. I highly recommend reading Theodore Schultz's 1963 *The Economic Value of Education*, Gary Becker's *Human Capital Theory* (1964), and Mark Blaug's *An Introduction to the Economics of Education*, a classic published in 1970. Whether or not one agrees with human capital theory, it plays a dominant role in comparative education analysis. Besides its influence on World Bank analyses of education across countries, it is the underlying rationale for motivating nation-states to pay close attention to international test-score rankings, now the most important form of comparative and international education. More about international tests in Chapter 11.

CHAPTER 4

The 1970s
Comparative Education and Modernity

ALEX INKELES ARRIVED at Stanford and SIDEC from Harvard in 1971, and he brought with him the data gathered in an innovative six-country project on "modernity." The project focused on what educators and social scientists today call the "affective" or behavioral skills that children are presumably taught systematically in their families and schools. The main hypothesis of the modernity project, however, was that these "skills" or worldviews or attitudes that shape behavior are learned more indirectly through the social structures in which people live and work; they are not specifically taught in a formal sense. The results of the research, published in 1974 as *Becoming Modern*, showed that although we think of learning as taking place mainly in families and schools, individuals showed about half as large a gain in "modernity" from working one year in a factory or agricultural cooperative as did a student in the same country from a year of schooling.

Because these ideas were so new at the time, they were not immediately absorbed into conceptions of comparative education or economic and social development. Indeed, even though the motivation for the project was to understand the formation of attitudes that were important for economic development, there was political backlash against the modernity scale—the key outcome measure used in the project. Remember, this was still the era of the antiwar and anti-American intervention in Vietnam. Critics argued that the modernity scale was essentially a measure of Western values and behavioral norms and was an attempt to define human progress and development in terms of such norms.

In retrospect, it is fair to say that the critics had a point. At the same time, the criticism overshot the mark and missed the important contribution of *Becoming Modern* to understanding the way education and other social structures contribute to learning. Years later, in the twenty-first century, there is a new focus on the importance of "affective skills" as an output of schooling and as a predictor of future economic success (Heckman et al., 2006; Cunha and Heckman, 2008). There is also an increased awareness that educational systems in different countries may produce very different mixes of cognitive and affective skills (Hulbert, 2007). It is probably time that social scientists and comparative educators revisit *Becoming Modern* and Inkeles's earlier work, "Social Structure and the Socialization of Competence" (1966), to understand whether other social structures, such as workplaces and sports teams, in different nations also produce similar differences in affective skills as do various nations' schools.

At Stanford, Inkeles immediately attracted PhD students to SIDEC. They extended his work to other contexts and made important contributions to comparative education over the next four decades. His research later in the 1970s, 1980s, and 1990s focused mainly on the global convergence of social structures and institutions such as family and schooling (see, e.g., Inkeles and Sirowy, 1983). Chapter 6 discusses the connection of this work with world society theory. World society theorists critiqued Inkeles's views of convergence as functionalist. Inkeles argued that modernity theory represented convergence as a function of new social roles developing in response to the needs of new institutions (e.g., industrial manufacturing). In contrast, world society theory characterized convergence as a response to pervasive ideologies (environments) that permeate all institutions and therefore all ideas of what modernity is.

Modernity theory also focused on the formation of individual beliefs and behavior because of individuals' exposure to "modern" institutional structures and what that meant for the development of society as a whole. That is, modernity theory is based on aggregating the relationship of individual attitudes to institutional structures: "The socio-psychological approach to modernization treats it mainly as a process of change in ways of perceiving, expressing, and valuing. The modern is defined as a mode of individual functioning, a set of dispositions to act in certain ways" (Inkeles and Smith, 1974, p. 16). In contrast, as we shall see, world society theory viewed the formation of individual beliefs as the result of ideological "environments" developed historically on a global scale—individuals, in turn, shaped nation-state "behavior," including the development of institutions (organizations).

Because Alex Inkeles died in 2010, at the age of ninety,[1] I was not able to interview him about his work. But his coauthor of *Becoming Modern*, David H. Smith,[2] was kind enough to provide a detailed history of the international research project that developed modernity theory and gathered extensive data in six countries to test it. In the next section, I combine Smith's recollections recounted to me firsthand (personal communication with David H. Smith, December 2016) about the development of modernity theory and the research for *Becoming Modern* with quotes from the book that fill out Smith's narrative. To make clear which is which, I provide one- or two-sentence introductions to the supporting quotes from the book.

DAVID H. SMITH'S HISTORY OF BECOMING MODERN[3]

"I had the privilege of being the co-author of Inkeles's book, *Becoming Modern* (Harvard University Press, 1974) and of being Associate Director of the underlying research project, begun at Harvard and later completed at Stanford. I had chosen Inkeles as my Faculty Advisor before coming to Harvard as a graduate student in sociology in 1960, mainly because of his work on the topic of personality and social structure (e.g., Inkeles and Levinson, 1954; Inkeles and Levinson, 1969), but also because of his interest in socioeconomic status, as one social structural aspect of societies, and its impact on psychological factors like happiness (Inkeles, 1960).

"As I have written in my posthumous appreciation of his life and scholarship (Smith, 2012), Alex Inkeles had a deep personal interest in psychology and particularly in psychiatry, and had undergone at least two years of psychoanalysis. But he was not a doctrinaire Freudian. He simply appreciated the role of psychology in human behavior, as well as the role of social systems. I did also, and still do.

"Inkeles was seen by many as a social psychologist, not as a usual sociologist, but saw himself as a psycho-sociologist, affirming his professional identity as a sociologist. He was a faculty member in sociology for much of his career, and was a candidate for the presidency of the American Sociological Association twice, but not elected (perhaps because of his being a maverick psycho-sociologist).

"Social psychologists often saw Inkeles as one of their own, such that he was invited to author a chapter in the first *Handbook of Social Psychology* (Lindzey, 1954). That chapter was entitled, "National character: The study of modal personality and sociocultural systems" (Inkeles and Levinson, 1954). A revised version was published in the 1969 edition of the handbook by these two authors.

"Within the category of sociocultural systems, he was particularly interested in how various aspects of *social structure*, rather than culture, affected the behavior of individuals. By social structure he understood social system elements that could be common across such systems/societies, whatever level of socioeconomic development was present. For instance, social structure involved various kinds of organizations (e.g., schools, factories, mass media systems, agricultural cooperatives, etc.) as well as a variety of social roles (e.g., socioeconomic status, gender, age, occupation, religion, associations, etc.). This was quite unusual at his historical time, for then and even now, the various socio-behavioral science academic disciplines tended to act as silos or islands, avoiding cross-disciplinary entanglements.

"Probably based on Inkeles' prior work on the relationship between personality and social structure, the Rockefeller Foundation approached him circa 1960 with a million-dollar grant if he would study the 'noneconomic aspects of economic development.'

"Much prior work had already been done on *economic* aspects of such development, but very little research attention had been given to noneconomic, especially the *psychological* aspects of such development. Alex accepted the challenge, and saw it as a major empirical opportunity to test his basic theory that social structure has crucial impacts on individual psychology. He was able to get some additional grant money from the Ford Foundation, and possibly other funding sources (I was too junior initially to be involved in the funding directly).

"The central organizing thrust of the project was twofold; (1) To identify various psychological factors that seemed to characterize modern individuals vs. traditional agriculturalists (farmers of various scales of ownership and land tilled), and (2) to identify major social structural influences on such individual modernity patterns, referred to as Overall Modernity/OM.

"As we stated in our Introduction [to *Becoming Modern*], '*It seemed to us that there was no more relevant and challenging task for social psychology than to ex-*

plain the process whereby people move from being traditional to becoming mod-
ern personalities. . . . We started, then, with the conviction that men are not born
modern, but are made so by their life experience' (Inkeles and Smith, 1974, p. 5).

"We undertook a massive review of the modernization research literature,
identifying potential elements/themes/variables that might be part of Overall
Modernity/OM, as a theoretical construct. Then we translated these themes/
variables into interview items, leading to a very long (4–8 hour) interview, when
translated into local languages. Chapter 2 of Inkeles and Smith (1974) lists the
most important aspects of Overall Modernity we want to examine."

[Thus, as Smith suggests, the definition of modernity and the list of its most
important aspects can be found in Chapter 2 of *Becoming Modern*, and this is
how modernity is spelled out there:]

From the start, we operated with the assumption that no single quality
could adequately define the modem man. We believed that individual modernity
could be, and generally would be, manifested in a variety of forms and contexts.
In other words, we thought of it as a syndrome or complex, of qualities rather
than as a single trait. An outstanding feature of our approach to defining the
modern man was, therefore, the development of a long list of themes each of
which we felt might reasonably be reflected in the attitudes, values, and behavior of the modern man. Each theme was assigned a pair of code letters, such as
EF for efficacy, and each question carried such code letters before its number
to indicate the dimension it was assumed to measure. Eventually we nominated
twenty-four dimensions of individual modernity for consideration as part of
the syndrome. These constitute the main themes we eventually built into our
measures of the modern man.

Although each theme was expected to make its case on its own merits, we
did not come upon them as completely independent, unrelated entities. Rather,
they were selected more or less as sets, each representing a different perspective or organizing principle. As it turned out, the distinctions we initially made
among these sets did not consistently shape the subsequent analysis presented in
this book. (Inkeles and Smith, 1974, p. 17)

"[The themes] included openness to new experience, social change readiness,
diversity of opinions, information about the world, punctual time orientation,

efficacy (sense of internal control vs. fate), tendency to plan and value planning, trust in others or calculability, valuing of technical skill, higher educational and occupational aspirations (for self and children), respect for others' dignity/ feelings, and understanding production. A second set of topical themes included weaker extended family ties, favoring more rights for women, favoring birth control, greater secularism (vs. religiosity), less reverence/respect for the aged, more interest in politics, more confidence in mass media, favoring consumerism, favoring a more open social class system, and greater commitment to one's job/occupation (e.g., factory work vs. agricultural work).In addition, there were several themes dealing with behavior, such as political activity, consumption behavior, religious activity, family behavior, verbal fluency, etc.

"Table 2-1 of Inkeles and Smith (1974, p. 34) lists 37 key OM themes we measured in our interviews. We created indices of the various themes to the extent feasible. Then, using Principal Components factor analyses, we assessed the degree to which these many themes of OM held together empirically in a general OM factor (ibid., Chapter 6). A general factor was found for OM in each of our six country's samples, and OM indices of varying lengths were constructed [Smith and Inkeles, 1966]. The key point was that the Overall Modernity concept/construct was clearly valid in all six nations in our data. Hence, it made empirical sense to try to explain these various reliable OM indices."

[Despite its validity in all six countries, however, Inkeles and Smith anticipated in the book that their concept of modernity could easily be confused with "European standards of value," and that the study could be criticized for imposing this set of values on the individuals they were interviewing in developing countries:]

In formulating our conception of individual modernity we wished to avoid blindly imposing European standards of value upon the citizens of developing countries. To do so would have been not only arrogant, but also totally inappropriate for a cross-cultural study done simultaneously in Asia, Africa, and South America. Yet it did not seem to be possible, or even meaningful, to think of a "value-free" measure of individual modernity.

[And s]ince industrialism first arose and received its widest diffusion in the countries loosely classified as capitalist, there was in this some risk that our modern man might be cast too much in the image of "capitalist" man. We felt we could reasonably well guard against this tendency, however, because the senior author of this study had spent some twenty-five years in research on the social structure and the people of the Soviet Union. By drawing on this experience he was able to identify modern personal qualities of more general significance, that is, those which were equally important to effective functioning of both capitalist and socialist societies. (Inkeles and Smith, 1974, p. 18)

"We also reviewed the literature to identify potential factors/variables that might explain Overall Modernity/OM. As control variables, we measured such demographic factors as 'age, religion, ethnic membership, and rural origin' (Inkeles and Smith, 1974, p. 8). But our theory of the social structural influences on OM led us to emphasize particularly work experiences, hypothesizing that the factory was a kind of school for modernity. 'We believed that employment in complex, rationalized, technocratic, and even bureaucratic organizations has particular capabilities to change men so that they move from the more traditional to the more modern pole in their attitudes, values, and behavior' (ibid., p. 6)."

[Inkeles and Smith's focus on the "factory" as the symbol simultaneously of industrialization and modernity is a key element of their study. They saw the factory as an institution whose very structure made those who worked there internalize modern values because those values were consistent with productive efficiency in the factory setting:]

We will encounter little argument, we trust, when we propose that the factory is one of the distinctive institutions of modern society. Industrialization is a very large part of the modernization process; indeed, many would claim it to be the *essential* element. Industrialization, in turn, rests on the factory—the large-scale productive enterprise, bringing together large numbers of men in one work place, systematically ordering their relation one to the other according to rational considerations expressed in formal rules, relying on concentrations of inanimate power and the innovative application of technology, and guided by a hierarchy of authority largely resting on technical skill and administrative competence.

The factory as an institution has no nationality: it is not English or French, or Dutch, or, for that matter, European. It played as great a role in the development of the Soviet Union as it had done earlier in the United states, was as important in the emergence of Japan as it had been in the Rise of Great Britain. The factory does not inherently violate the important taboos of any religious group, major or minor. No general proscriptions against entering or working in such a place are posed by the Islamic, Hindu, or Buddhist religions, and representatives of all these persuasions have found it easy to take up work in factories. We *proposed, then, to classify as modern those personal qualities which are likely to be inculcated by participation in large-scale modern productive enterprises such as the factory, and, perhaps more critical, which may be required of the workers and the staff if the factory is to operate efficiently and effectively.*

There are, of course, many ways of looking at the factory as an institution. We do not claim that our list of qualities and requirements of factory life is exhaustive or even definitive. In fact, we narrowed the range of the themes we would consider by focusing particularly on those features of factory organization which we assumed would be notable to and would most influence a naïve worker fresh from the countryside. This was justified by our special interest in the factory as a learning setting, as a school, if you will, in new ways of arranging things, of thinking, and of feeling which contrast markedly with the traditional village. In any event, we assumed that each of the themes we selected was a salient feature of the factory, and one likely to be influential in shaping men's response to their environment. (Inkeles and Smith, 1974, pp. 18–19)

"Based on prior modernization research, we naturally included formal education as a social structural influence. We also hypothesized that urban experiences (the city as a social structural factor) might have a distinctive influence on rural origin agriculturalists. Further, we included mass media exposure as such a potential influence. Our multivariate empirical findings strongly supported our theory of modernizing experiences (Smith and Inkeles, 1975). 'The multiple correlation between our small set of basic explanatory variables and individual modernity scores went as high as 0.79' (Inkeles and Smith, 1974, p. 7). We state (ibid., p. 7): 'Of the men fully exposed to the institutions our theory designated as modernizing, some 76 percent scored as modern, whereas among those least under the influence of such institutions only about 2 percent achieved modern scores on our scales.' Put another way, we found that two years of factory experience had the same modernizing influence as one year of formal education. Nobody had ever shown this before in large samples of agriculturalists, urban non-industrial workers, and factory workers, especially in data gathered with the same careful, comparable methodology in six modernizing nations from various world regions.

"Broadly interpreting *personality* as the total psychological system of an individual, *Becoming Modern* was able to demonstrate the validity of the Inkeles and Levinson's (1954, 1969) general theory of social structure and personality when applied to individual psycho-social modernization. Cultural values likely also play some role in becoming a modern person, as suggested by Hofstede and McCrae (2004), who showed that cultural factors are related to modal personality in many societies. But social structural influences dominate in our modernization research on men in India, Bangladesh, Chile, Argentina, Nigeria, and Israel. We studied only men because, at this historical time period, there were very few women in factories. Our theory suggests that the modernity of women is similarly influenced by our main set of social structural factors.

"Again, from my memoir of his life (Smith, 2012): One of the greatest lessons I learned from working with Alex was the power of theory and persistence. During the early process of analyzing the vast amount of HUPSCAD data back in Cambridge, we came to a point at which five of the six nations demonstrated Alex's theory about the impact of factories in making their participants more modern in terms of their values and traits—sense of efficacy, trust, punctuality, high aspirations, tendency to plan, et cetera. We developed an index of 'Overall Modernity' (the OM Scale) that measured the current level of 'psychological modernity' of our respondents.

"Chile was the problem. In the other five nations—Nigeria, Israel, India, Argentina, and Pakistan (at that time, East Pakistan, now Bangladesh)—length of factory experience correlated significantly with Overall Modernity. But in Chile, the relationship was weak and insignificant. We checked and rechecked everything we could think of—everything *I* could think of. Nearly anyone else but Alex would have given up and just said, 'Well, Chile is an exception.'

"*Not Alex*. He believed in his theory and in the quality of our methodology, and he was very persistent. He sent us back to every single bit of relevant raw data on the thousand interview schedules for Chile. It took many person-months of effort. That process seemed to be a "wild goose chase" to the rest of the project staff, but we trusted Alex and did the tedious checking.

"Eventually, we found the problem. It was a *single* inaccurate number for *one* respondent on *one* variable. But it was an absolutely crucial error. For one Chilean factory worker, the months of factory experience were entered as "999." When this case was combined with the other 999 respondents in our sample (actually 1,018, as I recall), the Pearson correlation was quite distorted, reducing substantially the apparent correlation of factory experience with modernity in Chile. When this one number for one case was corrected, the key correlation for Chile became strong and statistically significant, as in the other five nations.

"How could one erroneous case in a thousand have had such a distorting effect? There were three key reasons: (1) The error occurred on the single most crucial explanatory variable in our study, factory experience; (2) Factory experience was measured by only one interview item, so there were no other items measuring factory experience to counteract the error; (3) Pearson correlations have the mathematical property of being strongly affected by a single number that is very far from the mean (average) of its distribution. The error for that one case in Chile was indeed very far out, in terms of standard deviations.

"The general topic of personality and social structure continues to attract attention from social psychologists (McLeod and Lively, 2006; Schnittker, 2013), but not from many sociologists. In the last half of the 20th century, even social psychologists neglected sociology (Oishi, Kesebir, and Snyder, 2009). However, my own career as a psycho-sociologist has persistently demonstrated the explanatory value of the personality and social structure approach in studying volunteering (e.g., Smith, 1994; Smith, Stebbins, and Grotz, 2016)." (Correspondence with David Smith, December 2016)

David Smith's detailed description of *Becoming Modern* ends here. It is important for those of us interested in comparative education to assess this work's contribution to our field and to relate it to the role of education in society more broadly. This is what I try to do in the rest of this chapter.

MODERNITY AS A CONSTRUCT

The major contributions of Inkeles and Smith's modernity were the detailed list and descriptions of the attributes of modern men (the study focused on men) and the authors' translation of those largely abstract conceptions into questions intended to measure the degree to which individuals held "modern" beliefs. As noted, they nominated twenty-four dimensions of individual modernity that defined the "modern man."

The discussion of these dimensions is more than just the basis for constructing a modernity index. The notion of modern man or modernity and its components constitutes a definition of changing humans' beliefs and understanding of time, space, and their relation to nature, power, and other humans. In listing the various dimensions, *Becoming Modern* categorized the way societies were changing, largely because of industrialization and urbanization, and, in some sense, by using the word "modern," how societies should change.

As mentioned earlier, modernity theory faced resistance on several fronts when it was published. Inkeles and Smith certainly anticipated the critique that their modernity scale fundamentally represented European (Western) values and norms and ranked those above "traditional" values: "In formulating our conception of individual modernity we wished to avoid blindly imposing European standards of value upon the citizens of developing countries. . . . Our solution to the problem was to derive our list of modern *personal* qualities from the presumed requirements of daily living in a modern and complex *society*, and, in particular, from the demands made on a worker or staff member in a modern industrial establishment" (Inkeles and Smith, 1974, p. 18).

Even so, it was extremely difficult to disassociate the modernity scale from a set of values identified with the European enlightenment and long held up by nineteenth- and twentieth-century imperial powers as "superior" to precapitalist values, especially in terms of economic development and a specific concept of progress. The notion of a factory as the defining context of modernity was also controversial because it could be argued that many of the themes defining modernity listed by Inkeles and Smith developed in Europe well before factories were common organizations. True, *Becoming Modern* focused on individual attitudes, not overall societies, although for a society to be "modern," its members, would, on average, have to hold modern attitudes—they would need to be open to change, look to the present and future rather than the past, be willing to make changes to become better off, be aware and open to diverse opinions, sense that they can control their environment rather than be controlled by it, and so on. At least some of these ways of thinking are associated with Western-style democracies and with certain definitions of progress and morality. This is where Inkeles and Smith ran up against the argument that their measures were culturally biased. Yet at least in economic terms—looking to the future, seeking a better life, being willing to make changes to be economically or physically better off and to feel that one can make those changes—these are attitudes that have, for better or worse, been "voluntarily" adopted by most younger people everywhere in the world when given a chance. The clearest examples of this are the worldwide increase in demand for Western schooling and the massive migration from rural areas to cities.

In a later chapter, I show how other scholars took up the general theme of modernity as an ideological construct (beliefs and values) but rejected the notion that these beliefs and values were primarily the result of industrialization—of the organization of work in factories and factorylike institutions. A notion of modernity very similar to that detailed by Inkeles and Smith, but defining modernity as an ideal associated with the legitimacy of the nation-state, became the foundation of world society theory.[4]

Two of the most controversial aspects of modernity, as articulated in *Becoming Modern,* are the "threats" it poses to family-kinship ties and to religion. Kinship ties and religion are considered valuable supports for individuals, especially in economic terms (kinship) and in moral terms (especially religion). For example, the authors write: "We concluded that there was certainly some truth to the frequent assertion that increasing urbanism and industrialism tended to diminish the vigor of extended kinship relations. We had little reason to doubt that when urbanism increased the physical distance between kin, and industrial employment decreased their economic dependence, the strength of kinship ties as manifested in common residence, frequent visiting, and mutual help in work would decline" (Inkeles and Smith, 1974, p. 26). Furthermore, "many students of the subject argue rather vigorously that the individual's adherence both to fundamental doctrine of his traditional religion and to the religious ritual and practice it requires of him will inevitably be undermined by urban living, industrial experience, and scientific education" (Inkeles and Smith, 1974, p. 27).

The fact that the factory, industrialization, and urbanization would tear down these two "foundations of moral behavior" and psychological support could mean that it is rational for societies to oppose modern beliefs of tolerance for individualism, of the value of indiscriminate innovation and change, and even of political democracy when it might lead to increased "immoral" behavior or reduced influence of family hierarchies.

Inkeles and Smith questioned both of these commonly held notions and argued that it might be possible that living in urban, industrialized contexts allows for greater possibilities for religious observance, and that, where kinship ties might decline, families as such might strengthen, particularly the relationship between husband and wife. Given the steady decline of religious observance in modern industrial and postindustrial societies, it is difficult to make the case that modernity—especially the way that Inkeles and Smith define it—has not cut sharply into institutionalized religions. However, although they did not explicitly discuss this point, it is possible that organized religions adapt to the changing values of their potential adherents to "modernize" and to make themselves more attractive to individuals with modern beliefs and values. Inkeles and Smith discuss the rise of Protestantism as it split off from still-feudal Catholicism (well before factories appeared in Europe), but, with some delay, all religions have modernized, even as ultra-traditional versions of each have held on to resist change, even violently, and, in some cases, using the nation-state to enforce traditional values.

The case for the possible beneficial effects of modernization on family ties may be easier to make, particularly in terms of the increase in women's rights unleashed initially in the industrial era and accelerated in postindustrial societies and the effect of greater equality for women on the nature of the family. One might argue that a significant proportion of families has always been dysfunctional—always a highly imperfect source of producing either traditional morality or modern efficacy—and that the ties between religion and the family could be harmful to modernity or spawn just the right amount of resistance and rebellion and support for its members so that modernity benefited from these ostensible traditional institutions.

Inkeles and Smith's analysis of education provides numerous insights into the educational system and its relationship to shaping individuals' values and beliefs. They are concerned mainly with the statistical correlation between their modernity scale and the number of years an individual went to school, a correlation that continued to play a dominant role in world society theory, but in the opposite direction—the ideology of modernity as a driving force behind the expansion of schooling. In addition to this strong association between schooling and modern values, Inkeles and Smith also introduced an important discussion about how schooling implicitly developed modern values and beliefs in young people even as formal education did not explicitly teach students to be modern.

The thesis proposed in *Becoming Modern* is that individuals acquire modern values and beliefs in certain institutional settings characterized by certain organizational characteristics. Formal education, or schooling, is one of those settings: "In large-scale complex societies no attribute of the person predicts his attitudes, values, and behavior more consistently or more powerfully than the amount of schooling he has received. . . . In the light of this experience we considered it an essential test of the soundness both of our conception of individual modernity and of OM as a scale that scores on it be significantly related to measures of education" (Inkeles and Smith, 1974, p. 133).

Inkeles and Smith found a high correlation in each of the six countries where they conducted their survey—Argentina, Chile, East Pakistan (Bangladesh), India, Israel, and Nigeria—even though the average level of education varied across several of these countries in the early 1970s but was generally very low: "Each step up the education ladder generally brought with it fairly regular and substantial increment in the proportion of modern men. Moreover, this tendency was consistently manifested in each country, regardless of the segment of the educational range it represented" (Inkeles and Smith, p. 134). Even when other variables that could also explain individual modernity, such as the early socialization factors of father's education, rural origin, and ethnicity, plus adult experiences, such as factory experience, mass-media contact, living standards, urbanism of residence, and modernity of workplace, were included as controls, years of schooling continued to be robustly correlated with the modernity scale, with a median correlation of 0.40: "The fact that education so well survived a quite rigorous process of partial correlation also tells us that it was, in its own right, a very powerful *direct* and independent factor in determining men's modernity" (Inkeles and Smith, 1974, p. 136).

Thus, *Becoming Modern* explicitly argued that more years of schooling was a causal factor in increasing individuals' modernity in a broad range of developing societies and implicitly argued that as access to schooling expanded in developing societies, they would become increasingly modern—that is, the people living in those societies would hold the values and beliefs associated with modernity. The parallel with human capital theory is striking: just as economists in the 1960s saw in education a source of increased labor productivity, modernity theory argued that schooling also produced modern values that contributed to a modern society, characterized by increased secularism, greater interest in progress and change, increased tolerance of others not like themselves, and greater willingness to critique and to take criticism—that is, social and political "skills" associated with more democratic and "effectively" governed nations.

Inkeles and Smith argued that their modernity scale captured schooling's contribution to this change in values, and therefore an individual's social capacity: "To give the most concrete form to our measure of the effectiveness of education, we computed the number of points on the OM scale a man gained for every additional year in school. In effect, this treated the OM scale as if it were an achievement test of the kind commonly used to assess progress in school. Indeed, the OM scale can be viewed as measuring some kind of social capacity or skill" (1974, pp. 137–138). Without controlling for other factors, it appeared that each year of schooling produced 4 points on the modernity scale, and when controlling for other factors that could increase modernity, the gain per year of school was about 2 points: "Just as people presumably improved their scores on arithmetic and vocabulary tests for each year in school, just so did our men improve their overall modernity score by approximately 2 points per year of schooling" (Inkeles and Smith, 1974, p. 138).

This notion that schooling affects attitudes and values associated with modernity has great importance for comparative and international education. It has always had some importance in social science research on education but has been increasingly overshadowed by the focus on academic achievement. Yet in recent years, with more research on the affective skills learned in schools—behavior, discipline, values and norms—that seem to be as or more important than mathematics and language skills measured by achievement tests (Heckman et al., 2006; Duckworth, 2016), analyses of the outputs of education have come full circle. Many of the dimensions of the modernity index are associated with the social skills needed to negotiate complex organizations, to network effectively, and to be more productive in any situations requiring social interactions.

The other aspect of Inkeles and Smith's analysis that had impact on comparative and international educators was their explanation for why schooling produced greater modernity. They argued persuasively that the school curriculum, other than verbal fluency, had little to do with the dimensions of modernity composing their index:

One could not account for the higher OM scores of better-educated men on the grounds that the formal curriculum of the school *directly* prepared for high performance on our test of modernity. Even when our measure of modernity excluded any test of information or verbal fluency, the fields in which the formal curriculum specializes, education still showed as a substantial independent cause of individual modernity. . . . Indeed, we know of no curriculum which provides significant *formal* instruction in how to join public organizations, to be open to new experience, to value birth control, or to develop a sense of personal efficacy, to name but a few of the themes measured by the OM scale. Since the men who received more education displayed these qualities in greater degree, there must have been a good deal of learning in the school *incidental* to the curriculum and to formal instruction in academic subjects. As children in school these men not only learned geography and acquired skills in reading and arithmetic they evidently also learned new attitudes and values, and developed new dispositions to act, whose full significance would not be manifest until they were adults. (Inkeles and Smith, 1974, pp. 139–140)

The explanation for this outcome, they went on, was that the school as an organization inculcated students with behavior and other aspects of socialization that were associated with or laid the groundwork for modern values in adulthood:

In our view, the school is not only a place for teaching; it is, inevitably, a setting for the more general socialization of the child. The school modernizes through a number of processes other than formal instruction in academic subjects. These are: *reward and punishment, modeling, exemplification,* and *generalization.* These learning processes are not unique to the school. They occur in other formal organizations, and also in informal settings such as the family or the play group. However, the special nature of any organization gives distinctive form and content to the socialization process which goes on within it. (Inkeles and Smith, 1974, p. 140)

Inkeles and Smith illustrate each of these processes and provide a strong warning that not all schools and teachers provide the same degree of successful socialization that leads to modern beliefs and behavior:

The flow of work in the classroom may be chaotic, the school day subject to constant disruption, the annual schedule erratic, and the very continuance of the school uncertain. Such a school will not effectively exemplify the virtues of planning and will provide little training in developing fixed schedules. Moreover, either the conditions of a pupil's life outside, or the nature of the school itself, may lead his school experience to be one of continuous frustration, failure, and rejection. Insofar as this pupil generalizes from his school experience, therefore, it will hardly be by way of feeling more efficacious or more open to new experience. (Inkeles and Smith, 1974, p. 143)

Nevertheless, as a whole, schools apparently do have a socialization effect on students that is related to adult modernity, at least as measured by Inkeles and Smith's scale:

Our data show unambiguously that the schools in each of our six developing countries, flawed as they undoubtedly were, clearly had a substantial effect on the pupils exposed to their influence. Their pupils did learn. Furthermore, they learned more than reading, writing, and figuring. Our tests show that they also learned values, attitudes, and ways of behaving highly relevant to their personal development and to the future of their countries. Those who had been in school longer were not only better informed and verbally more fluent. They had a different sense of time, and a stronger sense of personal and social efficacy; participated more actively in communal affairs; were more open to new ideas, new experience, and new people; interacted differently with others, and showed more concern for subordinates and minorities. They valued science more, accepted change more readily, and were more prepared to limit the number of children they would have. In short, by virtue of having had more formal schooling, their personal character was decidedly more modern. (Inkeles and Smith, 1974, p. 143)

This analysis was considered by others, such as John Meyer, Francisco Ramirez, and their Stanford colleagues, as a classic example of functionalism. I discuss their alternative take on modernity and schooling in a later chapter—their main objection was that the ideology of modernization shapes organizations rather than organizations "creating" modern values. Despite this objection, if we abstract from the "origins" of what the school should look like and do, Inkeles and Smith's claim that the organization of the school shapes important aspects of students' behavior and social skills makes a lot of sense.

In the 1980s, Jean Anyon (1980) and I and Henry Levin (1985) took versions of Inkeles and Smith's analysis to suggest that there could be differential socialization in public schools serving youth from different social class groups. This differential socialization was not necessarily coercive but conditioned by the experience of parents and the convenient agreement of teachers and schools on the values and norms desired by parents for their children. Similarly, the voucher and charter school movements create even more possibilities for diverse socialization by expanding the number of privately run schools offering various academic and socialization options.

CHAPTER 5

The 1970s

Colonialism, Neocolonialism, and Comparative Education

THE ACADEMIC ATMOSPHERE in the 1960s and early 1970s in the United States and other developed countries was deeply influenced by the Cold War and how it turned the US away from democratic ideals and into the protector of US corporate interests globally. Americans had fought to liberate Europe and Asia from authoritarian, militaristic fascism, so the reaction of most of the World War II generation to Soviet communism is completely understandable. Nevertheless, as the US postwar idealism that reconstructed Europe and formalized American democratic institutions in Germany and Japan morphed into a broader effort to spread these institutions (and US influence) into the former European colonies and into Asia and Latin America more generally, American ideals rapidly turned into a geopolitical conflict with the Soviet Union and communism, also involved in spreading its ideology into the same regions. The US, for all its "idealism," sided with "its" dictators against any movement that seemed to conflict with US economic interests. By the early 1950s, the die had been cast in China, Guatemala, Iran, and Indochina (Barnet, 1968).

The US war in Vietnam was the logical outcome of these policies. Whereas in a divided Korea, the US had mobilized the United Nations to combat an invasion into the south from the north, in Vietnam, the objectives of intervening in a postcolonial civil war were much less clear. By the mid-1960s, a growing movement had formed against a Cold War American neocolonialism of the previous two decades that had lost its idealistic roots. This was a time of rebellion in the US, Europe, and Japan, and, of course, in various places in the developing world, including Indochina. But the protest movements were contradictory. At the same time as youth in Eastern Europe were rebelling against Soviet occupation and hard-line communist authoritarianism, US, Western European, and Japanese students—in their anticolonial fervor—supported idealized communist revolutions in Asia and Latin America that would end up being as authoritarian as their Soviet and Chinese predecessors.

The late 1950s and 1960s were also marked by a surge of neo-Marxist analyses of economic and social development (Baran, 1957) in what were then called "Third World" countries, particularly in Latin America (Frank, 1967; Cardoso and Faletto, 1979; Dos Santos, 1970) and Africa (Amin, 1957, 1974; Fanon, 1963; Memmi, 1965). This literature was not widely read in schools of education, but it was filtering into the civil rights and antiwar movements in US universities. The analyses spurred a wave of critical writing that viewed education as part and parcel of "capitalist reproduction" in the developed countries, and in developing countries, as rooted in the neocolonialist project of American capitalism's post–World War II expansion. Writers in the US such as Paul Goodman, Charles Silberman, Jonathan Kozol, and Marcus Raskin; in France, Christian Baudelot and Roger Establet, and in Latin America, Paulo Freire, developed a new explanation for why the idealized vision of education created by Horace Mann, Jules Ferry, John Dewey, Domingo Sarmiento, and Anísio Teixeira was not likely to be realized without radical changes in capitalist society, and even more so in dependent capitalist societies.

As part of my research at the Brookings Institution in the mid-1960s, I traveled often to Latin America, and I was also deeply involved in a nonradical, middle-class version of the anti–Vietnam War movement in Washington, DC, called Concerned Citizens for Peace. In 1966, a group of us living and working there decided to organize door-to-door, precinct-by-precinct in DC, getting people out to marches and preparing for the 1968 elections. I ended up as the head organizer of Robert Kennedy's DC primary campaign, and then went to California to work in the Los Angeles headquarters on his primary campaign there. The Latin American experience, organizing against the war, and my involvement in the tragically ended Kennedy campaign certainly affected my worldview and my scholarly approach to economic development.

Once at Stanford, I quickly joined the many other faculty at Stanford who were engaged in the antiwar effort. I also brought a more critical approach to the economics of education and the economics of development. As I described in Chapter 3, in the introduction to the work I did on rate-of-return analysis, I no longer believed that markets necessarily allocated resources efficiently or "equitably." I had come to think that politics and power mattered a great deal in determining which groups got what, and this reshaped how I thought about education's role in the larger framework of economic and social systems.

Marx's writings became very fashionable in the 1960s, and I read and discussed them extensively with my friends in the antiwar movement. But the books that had the most influence on me at the time were Albert Memmi's *The Colonizer and the Colonized* (1965) and my close friend Marcus Raskin's *Being and Doing* (1971). Memmi was a psychoanalyst and Raskin, a legal scholar and government official turned US foreign policy and social critic. Neither was a social scientist, and they were influenced far more by the existentialist philosophy of Jean-Paul Sartre, in Memmi's case, and by the antinuclear and peace movements, in Raskin's, than by the economic philosophy of Karl Marx. Memmi's work touched me because he analyzed the colonial condition in a country, Tunisia, which I had visited several times, and where I had just spent a month studying high school education. Its appeal also lay in the hold that Sartre's writings had had on me in college. Yet beyond that, Memmi wrote from his own personal position of a Tunisian Jew growing up "between" the French colonizer and the colonized Arabs—the very position my parents had been in as Jews in Poland between the Polish aristocracy and bourgeoisie and the mass of Polish peasantry and workers in the years before World War II.

Raskin's work was inspiring because it was rooted in a humanistic anti–Cold War militarism—a search for fundamental human rights in highly bureaucratized society—at a time, the 1960s, when the "military-industrial" complexes in the US and the Soviet Union placed the world under threat of a nuclear holocaust. Part of the problem for Raskin was educational systems that taught young people to accept their fate in such a world as "natural" and "logical." He characterized these educational systems as "channeling colonies":

On all levels in the school, whether public or private, progressive or traditional, the young person is expected to learn the *basic* economic and political lessons [that] the modern nation-state teaches and requires so that it may remain authoritarian and pyramidal. The school thus serves as the training instrument for the state. The substance of what is learned—Plato, zoology, *Silas Marner*, quadratics, woodwork, and music appreciation—is less indelible in the young person's mind than other lessons which are taught and internalized. The student is taught and usually learns the importance of identification papers, records, tardy slips, no whispering to your neighbor, the acceptable dress, signatures, forms, and tests. He comes to learn and respect the idea that in the colonized society authority dictates and individuals internalize the notion that papers are more important than the person himself. (Raskin, in Carnoy, 1972b, p. 25)

In the winter quarter of 1972, Fernando Henrique Cardoso, a brilliant Brazilian sociologist, came to Stanford as a visiting professor. With assistance from the Ford Foundation, a group of us organized a seminar around his visit. The seminar was run by faculty and students interested in Latin America and we self-published a set of essays—*The Structure of Dependency*—that we distributed around Stanford and to colleagues in other universities. The papers challenged traditional thinking about economic development, using many of Cardoso's ideas about dependency. Cardoso was an intellectual force, and the discussion in the seminar added to the influence of Memmi's and Raskin's work. All this pushed me to think about an alternative theory for comparing the evolution of educational systems.

That same year, I happened upon a book by Don Adams and Robert Bjork, *Education in Developing Areas* (1969). It made the argument, among many others in the broad sweep of their analysis, that although British colonialism in India (and Africa) had had many negative effects on the colonized populations, British education had at least created the positive intellectual conditions for postcolonial democracy and social modernization. I found this argument strange. Why would British colonial education produce outcomes that were contrary to the clearly expressed intent of British colonialism to subjugate Indians to British economic and political interests? As I read more about India and Indian education under the British, I found that Adams and Bjork's notion that Western education inherently developed democratic and critical thinking independent of the British colonial context did not hold up to scrutiny.

Rather, I concluded, colonial education was structured to reproduce the colonizer's power over the colonized, and in postcolonial situations, to reproduce the power of the powerful over the less powerful. Furthermore, dependency theory suggested that direct colonialism, where the "core" European powers militarily controlled the "periphery" territory, was not required for the core to shape institutions in the periphery. I reasoned that even in "independent" nineteenth- and twentieth-century Latin America, for example, the situationally dependent position of each Latin American country in the world economic system enabled core elites and governments to exert power over periphery elites and the way periphery elites organized themselves politically to maintain their local power. This in turn affected the shape of education in periphery countries.

The notions of core and periphery emerged from the dependency literature and, by the early 1970s, had been also formalized by Immanuel Wallerstein (1974) into world systems theory. I raise this point because material relations of capitalist production that were the basis of dependency and world systems theory were key to my understanding of how education developed in different nation-states and within nation-states. In other words, how various groups were situated within the world capitalist system had an important impact on how they would participate in access to knowledge and also interpret and use the knowledge they did acquire. There were important intellectual reactions to this "dependency" understanding of comparative education—namely world society or world culture theory—as I discuss in the next chapter.

In the period 1972–1974, I focused on two projects that explored alternatives to the prevailing ideology that the modern education system is organized to be an institution of enlightenment and upward mobility. The first was an edited book, *Schooling in a Corporate Society* (1972b). It collected work from eighteen writers who were challenging that ideology, including Paulo Freire, Marcus Raskin, Samuel Bowles, Herbert Gintis, Henry Levin, Michael Reich, and Ivan Illich. It is difficult to imagine, in today's comparative education environment dominated by country rankings on the international tests, the OECD's Programme for

International Student Assessment (PISA) and the Trends in Mathematics and Science Survey (TIMSS), how exciting and rich these critical discussions were and how—between the new empirical work being carried out at the University of Chicago, Inkeles's controversial ideas on education and modernity, and the challenges raised by great intellectuals such as Paulo Freire and Ivan Illich and Samuel Bowles and Herbert Gintis—this created a sort of first golden age of comparative education in the mid-1970s. Ironically, this golden age occurred just as British and US politics began to turn right, engendering the neoliberal wave that swept comparative education in the 1980s.

My ideas in *Schooling in a Corporate Society* and the ideas of other critics writing about education at the time, were that the inequalities observed in education systems in both developed and developing countries were not mainly the result of "inefficiencies" of educational bureaucracies but were built directly into the class and racial reproductive nature of the educational system itself. This implied that educational inequalities largely reflected the inherently unequal nature of capital societies, the degree of inequality of economic and power relations in these societies, and the role that education was assigned in helping to reproduce such inequalities. This conclusion was not warmly embraced by academics arguing that education was fundamentally meritocratic, or if it were not as meritocratic as it should be, this problem could be fixed with better information for students and their parents or more effective educational bureaucracies.

The introduction to *Schooling in a Corporate Society* spelled out my underlying view in the early 1970s:

Throughout the history of educational research . . . educators and, more recently, social scientists, have tacitly assumed that the goal of both socioeconomic and educational systems . . . is the maximization of every individual's potential. This view is consistent with both the concept of education as a liberator of men's minds and with the later idea that the modern, industrial state requires a socially mobile population. . . . These are deeply ingrained beliefs. It is not surprising that those who are successful in any society orient their thinking to praise the system that allowed them to succeed, rather than question or condemn it. . . . Research has therefore assumed away the issues of goals, the institutional structure of schools, and the *reasons* for public education.

Starting from visionary American "ideals," the research has taken as its primary aim to improve the efficiency of *achieving* these ideals. The existence of 'distortions' and inefficiencies in the school system were (and are) taken as impediments to *desirable* objectives. It is these impediments, not the goals of the socioeconomic and educational structures, that are the object past research.

But what if these ideals are *not* the goals of the system? Perhaps the real goal is not that "maximization" of everyone's potential, that only the potential of the few. . . . The American dream of social mobility may become a reality for a limited percentage of low- and middle-income families, while the majority [is] held in place, to a large extent by the school system itself. If these are the goals of the system, "distortions" and inefficiencies as seen by those who assume the objective of the American dream would not necessarily be distortions at all, but rational and efficient parts of the system with very different desired outputs. (Carnoy, 1972b, pp. 1–2)

The second project I undertook, two years later, was *Education as Cultural Imperialism* (1974), which developed a new version of comparative education analysis based on education as an institution whose primary function was to reproduce and shape the existing, complex power relations in colonial and class societies, in the context of Western colonialism, postcolonial imperialism, and nineteenth-century United States. In the book, I analyzed historically how educational systems in India, West Africa, Latin America, and the United States were organized primarily to achieve such reproduction, not social mobility or critical thinking about the nature of the society in which students lived. I argued that the main function of education in unequal colonial-"periphery" or developed-"center" capitalist societies was to reproduce inequality by acting as an institution of "legitimizing" the very inequality that the educational system was supposed to undo by providing the "opportunity" to everyone to succeed.

In *Education as Cultural Imperialism*, I characterized the educational systems designed by colonialist Britain, by dependent Latin American countries' local elites, and by US elites for their own mass educational system, as functionally reproducing colonial and class hierarchies even as the elites "sold" the systems to their subjects or citizenry as intellectually uplifting and contributing to social mobility:

The concept of individual material and moral improvement combined with so-cial mobility—all purportedly due to schooling—is generalized into *national* economic growth and improvement, into nations—through expenditures on schooling—increasing their income per capita, "civilizing" themselves, and raising their status among nations in a competitive, industrializing world.

The legitimization of schooling in this way is particularly important be-cause it is a link between the economic and social structure and the minds of children—the future work force and political participants. We are currently pre-sented with an explanation of schooling's function which implies that in unjust, inequitable, and economically stagnant societies, schooling has provided and continues to provide the means for individual and societal liberation. The for-mal education system—according to this view—acts to offset social inequities and inefficiencies by being an objective selector of intelligent and rational indi-viduals for the highest positions in the social, political, and economic hierarchy.

. . . We argue that this explanation is misleading. Our thesis is that educa-tors, social scientists, and historians have misinterpreted the role of Western schooling in the Third World and in industrialized countries themselves. We ar-gue that far from acting as a liberator, Western formal education came to most countries as part of imperialist domination. It was consistent with the goals of imperialism: the economic and political control of the people in one country by the dominant class in another. The imperial powers attempted, through school-ing, to train the colonized for roles that suited the colonizer. Even within the dominant countries themselves, schooling did not offset social inequities. The educational system was no more just or equal than the economy and society itself—specifically, we argue, because schooling was organized to develop and maintain, in the imperial countries, an inherently inequitable and unjust organi-zation of production and political power. (Carnoy, 1974, pp. 2–3)

Thus, I claimed that the spread of schooling into the African and Asian colonies of European countries, and even into Latin America, which by the early nineteenth century was—except for Brazil and the Guianas—formally independent of direct European colonial control, part and parcel of European and US imperialism, and could not "in *its present form and purpose be separated from the context.* This is not to say that schooling was not affected by the cultures into which it was introduced; however, the effect was small relative to the principal relationships that schooling was designed to promote" (Carnoy, 1974, p. 15). In addition:

The structure of schools, since it came from the metropole, was based in large part on the needs of metropole investors, traders, and culture. As I shall show in later chapters, Western schools were used to develop indigenous elites which served as intermediaries between metropole merchants and plantation labor; they were used to incorporate indigenous peoples into the production of goods necessary for metropole markets; they were used to help change social structures to fit in with European concepts of work and interpersonal relationships; and, within advanced capitalist economies such as the United States, schools were used to fit white workers and, later, disenfranchised minorities into economic and social roles defined by the dominant capitalist class.

Since schooling was brought to non-Europeans as part of empire, and to workers in the metropoles as a function of capitalists' needs, it was integrated into an effort to bring indigenous peoples into imperial/colonial structures. But was the spread of schooling harmful? After all, did not the European teacher and the school built on the European capitalist model transmit European values and norms and begin to transform traditional societies into "modern" ones, ready to industrialize and compete in world markets? In order to accept the interpretation of many Western writers that schooling in the colonial period— which in Asia and Africa lasted until after World War II—contributed to development, we have to accept that imperialism and colonialism were in the long run beneficial to colonized peoples. Even if we are not willing to go that far, we would have to believe that four centuries of colonizing and exploiting Africans, Asians, indigenous Latin Americans, and white European workers themselves was, if not justified, at least *attenuated* by bringing them Western schooling. We would have to be convinced that, despite the negative aspects of imperialism and colonialism, formal schooling enabled the blacks, yellows, browns, and poor whites of the world eventually to emerge from their backwardness and ignorance to join the modern world. (Carnoy, 1974, p. 16)

In writing *Education as Cultural Imperialism*, I faced an intellectual struggle that was shared by my contemporaries. After all, Western education could and did have positive effects on the colonized, the marginalized, and the working class—for example, it served as one of the key institutions of transition from traditional to market economy and this had potential benefits for those locked into roles determined by birth or caste. This is what gave schooling its legitimacy. It could and did provide social mobility for some, and these individuals served as examples of modernity and progress. However, despite these "progressive" aspects of formal education as it was brought to these groups, I and other observers of "modern" educational systems insisted that this was not the most important function of schooling in a colonized, dependent, or even developed-country class society. Because education was rooted in a particular colonial, class, and racial hierarchical structure, it was designed, by its very nature and (more difficult for most readers to accept) intention, to reproduce that structure:

We argue that even though European or U.S. schooling brings people [in low-income, developing countries] *out of* a traditional hierarchy, it also brings them *into* a capitalist hierarchy. While this process has elements of *liberation*, it includes elements of *dependency* and *alienation*. More important, the school does not create the conditions in which the pupil can begin to liberate himself or herself. Rather, the degree of liberation allowed by the school is *controlled* by those who are the most influential in setting goals for the society. In most cases, the modern, capitalistic society [in these developing countries] was/is controlled by foreigners (different culture, history, social structure) either directly or indirectly, and/or by a class of people who represent very different interests, consumption patterns, and cultural identity, from the bulk of the population. So schooling brings people out of a hierarchy in which they may be servants rather than their own masters . . . into a different hierarchy where their roles are determined on the bases of different criteria, but in which they are still dependent on working and social conditions determined by others. Through that dependency, they [still lack] personal choice and, therefore, [still lack] . . . freedom. . . .

Thus, we observe that schooling is an institution for change in non-Western, feudal societies, and from the standpoint of a Western observer or a non-Western native struggling to better his economic condition, change may be positive and may increase human welfare. But an important characteristic of this change is that schooling brings people from one hierarchy into another. Even those who do not go to school are affected by this transformation because they *lack* schooling. They fall into the category of those with no schooling, putting them near the bottom of the social structure.

The school system, because of the nature of the new hierarchy it represents, we argue, is not available to everyone in equal doses. This means that the quantity and the nature of the schooling process can be and is used to maintain the hierarchical roles of different groups in the society from one generation to the next. Once the transition from feudalism to capitalism is made, therefore, the school system becomes less an agent of change and more and more an agent of *maintaining* the social structure. In that structure, people may have even less to say about their lives and the amount of goods they receive than before, but even if they have more say, they are far from benefiting fully from the wealth of their society and are far from controlling its direction. (Carnoy, 1974, pp. 14–15)

Even in less-developed capitalist societies, I suggested, the positive effects of schooling on the incomes of the "fortunate" minority who completed higher levels of schooling would likely work to their benefit. Although, again, it was much less clear that should the average level of schooling increase more generally, this would result in higher incomes on average:

There is ample evidence that schooling increases the incomes of those who go to school, and increases their ability to function in a "modern," complex society. From the standpoint of material advancement, these are positive effects of schooling on *individual* material welfare. When the individual goes to school, he or she has access to a larger slice of the economic and social pie, *provided that everybody else has not gone to school with him*. As one individual gets more schooling than another, he will have greater access to the physical resources of the economy, enabling him to raise individual income. Can this type of argument be extended to entire nations in a world economy? If everyone in a society gets more schooling, does that mean that everyone will produce and earn more? Some studies have shown that people in high-income countries have a higher observed average level of schooling. From such data it is too easily concluded that increased schooling leads to increased per capita income.

Other studies purport to show that a more highly schooled society is likely to be a more politically democratic society. Like the income-schooling studies, these analyses are based on international data. The analyses observe chat countries with more schooling per capita arc also more likely to have Western-style democracies, i.e., free elections and representative government. It is concluded that raising the average level of schooling in a society will create more democratic institutions. Such notions may be correct when more schooling per capita is accompanied by other, simultaneous occurrences, such as concurrent investment in physical capital and increasingly equitable distributions of wealth and income, but these factors do not follow from higher schooling expenditures. (Carnoy, 1974, pp. 6–7)

My analysis also recognized some possible contradictions generated by educational systems in the reproductive process—for example, if education intended to "fit" students into particular hierarchies, it might also create in some students the intellectual capacity to question the hierarchies, and even provide them the analytical tools to overthrow the very social hierarchies they were supposed to support and reproduce. Western schooling could thus possibly contain the seeds of contradictions in the reproduction of colonial capitalism, dependent capitalism, or capitalism in the developed countries themselves. But my purpose in the book was to show that, historically, this was a minor factor in the overall role of schooling. That role was to support the colonizers and core country capitalists in meeting their needs, not the needs of the larger population. I therefore tended to downplay these possible contradictions in the face of the predominantly (successful) reproductive role that schooling plays in colonial and capitalist societies:

Schooling in capitalist societies *does* serve as a means to higher status for a *small percentage* of the urban poor and an even smaller number of rural poor, and it also may contribute to dissent and original thinking, which may be important intellectual forces for societal change. Nevertheless, these are not the *primary purposes* or functional characteristics of school systems. They are by-products of schooling which occur as it attempts to achieve its main function of transmitting the social and economic structure from generation to generation through pupil selection, defining culture and rules, and teaching certain cognitive skills. (Carnoy, 1974, p. 13)

And:

When Western writers ascribe to imperial school systems the seeds of revolution and independence "in spite" of colonial economic and political structures, they ignore this basic understanding of the school system. Although it is possible that people acquired revolutionary ideas in schools, this was far from the schools' purpose. It is much more convincing to argue that schools put some working-class Europeans and some non-Westerners in positions of relative authority in the colonial structure.

A few of the Africans, Asians, and Latin Americans drew on deep-seated anti-European feelings in the *unschooled* population to lead pro-capitalist in-dependence movements; an even smaller number recognizing the intimate con-nection between capitalist economic institutions and the European domination of their culture, went further to lead anti-capitalist independence movements. But the vast majority of the tiny proportion of highly educated non-Europeans in colonized countries chose to emulate Europeans and leave their own people behind. The success story of colonial schooling is the small number of Third World "independence" leaders who chose to break the economic and political ties by which industrial countries control them.

. . . Analogously, white workers and people of color in the United States also acquired revolutionary ideas inside and especially outside schools. They organized anti-capitalist movements such as labor brotherhoods and political parties, largely among the unschooled. Nevertheless, other leaders arose among the poor who cooperated with northern capitalists. As we shall show, schooling became one mechanism by which poor whites and blacks could be temporarily appeased through this group of coopted leaders while their position in the so-ciety remained essentially unchanged. Rather than building independence and self-reliance among the poor in America, schools are used to ensure, as much as possible and apparently with some success, that those in the worst economic po-sitions do not rebel against the system which represses them and identifies with leaders who would work within the framework of action set by the dominant ruling class. (Carnoy, 1974, pp. 16–18)

The book's methodology in making this case was historical. I had never done historical research before, and most historians would probably not consider my research as meeting historiographical standards. I used secondary sources, a method that could be questioned, and I covered a lot of territory in each chapter—one on India during the colonial period, another on West Africa under British and French colonization, yet another on nineteenth-century Latin America, one chapter on black education in the post–Civil War South, and yet another on the extension of US internal colonization to the Third World, particularly after 1945. It could easily be argued that I gave too much weight to the role of Western education as a key institution in serving colonial powers and capitalist elites and too little to the contradictions of expanding education to the masses. I certainly recognized the other side of schooling as a force for "liberation," progress, mobility, and societal modernization—that was the prevailing view in comparative education at the time and was precisely the mainstream view put forth by Adams and Bjork (1969) that I was criticizing. Yet the historical literature I reviewed in each chapter showed a consistent pattern: those in power, whether the colonialist elite back in England or France or Portugal or the capitalist core countries dominating world trade and monopolizing military power and finance capital defined how educational systems would function, including who would get how much and what kind of schooling. If schooling had a "liberating" side, it seemed to me to be a distinctly unintended side effect of the educational system as defined by economic and social elites. To me, the historical literature strongly suggested that the main intended effect of these educational systems was to successfully promote and maintain hierarchical class structures. As I wrote at the end of the introductory chapter:

The use of schooling to promote and maintain class structures in capitalist development, whether in the colonies or in the metropole, was not the result of "conspiracy." We do not contend that certain men and women conspired to organize schools for colonizing little boys and girls. To the contrary, the theory spells out that powerful economic and social groups *acting in their common self-interest* succeeded through legislation and influence to use schooling to further their own ends. Important conflicts occurred in the power structure in times of economic and social change, and schooling often changed with the outcome of these conflicts to serve the needs of those who prevailed. But these conflicts were largely among powerful groups themselves, not between the mass of people and those who ruled. In imperial conditions, the struggles were centered on various colonial interests: for example, domestic manufacturers vs. merchants. Once colonies gained independence, conflicts emerged between metropole economic interests and the interests of at least part of the dependent country elite.

Within industrialized nations, struggles for political and economic power also shape the design and function of schooling. This is not a conspiracy of the powerful against the weak. It is the wealthy supporting institutions and ways of life which maintain their position of wealth and power in their own country and in the world. They are obviously not going to *help* the poor of the world take *control* of the world's resources for their own use, by schooling or by any other means. Schooling as a colonial and imperial institution is eminently reasonable once we understand who influences it and who controls the public funds which support it.

Is schooling inherently colonizing and imperialistic or can it serve to develop liberated, creative adults? The answer is not obvious and depends on the objectives of the society and its economic and social structure. We argue that, until now, formal schooling has helped a few to control more effectively the lives of many rather than the many to understand and control the nature of progress and changes in their own lives. (Carnoy, 1974, pp. 24–25)

My structuralist approach was also flawed in not incorporating adequately Cardoso and Faletto's more dialectical method in *Dependency and Underdevelopment* (1979). Cardoso and Faletto characterized dependent development as a dialectical process by which local "history" ran up against the "structure" of the world economy. Change occurred as local "agents" developed local histories that were shaped but not determined by the hierarchy of the world economic structure's relation between core and periphery. I probably should have analyzed education in each of the contexts I studied to examine how colonial and, later, postcolonial capitalist educational systems, were parts of local "histories" and therefore developed inherent contradictions within their reproductive functions defined by the economic relation between core and periphery and the economic class-race structure in core and peripheral countries.

Ten years later (1985), Henry Levin and I corrected these theoretical problems in another book, *Schooling and Work in the Democratic State,* that had a US focus but nonetheless introduced a more dialectical approach that had important implications for and application to comparative analysis. I include an analysis of that book later in this volume. Parenthetically, Bowles and Gintis also wrote an insightful book in 1986, *Democracy and Capitalism,* which focused less on education but did provide an analysis of the contradictions between democracy and class relations in capitalist development—with important implications for the role of education in that dialectical process. I refer to this work in a later section as well.

Despite its flaws, I believe that the critical approach many of us took in the 1970s is still useful in understanding why education reforms have limited impact on the underlying unequal and inequitable structures of educational systems. This approach is also key to understanding why educational systems may be more "efficient" in fulfilling meritocratic or equity ideals in some societies and not in others. To put it simply, those societies in which education is more meritocratic or equitable are societies that are organized politically to be more meritocratic and equitable. Education is a reflection of the "real" society in which it is situated, not the "ideal" society of anthems and social studies textbooks and political speeches. In later years, my position, and that of other critical analysts, "softened" to include potential contradictions between education's "ideal" role and its "reproductive" role, but the basic premise that education reflected political economic "reality" was still the starting point of our analysis.

CHAPTER 6

The 1970s and 1980s

World Society Theory and Comparative Education

THE 1970S SAW the birth of another important theory of how to approach international and comparative education—world society theory. World society theory, or world culture theory, as its creators sometimes call it, quickly had an enormous influence on comparative education.

Like many new, influential ideas, world culture theory came about because of the synergy among individuals who happened to be at the same place at the same time. Stanford's sociology department in the late 1960s and early 1970s included three scholars—Richard Scott, John Meyer, and Michael Hannan—interested in organizations and how they are shaped by their institutional environments.[1] Working with them was an unusually talented group of students, including Francisco Ramirez, Chris Chase-Dunn, John Boli-Bennett, and Richard Rubinson. Together, they expanded institutional theory to try to understand global change.

As do such new ideas, world society theory emerged in response to other theories—in this case, functionalism, in which the expansion and shape of educational systems was dictated by its "function" in society (e.g., to produce behavior and beliefs consistent with the industrial system, as in Inkeles and Smith), and to world systems theory, which rooted knowledge and ideas and the development of educational systems in the unequal material relations of capitalist production on a world scale (Wallerstein, 1973). It is no accident that Wallerstein was teaching at Columbia when Meyer was also teaching there.

World systems theory incorporated dependency theory in explaining how institutional development, including education, in developing countries was "conditioned" by those countries' material subordination to developed countries' economies. In contrast, world society theory focused directly on global ideology and on education as an important element of this ideology. The global ideology in world society theory is "inclusive" rather than hierarchical—it posits an all-encompassing ideological environment that defines modernity and progress and encourages all nation-states to embrace the institutions that conform to that environment:

The world environment is a symbolic universe in which theorized models of progress and justice provide a narrative that links several rationalizing and legitimating myths. Central to this narrative is the role of education as a means to progress and justice. Education is in fact the most legitimated and most scripted means to attain these goals. All sorts of educational and related principles, policies, and practices make sense given the triumph of a world educational culture. All sorts of expertise are aligned to this culture, both gaining legitimacy from it and strengthening it as well. Actors, interests, and goals are thus socially constructed. Their legitimacy is contingent on the wider world, and its privileged models and scripts and the legitimated identities that follow from their enactment. (Ramirez, 2012, p. 431)

Meyer, Ramirez, and their colleagues tried to show that this inclusive ideology provided a better empirical explanation than world systems theory and other functionalist models for how institutions—starting with mass education—developed globally. As John Meyer tells it:

I began to think a little bit in the 1960s and a lot in the 1970s about the way organizations and individuals are shaped by their environments. Organizational structures and routines reflect rules and structures institutionalized within their environments, and these environments include not only direct state regulation, but also meaning systems that are important in defining what organizations do. This explains why organizations in a similar environment conform to each other but are quite loosely internally integrated and subject to change as cultural values (such as citizens' rights) that have little to do with "organizing" change.

I wasn't contemplating world society in that sense. At the same time, I was involved in a very large empirical project with Michael Hannan in the early 1970s to collect data on nation-states over time and to explore the standard ideas about the effects of institutional development and economic growth [This resulted in the edited book by Meyer and Hannan, 1979]. People had tried to use these emerging cross-national data sets to draw inferences about these relations, and they had done badly, and argued that it was because the data were bad, but we thought that it was that they were not methodologically sophisti-cated. (Interview with John Meyer, March 2017)

WORLD SOCIETY THEORY AND THE
EXPANSION OF EDUCATION

A graduate student working under Meyer, Francisco Ramirez, played a crucial role in the use of these data, and one of the main variables he and Meyer, Rubinson, and Boil-Bennett focused on was education. They viewed schools as embodiments of collective myth and ceremonial administra-tion, tied to modernity and its conceptions of progress and justice. This framework explicitly argued that schooling's form and function reflected the norms and values of broader social institutions.

Ramirez writes:

The turning point for me came in 1971 as a teaching assistant in an introduc-tion to sociology course taught by John Meyer. This course focused on large-scale social change and its impact on institutional, organizational, and inter-personal dynamics. In this course modernity was not imagined as a bundle of virtues that all people everywhere should aspire to attain. There were costs and tensions and paradoxes. I continued to be interested in development, though it was increasingly difficult to figure out exactly what development meant.

The initial goal was to address the chicken and egg problem—did education lead to economic development or was it the other way around. Much to our surprise we found that primary educational enrollments grew dramatically just about everywhere. There were no obvious economic or political triggers. What was increasingly obvious is that schooling the masses had emerged as the path favored throughout the world. A process that had been contentious in earlier eras in Western Europe was now called education for development and was very much globally legitimated. In the post-World War II world a legitimate nation-state was expected to pursue progress via educational expansion. This pursuit would also be in the interest of justice, as the masses that would become citizens via schooling increasingly included girls. Earlier fears about over educa-tion would give way to the enthusiastic endorsement of expanded higher edu-cation. The underlying idea was that nation-states would develop educational policies and structures and undergo educational changes to enact the proper nation-state identity. External legitimacy had become crucial in an increasingly integrated world of nation-states. These ideas lead to varied research directions but the first step was the empirical generalization we called a "world educational revolution." (Personal communication from Francisco Ramirez, April 2017, drawing on Ramirez, 2016, pp. 172–173)

John Meyer sees the evolution of these ideas similarly:

There had been an earlier history of educational expansion in the core countries, but now there was a new history. Forces were emanating from an imagined center in world society rather than endogenous forces. In 1978, in another paper with John Boli-Bennett [Boli-Bennett and Meyer, 1978], we looked at constitutions historically—what did they say about children, including education. What they said about children had nothing to do with economic development. The new poor countries were more "modern" on this issue than the older developed countries. The story of a dramatic world change. The new countries were more susceptible—they were more modern about child labor and state responsibility for education. A self-perception was promulgated somewhere and spread everywhere. The nation-state became a creature of a global environment. This was true of variables that you could really measure—educational enrollment, constitutional structures, etc.

We overturned the idea that endogenous processes and decision-making were the driving force behind the development of educational system—we argued that it was exogenous forces that were shaping these systems. At the end of the 1970s, we were arguing that there is one system, but we distinguished ourselves from Wallerstein's economic *world system*—his was formulated in a very tight ideological model of economic structures driving relations. The contrast with Wallerstein is quite clear: the world systems people thought that the world is a stratification system that forced inequalities. They also see the national development as shaped by exogenous forces, but forces rooted in unequal economic relations. They understood the world as, for example, colonial powers prohibiting universities, but that is not what happened. In fact, Wallerstein's students tried to do analyses of educational expansion, showing that education was restricted in colonized countries. But as we were showing, it was expanding everywhere, colonial or not. It was not responding to the world stratification system; it was responding to a world polity. Thus, we start to use the terms world society or world polity, or world culture.

Another influence that is more esoteric is the strong emphasis on the model of education as ideology as opposed to education as practices. Education as a vision of the world, and that vision is an ideological construction—a vision of society not a response to what actually goes on in society. Schooling was not designed to train people to live in Smithville, Ohio. Education was uniting people with a big knowledge system. Education spreads as an ideology. It spreads as a general model of both the individual and society, not as a technical training system. One of the reasons that the field of higher education is so boring is all the talk is about structure (organization) not about the actual content. One of the most powerful slides I show is of professorships at three universities on different continents, and the list of professorships is all the same. The fields of knowledge are the same. The issue of the power structure in the university is not as important as the fact that the cultural knowledge system is dramatically universalized—this is a creature of culture/ideology. (Interview with John Meyer, March, 2017)

Beginning in 1977 with the publication of the "World Education Revolution, 1950–1970," Meyer and Ramirez (and two of Meyer's other graduate students, Rubinson and Boli-Bennett) developed this conception of education as a symbol of a modernized society, with mass education spreading as part of the spread of the enlightenment conception of progress and of what it meant to be a nation-state. Ramirez later (2012) argued in a piece on world society theory that earlier writers had claimed either that mass schooling was a response to the functional needs of growing industrialization and urbanization (Dreeben, 1968), or—from a Marxist functional perspective—that mass schooling was needed to reproduce the class-stratified society; that is, schooling served to successfully incorporate alienated workers into an unequal social structure dominated by the capitalist class (Bowles and Gintis, 1976). Although each of these explanations is persuasive, Ramirez contends, none is able to account for the enormous worldwide growth of primary schooling, compulsory school laws, and the formation of national educational ministries after World War II, as this took place in a variety of economic conditions and in capitalist and noncapitalist societies:

One needed to think about the wider world and its influence on nation-states and primary education. . . . It is a standard sociological strategy to assume that if different sub-units behave in common ways, one should look to the larger unit to make sense of the common patterns. This strategy leads to thinking about groups, organizational environments, and the wider world to make sense of common patterns of activity among individuals, organizations, and nation-states . . . it suffices to point out that the first effort to deal with the empirical puzzle is to make the following assumptions: (i) nation-states are embedded in and influenced by a wider world; and (ii) that wider world legitimates the pursuit of mass schooling as a nation-state project. From these two assumptions it follows that nation-states that undertook mass schooling were regarded as more legitimate than those that did not. The pursuit of mass schooling was thus closely related to the proper enactment of the nation-state identity. External legitimation and proper enactment of nation-state identity would become key concepts in the world society perspective. Further educational and related developments would be linked to these concepts instead of to ideas about functional solutions to systemic problems. From a world society perspective, education emerged and expanded not primarily because education solved problems but because education generated legitimacy for the nation-state and for its leadership. (Ramirez, 2012, pp. 424–425)

Thus, world society theory rejected the functionalist theories that explained the rise of mass schooling as a response to the imperative of filling particular social functions, such as incorporating youth into industrial production, with its need for particular kinds of human skills and behavior, and also those theories that explained mass schooling in terms of its crucial role in reproducing class relations of production in a broader economic-political functionalism, as expressed in Chapter 5 in this book, describing my work on colonialism and class reproduction. For Meyer and Ramirez, the nation-state is an ideological project that is abstracted from any single economic system or the interests of any social group, and the expansion of mass schooling is the expression of a "modern" nation-state's drive for legitimation within a wider world environment that defines progress and modernity:

In sum, mass education became a core component of the nation-state model. Its collective standardization celebrates the unified sovereignty and purposiveness of the collectivity (the state), its individual focus and universality enact the integrated and universal character of society (the nation of citizens), and its secularized culture defines the character of the nation-state as an enterprise that is designed to attain progress. From this point of view, mass education is not primarily an adaptation to societal realities of function and power. It arose as nation-states and candidate states affirmed, enhanced, and thus legitimated nationhood within the broader Western civilizational network (Boli et al. 1985; Meyer, Boli, and Thomas 1987; Ramirez and Boli, 1987). The wider world environment and its models of the legitimate political organization must be central to the explanation of the striking similarities in the expansion of mass schooling across widely varying national circumstances.

We thus argue that the expansion of mass education around the world is dependent on the formation of unified sovereign projects that are linked to and recognized by the wider world society of nation-states and the formation of internal principles of nationhood within countries. Since both the nation-state principle and the linkage of mass education to it have gained intensity over the past century, we expect rates of penetration and expansion of mass education to have increased over time. (Meyer, Ramirez, and Soysal, 1992, pp. 131–132)

The crucial elements for world society theory, therefore, are its conceptions of a "wider world environment [i.e., a unifying ideology] and its models of the legitimate political organization" and a nation-state that arose as an "ideological enterprise that is designed to attain progress." This is a powerful theory, and, as I will outline further, Meyer, Ramirez, and others have been able to use it to explain a number of phenomena on a world scale. Implicitly, this underlying idea of the nation-state in world society theory is able to sustain itself because it has the support of its citizens, who believe in the "symbolic universe in which theorized models of progress and justice provide a narrative that links several rationalizing and legitimating myths" represented by the nation-state:

Actors, interests, and goals are thus socially constructed. Their legitimacy is contingent on the wider world, and its privileged models and scripts and the legitimated identities that follow from their enactment. These models and scripts are articulated through a range of organizational carriers that include scientists, consultants, and other educated experts. Much of the expert advice offered is

universalistic in tone and has the character of advancing abstract "best practices." (Ramirez, 2012, p. 431)

Yet it is important to note that whereas world society theory's conceptions of both this unifying ideology and the nation-state can provide
convincing explanations of many phenomena, other conceptions of the
world environment and the nation-state developed in the 1970s are also
powerful explainers of these same phenomena, including why education
expanded as it did and when it did. In Chapters 7 and 8, I summarize
two of these—compensatory legitimation, influenced by neo-Marxian
Frankfurt School political philosophical conceptions of the nation-state
(Habermas, 1975; Offe, 1972), and the second, a dialectical social movement state theory influenced by a different neo-Marxian unifying ideology
and conception of the nation-state developed by Nicos Poulantzas (1978).

Many of the state theories that underlie compensatory legitimation
define the nation-state as rooted in materially based capitalist power relations but mediated by a state bureaucracy charged with reproducing those
relations, mainly by effective organization of the economy and social institutions. The nation-state bureaucracy therefore becomes a center of power
itself, and it seeks to legitimize not only unequal relations of production but
also its own bureaucratic power. Poulantzas argued that capitalist nation-
states have a common ideological project, but rather than being driven
by an ideological abstraction of justice and progress as in world society
theory, the raison d'être for the project is an underlying materialism and
the reproduction of the power relations that are part and parcel of that
materialism. Mass education and other institutions of the capitalist state
are essential ideological elements needed to separate individuals from their
identities as members of a class and into a new identity as worker-citizens
in the historically, juridically, temporally, and territorially defined nation.

There are still other conceptions of the nation-state, including Foucault's (1977, 2006). Foucault's nation-state is a crystallization of political
power relations but is only one of many centers in which power relations
are crystallized: "Foucault wanted to push away from a focus on institutions and ideologies and toward how the state participated in more mal-
leable and porous relations between different ways of deploying power.

In short, Foucault's discussions of the state showed less of an interest in leaving the state behind entirely than in reconsidering its place in a larger set of power relations that penetrated far beyond the specific apparatus of the state" (Sawyer, 2015, p. 141). For Foucault, it is power relations in society that are "real," and the state is a convenient creation that formalizes those relations. The nation-state as a power center uses the law and its repressive apparatuses to express power and to shape individuals into subjects of the state. But for Foucault, schools, prisons, asylums, hospitals, and the family are also centers of power relations: "The state does not stand outside or determine the deployment of power, but is rather tied into and shares in a nexus of power" (Sawyer, 2015, p. 143).

All these theories—which unlike world society theory, see the nation-state as the expression of unequal power relations in society—agree with Meyer and Ramirez that the knowledge and expertise associated with formal education are key to legitimizing the nation-state, or at least play a role in shaping individuals through their expression of power.[2] The question is, Who defines knowledge and expertise and for what purposes? At least some of the alternative theories would also agree that the expansion of mass schooling was rooted in the legitimation of the nation-state. But the alternative theories see the need for that expansion either in contradictions in capitalist relations of production (e.g., compensatory legitimation, Poulantzas) or in the unequal distribution of power among different "permanent" social groupings.

WORLD SOCIETY THEORY AND OTHER IDEOLOGICAL PHENOMENA

Francisco Ramirez returned to Stanford, joining SIDEC in 1987. Since then, he and his students have greatly expanded the comparative empirical work of world society theory to the expansion of women's rights (Wotipka and Ramirez, 2008), the worldwide institutionalization of professions (Suárez, 2007), the analysis of textbooks (Bromley et al., 2011a, 2011b), and, most recently, the conceptualization of the university. In his words:

For the next two decades [after 1987], world society scholars examined different aspects of both the international human rights regime and the authority and influence of science. World models of justice and progress and their organizational carriers fueled both developments. The authority of science could lead to garnering resources but the influence of scientists was based on their authority, not on the resources per se. The rise of economics, for example, was less about its instrumental value or the inherent power of economists as a status group but instead reflected their successful appropriation of "the scientific method." Other disciplines linked themselves to the high ground of science. Environmental concerns gained traction when framed in scientific ecological terms, not simply love of nature. There were [also] many educational implications that followed from the growing centrality of science (Drori et al., 2003). (Personal communication from Francisco Ramirez, April 2017, drawing on Ramirez, 2016, p. 175)

The rise of gender rights became an especially important issue to researchers working with world society theory. The spread of women's rights and the growing importance of girls' education worldwide beginning in the 1970s provided another important example of nation-states seeking legitimacy by showing that they were "on board" with new conceptions of modernity. Ramirez recounts how he came to see the importance of this issue in his own research:

My interest in gender issues was personally motivated by a feminist worldview that was critical of the exclusion of women from the public sphere. This was a worldview grounded in the sixties and the rise of the second women's movement. My recurring finding of positive changes in the status of women often met with skepticism. The latter was often couched in the "half full or half empty metaphor." But I contend that inclusionary logics have triumphed and paved the way for the current debates about the terms of inclusion. Though inequalities between men and women indeed persist in some domains, it is egalitarian standards reflecting a century of women's movements that has increased the scope of scrutinized policies and the intensity of the scrutiny.

The current debates about gender go beyond demanding opening doors for women and focus instead on valuing differences and changing the culture of the organizations and institutions into which women have entered. Feminists critique the gendered character of these male dominated structures. Underlying this critique is the triumph of egalitarian standards. As experimental studies in social psychology show, inequity perceptions are greater when egalitarian norms are activated. It is precisely these worldwide egalitarian norms that made me skeptical of the positive impacts of mobilizing states, impacts my earlier studies emphasized. These mobilizing states may have more readily included women in the public sphere without affecting the greater workloads women shouldered in the familial sphere. The resulting double burden could not go undetected.

A world characterized by egalitarian standards is indeed one where more inequalities will be detected and experienced as inequities. Later, I made a similar argument as regards the rise and development of an international human rights regime. It is not that regimes have become more wicked but that wicked regimes are more likely to be identified, exposed, and critiqued. (Personal communication from Francisco Ramirez, drawing on Ramirez, 2016, pp. 174–175)

Ramirez sees the international spread of the gender equality ideology as at least in part reflected in increasing female enrollment in the sciences and engineering. This combines—in a sense—the ideology of mass schooling as a symbol of modernity with another symbol of modernity—the ideology of gender equality:

Here again my studies show that the global pattern is one of growth in women's share of enrollments in these fields, though they are nowhere near parity. The gender focus allows us to see how scientific authority and human rights emphases can be aligned. The former is utilized to lament the underutilization of female human capital due to lack of access to scientific and technical education and to barriers to their success therein. The latter is rooted in equity frames and leads to the contention that it is unfair to deprive women of their right to these fields of study, especially since these are gateways to higher paying jobs. (Personal communication from Francisco Ramirez, April 2017, drawing on Ramirez, 2016, p. 176)

A more recent "finding" in world society theory is that some countries are more likely than others to acquire these symbols of modernity—mass schooling, human rights, and gender equality—and that the convergence impact of these ideological symbols is greater now than it was in the past:

Throughout these studies, we often found that countries that were better integrated into the wider world were more likely to undergo the changes that made them look more legitimate. This is the case whether the outcome of interest is the likelihood of creating a human rights commission or the ratification of the [UN Convention on the Elimination of All Forms of Discrimination against Women]. We also found that the impact of world society was greater in more recent eras. That is, societal differences were more consequential earlier on and what other countries are doing is more influential in the more recent periods. This is the case whether one examines women's acquisition of the franchise or the establishment of UNESCO influenced associated schools. That is, world models are more available in a more compressed world, and there are more consultants and translators to facilitate dissemination. (Personal communication from Francisco Ramirez, April 2017)

In his summary of world society theory's contributions to our understanding of why phenomena diffuse worldwide through nation-states, Ramirez (2012) delves into several important issues regarding the theory and comparative analysis using the theory. One of these is the extension of the research to explain the expansion of women's rights—the "transformation of women's status"—the rise of science and the environmental movement, and in the emergence of international human rights and the increasing inclusion of human rights (and the changing view of women's roles) in educational textbooks.

I want to note here that the world society research into girls' education and women's rights forms part of a much larger literature in comparative education situated in the relationship between gender and education. This literature includes feminist approaches to comparativism and to comparative education that are embedded not in world society theory but in methods that contest traditional views of measuring education and education outcomes. In the last chapter of this book, with the help of Christine Min Wotipka, who writes on gender and education, I discuss the possibilities of such approaches to make significant changes in comparative and international education in the future.

REFLECTING ON WORLD SOCIETY THEORY

Ramirez also deals with what could be viewed as a critique of world society theory—the changing patterns of the rate at which nation-states expanded mass schooling or human rights, for example, in different historical eras.

He notes that early world society theory argued that once a society self-identified as a nation-state, it expanded schooling independently of its economic level, political regime, or local culture. However, as more data became available, expansion was shown to vary over time:

Meyer, Ramirez, and Soysal (1992) showed that prior to World War II, countries with fewer primary enrolments grew slower than those with greater enrolments, but that this was not the case after WWII. This finding suggested that paying attention to historical eras was an important consideration, as these would condition the likelihood of trends. Later, this idea led to the premise that nation-state characteristics would be more influential in earlier eras and, conversely, that world influences would be greater in more recent eras. This idea resonates with neo-institutional arguments that in the earlier eras differences between organizations matter more, but that over time organizational blueprints take over creating institutional isomorphism via diffusion processes.

One way of thinking about earlier versus more recent eras is to distinguish between when a policy or structure is contested terrain versus when it has become an institutionalized or taken for granted domain. The acquisition of the franchise by women illustrates this point. This was very much a contested issue in earlier eras, but has been taken for granted in recent years. Thus, one finds that in earlier eras national differences matter more in predicting whether women will gain the right to vote, but that what other countries are doing matters more in more recent eras (Ramirez, Soysal and Shanahan 1997). Furthermore, the gap between the date of male franchise and female franchise acquisition sharply declines over time. That is, in earlier eras, one could universalize the franchise for men but assume that women did not have the same legal persona. This has turned out to be an illicit distinction in the twenty-first century. (Ramirez, 2012, pp. 435–436)

Ramirez discusses other important aspects of schooling across nation-states—especially why, even if there exist generalized "ideal" conceptions in the citizenry of what schooling should be, and, as posited by world society theory, demands on the state from the citizenry to provide that ideal across varying local situations (institutional isomorphism), there can also exist considerable variation in the quality of schooling across nation-states and communities within nation-states:

It is not difficult to imagine how these processes separately or in tandem would lead to formally similar schools or universities. It is also not difficult to grasp that vast differences in resources would result in gaps between schools and between universities along many dimensions. These gaps would simply be differences and receive little attention if different schools and different universities had clearly different goals more in line with local conditions; but because different schools and different universities proclaim common goals and adapt similar policies and routines, the gaps have been conceptualized as loose coupling. (Ramirez, 2012, p. 432)

He continues with a reaffirmation of the larger argument of world society theory that whatever the variation in how educational change may occur in different national or subnational contexts, the key is that nation-states have a common goal of expanding schooling and the schooling they expand has similar goals and structure worldwide:

What really matters is how people experience common cultural flows and the institutional and identity implications of these flows. This point takes us back to the institutional isomorphism and loose coupling ideas as they were first developed. Nowhere in the initial formulations is there the assumption that schooling is experienced in the same way across different students or schools. Educational reforms and innovations are certainly experienced differently across different nation-states [Steiner-Khamsi, 2010]. *The question, though, is why some educational reforms and innovations diffuse and others do not.* Mass schooling may be experienced differently between and within countries, but its worldwide triumph cannot be ignored. (Ramirez, 2012, p. 433, emphasis added)

Indeed, the question is why some reforms diffuse and others do not. In world society theory, the answer lies largely in agreed-on conceptions of what schooling should be and whether reforms are considered to move those conceptions forward. But it may also be the case that these conceptions can be heavily influenced by powerful political groups, either national or global. Powerful groups at the national and international levels can shape ideology, and certainly in ways that benefit them. Experts participate in this shaping, and because they often do not agree, it is perfectly possible that some ideas diffuse and others do not because there is not a clear conception of what "ideal" schooling or environmental policy or even human rights are supposed to be.

We can also ask why, with a clear view of what schooling should look like and what it should do (institutional isomorphism), schooling for different groups even in a highly developed country such as the United States should not be the same, even in many aspects of its formal structure (e.g., curriculum). It may not be the case, for example, that different groups of parents have the same conception of good schooling—and that these differing conceptions are shaped by their position in the class structure (Anyon, 1980).[3]

Other theories of the nation-state provide answers that differ from Ramirez's and have, as discussed earlier, different views on why nation-states expanded mass schooling when they did.

WORLD SOCIETY THEORY AND HIGHER EDUCATION

Although world society theory has been largely concerned with mass schooling, in the past five or six years, with the expansion of higher education worldwide, Meyer and Ramirez have turned their comparative analysis to the tertiary sector. Ramirez writes that he was influenced in taking up questions in higher education by his experience teaching at Oxford for three months (how different it was from Stanford, yet how great the pressures were on Oxford "to look more like an idealized model of university excellence") and as associate dean in Stanford's School of Education. He describes these influences:

My experiences as associate dean led me to reflect on the university as an organizational actor. Much scholarship focuses on the growth of university administration. It is less clear why this is the case and whether one should expect similar developments globally. One idea is that as a university becomes more entrepreneurial and more empowering of different individuals within it, its organization increasingly includes more administrators to cope with a broader set of issues. [By examining] university websites [we can] ascertain whether and to what extent the university has a development or institutional advancement office, an inclusion or diversity office, and a legal office. We are also exploring an international data set to ascertain which of these organizational developments globalize and which are resisted. The overarching question is whether and to what degree universities remain historically grounded institutions or become organizational actors enacting models of excellence and inclusiveness promoted by consultants without borders. (Personal communication from Francisco Ramirez, April 2017)

SUMMING UP AND FURTHER READINGS

As I stated at the beginning of this chapter, world society theory has had a powerful impact on comparative and international education analysis since it was formulated in the 1970s. It was a reaction to both functionalist sociological theories of educational expansion and class reproduction theories (also functionalist), such as Wallerstein's (1973, 1974) world systems theory, or my and Bowles and Gintis's work described in the previous chapter. World society theory situated schooling in a global ideological environment and in a nation-state that necessarily needed to respond to that global ideology to be legitimate. This global ideological environment was based neither in capitalist class relations nor in other power relations (e.g., colonialism) between or within nation-states. Idealized notions of schooling and what it represented were an important part of the way nation-states defined themselves. Comparative education analysis in such a theory tended to focus on similarities in education systems rather than differences, on the reasons for such similarities, and especially on the convergences of differences when they did exist.

In this chapter, I have drawn heavily on two articles that are easily accessible and should be read to fully understand the intellectual underpinnings of world society theory. One, by Meyer, Ramirez, and Soysal (1992), is a more comprehensive version of the original article, "The World Education Revolution, 1950–1970" (Meyer et al., 1977) on the expansion of mass schooling that helped launch world society theory in the 1970s. The second piece is a recent summary of world society theory by Ramirez (2012). It discusses the underlying neo-institutionalism that forms the basis of the theory, its contribution to comparative education, and world society scholars' focus of research beyond the expansion of education.

CHAPTER 7

The 1980s

The Politics of Education: Legitimation, Reform, and Knowledge

ONE OF THE MOST important theoretical contributions to comparative and international education in the 1970s and 1980s was the application of theories of the state to understanding educational expansion and change in different societies. This application began with the simple assumption that every society has its specific political-economic context, and that the political organization of society—the state—is a reflection of that context and of the external and internal forces that have historically shaped it (Skocpol, 1982). Further, state theorists argued that educational systems are part and parcel of the state, and that, with the rise of capitalism, schools have been a main instrument for inducting young people into social and economic roles. For some who use state theory in analyzing education systems, that institutional role has put the educational system at the center of reproducing social relations and economic as well as political power in capitalist and postcapitalist societies. For others, the educational system has a more purely ideological relation to the state, serving to legitimate the institution of the state, or, as a tool in the hands of the state bureaucracy, to legitimate state power. The previous chapters touched on the implicit theory of the state inherent in the theoretical arguments presented there, especially in the discussion of dependency, neocolonialism, and world society theory. This chapter and the next review how, in the early 1980s, new work brought theories of the state out of the shadows into the forefront of the discussion of doing comparative and international education.

Much of the research at Stanford on political approaches to international and comparative education was, not surprisingly, carried out by faculty trained in political science. The political scientist Hans Weiler was one of the first faculty recruited by Paul Hanna, and Weiler taught in SIDEC for more than twenty-five years, until he retired in the early 1990s and became president of the newly unified Germany's Europa-Universität Viadrina in Frankfurt (Oder) and a founder of the Hertie

School of Governance in Berlin. Weiler had studied in Germany and Britain and conducted field research in West Africa, where, in his words, he was exposed "to the momentous transitions from colonial rule . . . in the late 1950s and early 1960s" (personal communication with Hans Weiler, February 2017). His mentor at the University of Freiburg was the political scientist Arnold Bergstraesser, who, in cooperation with colleagues in Britain and France, pioneered interdisciplinary research in Europe on Third World development processes.

In this same period of the early 1960s, comparative politics and a growing attention to the importance of "political culture" expanded traditional perspectives on the structures of governance. Stanford's Gabriel Almond, Harvard's Sidney Verba, MIT's Lucian Pye, and others played a major role in the development of this line of work in the 1960s and 1970s. Almond and Verba's 1963 book, *The Civic Culture*, had an enormous influence at the time. It argued that modern democracies required a political culture to sustain the democratic system of governance—that is, adults socialized into certain values of tolerance, participation, positive attitudes toward government and their nation. The authors also claimed that "educational attainment appears to have the most important demographic effect on political attitudes. Among the demographic variables usually investigated- sex, place of residence, occupation, income, age, and so on—none compares with the educational variable in the extent to which it seems to determine political attitudes" (Almond and Verba, 1963, p. 379). For Almond and Verba, schools could be important socializers of students into democratic, participatory attitudes if schooling itself was structured to be more participatory, and therefore modeled the influence that individuals could have later in life by participating politically.[1]

There was a lot to criticize about Almond and Verba's idealized view of Western democracy, especially the underlying pluralist conception that it produced outcomes that worked in the interests of all citizens (or at least in the interests of all those permitted to participate politically). Further, it was very much part of the post–World War II ideology of spreading the US version of democracy and capitalism to the rest of the world through institution (nation) building and using education to accomplish that goal. Not surprisingly, it fit perfectly with Paul Hanna's views—discussed in

Chapters 1 and 2—on shaping political values through schooling and implementing the "right" social studies curriculum. By coincidence, in 1962, while still at the University of Freiburg, Weiler, his adviser Bergstraesser, and Hanna all attended a meeting at the Rockefeller Foundation's Villa Serbelloni in Bellagio, Italy. The subject of that meeting was the role of education in development. As recounted by Weiler, he and Bergstraesser became acquainted with Hanna and had a chance to discuss Weiler's (1966) dissertation research, a historical analysis of educational policy in the transition from colonial rule to independent statehood in West Africa. Hanna liked Weiler's ideas and eventually recruited him to come to Stanford in 1965 to join the SIDEC program. There Weiler started teaching about political approaches to the comparative study of education. He writes about how his academic pursuits developed further once he was at Stanford:

My interest increasingly turned to the study of "political socialization," a growing *topos* in the "political culture" domain of political science. The center of attention in this domain was the acquisition and change of political attitudes and beliefs, especially among young people. Besides influencing some of my students' dissertations, this led to my empirical study of political beliefs among German high school students (Weiler, 1972), one of my earlier deviations from the Africanist path that I had pursued since my first explorations in West Africa in 1958.

A few other such deviations, including my experience as Director of UNESCO's International Institute for Educational Planning (IIEP) in Paris in the 1970s, rekindled my interest in the making of educational policy and, more specifically, in the political dynamics of educational reform. This interest was connected to my earlier work on colonial and post-colonial educational policy, but also to observing the range of educational reforms that, in the wake of student unrest and the allures of new conceptions of schooling, had swept over a number of European countries in the 1970s. [The 1983 piece] "Legalization, Expertise, and Participation: Strategies of Compensatory Legitimation in Educational Policy" [Weiler, 1983] is an outcome of this return to the study of educational policy. It is primarily an attempt to come to terms with the theoretical challenges that this kind of analysis presents, and to seek an organizing and unifying theoretical construct for understanding how states behave when faced with the (real or perceived) need for educational reform. The gravitational center of this paper is the notion of "compensatory legitimation." The argument underlying this notion is, briefly, that the modern state, faced as it is with serious and structural threats to its own legitimacy, seeks to orchestrate its response to major policy challenges (such as the need for reforming outdated educational systems) in such a way as to maximize the resulting ("compensatory") gains of legitimacy. Against the background of recent developments in European educational policy, I identified three such compensatory strategies: the invocation of (in terms of legitimacy relatively unscathed) legal systems, the use of professional expertise to buttress the credibility of policy decisions, and the use of (more or less) credible participatory arrangements for shoring up the state's democratic credentials. A particularly intriguing variant of this argument has focused on the utility of policy experimentation, where the experiment combines the advantages of holding off on a final, either-or policy decision with projecting the prestigious imagery of a scientifically demanding effort at generating incontrovertible evidence in the policy process.

In much of the work that followed from this set of theoretical propositions, I have sought to develop these arguments further in a variety of studies on educational policy and reform [Weiler, 1985, 1994; Eliason, et al., 1987]. Compensatory legitimation was perhaps most useful in my work on decentralization in educational policy [Weiler, 1989, 1993], where I advanced the claim that, in many instances, decentralizing educational decision-making was yet another expedient in that it combined shifting the locus of ubiquitous conflict over education away from the state's center and conveying the legitimacy-enhancing image of allowing broader participation in the policy process. (Personal communication from Hans Weiler, February 2017)

The underlying premise of the compensatory legitimation analysis of educational reforms is that the capitalist state faces a "crisis of legitimacy"— a crisis that derives from the class structure of capitalist society and the difficulty for the state to at once distribute social goods and services unequally yet legitimately (Offe, 1972; Habermas, 1975; Weiler, 1983):

It is clear to Offe (1972) as well as to other theorists in a Marxist tradition that the class structure of capitalist society lies at the very heart of the legitimacy problem of the modern state. Habermas (1975) sees the inherent difficulty of "distributing the surplus social product inequitably and yet legitimately" as one of the main sources of the state's legitimacy deficit. Along somewhat similar lines, Alan Wolfe casts his analysis of the legitimacy issue in terms of the inherent tensions between liberalism and democracy under conditions of capitalism. The crisis emerges, Wolfe claims, as the capitalist state exhausts solutions to these tensions and is "called on to solve problems at the same time that its ability to solve them is undermined" [Wolfe, 1977, p. 10]. The thrust of this argument is reflected in analyses of a more specifically educational policy context. Both Offe and Levin assess the dilemma of educational reform in capitalist societies as stemming from this same basic contradiction: reform policies with their associated rhetoric tend to generate expectations and needs which, given the highly limited capacity of the capitalist state for genuine change, they ultimately prove unable to meet [Offe, 1972; Levin, 1978]. (Personal communication from Weiler, February 2017).

Weiler built on Offe's "commodity" concept of the legitimation process and added a distinctly ideological dimension to it—namely, the role of educational policy making itself in the legitimation process. In Offe's model, the functions of the state emanate from the problem, on one hand, of ensuring continued economic growth and, on the other hand, of legitimating the state. Offe views government policy making as the attempt to establish a dynamic equilibrium among constituent elements. He argued that the advanced capitalist state—as opposed to the liberal capitalist state, which could be legitimized by noninterference with private markets—must exercise its power and intervene in the accumulation process. It must, at the same time, practice its class character by promoting private capital accumulation but act as if it were representing mass interests—the existence of the capitalist state presupposes the systematic denial of its nature as a capitalist state. The problem arises when there are difficulties of accumulation and legitimation. To overcome these difficulties—to ensure their legitimacy—the state apparatuses must improve the employability of labor, ensure that it is employed in the marketplace, and ensure that the individual units of capital find it profitable to employ that labor—that the rate of profit is high enough to promote increased investment and economic expansion. Offe (1973) argues, therefore, that the capitalist state will, out of its institutional self-interest—to ensure the continued existence of the state apparatuses—attempt to increase the employability of labor and to promote capital investment.

Investing in education and workers' vocational training, in Offe's model, are the mechanisms that the state uses to make labor more employable and, simultaneously, by increasing worker productivity and providing other subsidies to capital, to make capital more profitable. In this conception of legitimation, the state legitimates itself purely in terms of providing commodity value to both labor and capital. Weiler accepts the underlying idea of the self-interest of the state in legitimating itself through intervening in the capital accumulation process, but he expands this concept of legitimation to include the role of policy making and reform as having ideological value in the legitimation process:

Assuming, without extending this more general argument any further, that the modern state does face a more or less substantial legitimacy deficit, I contend that the state has a vital interest in making up for as much of this deficit as possible. If it did not, the continued existence and functioning of the state would be in serious jeopardy; without adequate legitimation, the state would either have to assert its authority through coercion, with the resulting danger of massive resistance, or it would continuously have to "purchase" legitimacy through various kinds of material gratification—an unrealistic strategy in view of the finite nature of the state's resources. Faced with this dilemma, the retrieval of legitimacy becomes a matter of central concern for those who hold the state's authority. The analysis presented in this article is predicated on the notion that this concern becomes a powerful determinant of the ways in which policies are designed and implemented. Policies are seen in this argument as strategies of compensatory legitimation or, in Habermas's terms, as "attempts to compensate for legitimation deficits through conscious manipulation" (Habermas, 1975, p. 71). This article suggests that such a theoretical perspective will help us better to understand the political dynamics of the policy process. (Weiler, 1983, p. 261)

Weiler then discusses the special role that education has in compensatory legitimation:

While this argument would apply to the state's behavior in various policy domains, both the intensity of the legitimacy problem and the state's desire to compensate for it seem particularly pronounced when it comes to education. Education has a key role in allocating statuses and in socializing different groups in society into accepting and sustaining existing structures of wealth, status, and power. In this role, education is particularly exposed to conflicting norms and thus in need of especially high levels of legitimation. At the same time, however, educational systems in many modern societies face an unprecedented crisis of confidence of their own which seems both to reflect and to compound the general legitimacy problem of the state.

Against this background of the erosion of legitimacy and of the state's preoccupation with regaining at least some of what has been lost, I posit that the state tends to adopt policy strategies that appear to be particularly well suited for this compensatory purpose. For the field of educational policy, three such strategies seem to be particularly conspicuous in the policy behavior of the modern state: (a) the "legalization" or "judicialization" of policy in terms of the increased invocation of legal norms and institutions; (b) the utilization of scientific expertise in the policymaking process, especially through such devices as experimentation and planning; and (c) the development and stipulation of client participation in the policy process. By implication, this argument also suggests that the state's preoccupation with policy strategies for compensatory legitimation is likely to be at the expense of other possible policy intentions, notably, those of reform and change. (Weiler, 1983, pp. 261–262)

The importance of public schooling in ostensibly allocating jobs and status in modern economies makes it a prime candidate for compensatory legitimation. The state seeks legitimacy in part through shifting public attention to reforms that would appear to create greater mobility and equality through "more and better schooling" (see, e.g., Bowles and Gintis, 1975). This despite the likelihood that such "reform policies with their associated rhetoric tend to generate expectations and needs which, given the highly limited capacity of the capitalist state for genuine change, they ultimately prove unable to meet" (Weiler, 1983, p. 260). Moreover:

There is, in principle, an almost unlimited array of devices and strategies that could potentially serve the state's quest for compensatory legitimation—and quite a number for which there are more tangible theoretical arguments and empirical evidence available.[2] The three strategies with which this article deals—legalization, expertise, and participation—have been identified on two grounds. First, they seem to enjoy particularly wide currency in the policy instrumentarium of the modern state, at least in advanced industrial societies. Furthermore, these three strategies represent variations on what, in the history of Western political thought, have been seen as the most powerful sources for the legitimacy of political authority: the principles of legality, of organizational rationality, and of democratic participation. (Weiler, 1983, pp. 262–263)

Weiler argues that education policy and practice had been increasingly shaped by the use of legal norms and judicial decisions in both the US and West Germany: "The range of educational issues that has been affected by this process in both countries has encompassed a wide variety, ranging from matters of discipline to the determination of educational objectives, and from teacher tenure to equity in access and resource allocation" (1983, p. 263). The entry of the judicial system into educational policy, Weiler suggests, is needed to bolster the legitimacy of the educational institutions as an efficient and fair producer of skills and allocator of social roles specifically because other state institutions (namely legislatures) have failed to act to provide that legitimacy—in large part because of competing interests in defining what is efficient and equitable in education.

Similarly, "To the extent that the erosion of legitimacy stems in no small part from the particular credibility problems of systems of representation, the state may attempt to regenerate its own legitimation by tolerating or actually instituting various schemes for citizen participation. While the potential relevance of this discussion ranges across a number of policy areas, education once again seems to have been a particularly eventful forum for trying out a number of participatory devices" (Weiler, 1983, p. 272). He focuses on the participation of parents, teachers, and students in the process of curriculum development and reform: "The argument is relatively straightforward: Given the erosion in the legitimacy of formal institutions of representation such as parliaments, curriculum decisions are expected to derive added credibility and legitimacy from the direct participation of those affected by the outcomes of the decision process" (Weiler, 1983, p. 274).

Finally, Weiler argues that experimentation, research, or new knowledge and expertise can serve as further forms of legitimation. "The notion of experimentally 'exploring' the strengths and weaknesses of alternative policy propositions thus exemplifies—in the eyes of the public as well as those of policymakers—a particularly powerful source of "organizational rationality" and thus a particularly rich and compelling source of added legitimacy for the policy process. Indeed, it seems that it is the legitimacy of the process, rather than that of its results, that stands to gain the most from the scientific connotation of the experiment" (Weiler, 1983, p. 270).

Weiler's conception of compensatory legitimation is a powerful tool for explaining the nation-state's use of educational expansion and quasi-reforms in both developed and developing countries to overcome various crises in capital accumulation and of state legitimacy. It therefore has important theoretical implications for comparative and international education. This can be illustrated by contrasting it with one of the oldest underlying ideas used in comparative education and recently more formalized—the notion of borrowing (e.g., Phillips, 2006; Silova, 2004; Steiner-Khamsi, 2006). Most of the early comparative work in education was justified in terms of borrowing educational ideas from other countries to "improve" education at home (Noah and Eckstein, 1969). In today's world of comparative education, reforms are "borrowed" from elsewhere—or are suggested as "lessons" to be "borrowed"—based on their "success" in improving student performance (OECD, 2011) or in terms of their political attractiveness (Phillips and Ochs, 2003). Such borrowing is analyzed as part of a policy-making process that meets rational policy goals or a political agenda abstract from the contradictions of the capital accumulation process and the underlying contradictions in the capitalist state. Because it is couched in the larger political-economic framework of state theory, compensatory legitimation provides a much richer set of constructs for understanding educational "borrowing" than does the borrowing literature itself.

In later chapters, I discuss other iterations of state theory that take somewhat different views of the state's and its education policies' role in attempting to smooth over the economic and social contradictions in capitalist development. The main takeaway of Weiler's conception of compensatory legitimation is that it provides an important theoretical foundation for understanding how and why educational policies are taking shape in a wide political-economic array of capitalist and post-capitalist nation-states.

COMPENSATORY LEGITIMATION AND THE CONSTRUCTION OF KNOWLEDGE

Weiler's professional career path changed in the wake of German unification. He was asked in the early 1990s to assume the presidency of Europa-Universität Viadrina in Frankfurt (Oder), on the border of what had been the German Democratic Republic and Poland. It was a major challenge, and in that new environment, his academic work also turned toward university policy. He writes:

A further stage in the development of my theoretical interests emerged and provided an opportunity to explore yet another facet of the relationship between legitimacy and education. This theme had already been important in how I had dealt with the role of expertise as a strategy of compensatory legitimation in my 1983 article. It also had provided a useful perspective in looking at such issues as the politics of foreign study and the role of organizations like the World Bank in shaping the production of knowledge about education and change [Weiler, 1984, 1991]. With the pressures of the founding years of the Viadrina behind me, this linkage between knowledge, education and power has occupied most of my thinking over the past fifteen years [Weiler, 2005]. The most complete renditions of the theme can be found in the 2011 article "Knowledge and Power: The New Politics of Higher Education" [Weiler, 2011].

The common denominator that connects this piece with my 1983 article is the construct of legitimation as a dominant factor in the making and the implementing of educational policy. The progression over this time span is the result of broadening the focus of the theoretical argument from the realm of educational policy to the realm of knowledge and of the political conditions for its creation, validation, and utilization. This conceptual journey has involved a rather extensive review of the profound changes in our understanding of what knowledge is, how it gets produced and used and, most importantly, "whose knowledge matters" (Guy Gran). This review has benefited greatly from the fertile discussion of "new ways of knowing" in the work of people like Ashis Nandy, Rajni Kothari, Paulin Hountondji, Homi Bhabha, Arturo Escobar, Zygmunt Bauman and others, as well as from my involvement in the brief but immensely creative "UNESCO Forum on Higher Education, Research and Knowledge" that, for the brief span of a few years at the beginning of this century, brought together an amazing group of thinkers about the world of knowledge from around the world [Neave, 2006].

Within the context of this debate, my own thinking about "the politics of knowledge" centered on four interconnected issues: the critical importance of hierarchies in the existing knowledge order, the relationship of reciprocal legitimation between knowledge and power, the transnational division of labor in the contemporary knowledge order, and the political economy of the commercialization of knowledge. Each of these four issues is developed in more detail in the 2011 knowledge paper. From a theoretical point of view, however, I attach special importance to the second of these issues, in which I posit a relationship of "reciprocal legitimation" between knowledge and power. This argument acknowledges, on the one hand, the legitimating potential of knowledge and expertise in the exercise of power. At the same time, it includes the important role of the state and its instruments of authority in validating and legitimating certain kinds of knowledge over others. It is this argument that provides the linkage to my preoccupation with "compensatory legitimation" in the 1970s. Yet, this same argument also opens that discourse to the wider realm of the mutually advantageous relationship between knowledge and power. (Personal communication from Hans Weiler, February 2017)

At the heart of Weiler's analysis of knowledge and its role in education is the relationship between knowledge and power. As he points out, there is "nothing new about recognizing the fact that knowledge and power are closely and symbiotically related; it has been dealt with in the works of Karl Marx and Karl Mannheim as well as in those of Emile Durkheim and Max Weber" (Weiler, 2011, p. 209). Major contributors to reframing our understanding of this relationship were Michel Foucault (1978), who elaborated in great detail on the order, stability, authority, and regulatory power of knowledge, and Nicos Poulantzas (1978), who argued that the "state takes knowledge and participates in its transformation into language and rituals that serve to separate knowledge from mass consumption and from manual work—from the process of direct production" and that "this legitimizes a particular ideology—the dominant bourgeois values and norms—by changing that juridical-political ideology into a set of technocratic 'facts' and decisions based on 'scientific' studies, on expertise,' etc." (Carnoy, 1984, p. 113).

Weiler's focus in this more recent work is less on *compensatory* legitimation—that is, on the need of the state to solve its crisis of legitimacy through various "ideological" (e.g., experimentation and participation) and "commodification" (notably, juridical interventions that force the state to allocate more resources to less legislatively powerful groups) interventions in the educational system—than on reciprocal legitimation between knowledge and power. After positing that there are competing conceptions of knowledge, he argues that knowledge hierarchies are shaped by those with the power to order those hierarchies. In turn, he argues that just as power shapes the "value" placed on different types of knowledge, political decisions—which reflect the exercise of power—are increasingly justified, in modern society, by using knowledge:

Knowledge and power are connected by a relationship of reciprocal legitimation—i.e., knowledge legitimates power and, conversely, knowledge is legitimated by power. There is ample evidence for this symbiotic relationship between knowledge and power, most notably the ever-increasing degree to which political decisions are justified by reference to a particular body of knowledge— from environmental and energy policies to the location of new industries and from the redistribution of wealth to decisions on how to manage financial crises. In our complex and knowledge-based societies, knowledge and science have virtually become the currency of choice in legitimizing state power. . . . But the relationship is far from being a one-way street. Just as knowledge legitimizes power, it also derives a great deal of its own legitimation from decisions of the state—decisions on, for example, what is to be learned and taught at schools, what sort of knowledge is required to qualify candidates for specific public offices and careers, what sort of research should enjoy public funding, etc. In all these and many other decisions that are subject to state authority, *one* type of knowledge is typically given priority over *another* and is accorded special standing and legitimacy. The close and often intricate relationship between knowledge and power reveals itself as an instrument of reciprocal legitimation. (Weiler, 2011, pp. 210–211)

Thus, the role of knowledge is to legitimate and justify the use of power but at the same time, power defines "what knowledge matters." Political (and economic) power strongly influences which knowledge is legitimate and which is not. This reciprocity between knowledge and power is, according to Weiler's analysis, increasingly played out transnationally, which draws interesting comparisons to world society theory. As discussed in the previous chapter, world society theory argues that, as far as educational expansion is concerned, such reciprocal transnational legitimation has been playing out since the nineteenth century. His analysis also resonates with the theoretical work on globalization reviewed in Chapter 10:

This international dimension is characterized not only by a worldwide information flow that is increasingly facilitated by technology, but also by its own kind of political dynamics. For the apparent openness of the international knowledge system tends to obscure the fact that there are extreme global disparities in the distribution of both knowledge production and consumption. Indeed, one of the salient features of the international knowledge system is its peculiar division of labor, in which key intellectual tasks, such as setting theoretical agendas and methodological standards, are the prerogative of a relatively small number of societies and institutions that play a disproportionately important role in this system—societies and institutions which are, almost without exception, located in the economically privileged (northern) regions of the world.

This particular type of hierarchy in our contemporary international knowledge system is by no means concerned only with knowledge, but reflects quite faithfully the international hierarchies of economic influence and political power with which the international knowledge system maintains a closely symbiotic relationship. This relationship in turn has parallels to the relationship of reciprocal legitimation between knowledge and power that I have described earlier. This is particularly evident in the case of institutions like the World Bank, whose role in the international system is by no means confined to exercising influence on economic activity and policy. Less well-known, but extremely effective is the influence the World Bank wields by imposing an orthodoxy of knowledge to which all countries and institutions that wish to enter into negotiations on financing and support with the World Bank must subscribe. (Weiler, 2011, pp. 211–212)

Because universities in almost all countries are important knowledge producers, how does this reciprocal legitimation between knowledge and power play out in the university system, especially in the context of the transnationalization of knowledge and power? Weiler sees greater separation between the national state and universities—that is, he views universities as gaining increasing autonomy from the state, largely because of the fiscal crisis of the state. If the state has fewer resources to allocate to higher education, and particularly in the context of higher education expansion, universities increasingly come to rely on other sources of funding, namely private tuition and donations. This process of privatization is evident worldwide. Yet Weiler also recognizes that the state is increasing pressure on universities to be accountable for the funds that they do receive from the state, and that this accountability exerts power over what is "valuable" university output, including the output of knowledge. In this sense, even as the state may implicitly be giving universities greater autonomy as state resources play a smaller role in funding the university system as a whole, the state plays its legitimacy card by appealing to citizen "demands" to have a clearer idea of what universities actually produce and instituting accountability measures that define university output and seriously curtail autonomy.

Compensatory and reciprocal legitimation are important concepts, as are the insights we can draw from Weiler's analysis of knowledge and its relation to power. At the same time, it is crucial to the meaning of these concepts to have a clear understanding of the configuration of state power, and therefore of the forces that define the field of play on which the conflicts over knowledge are fought out. In his analysis of compensatory legitimation, Weiler argues that there have been many reasons given for the state's crisis of legitimacy—for example, the increased load of tasks undertaken by modern capitalist governments, the phenomenon of overloaded politics, the shortcomings of existing modes of representation, the inherent difficulty of distributing the surplus social product inequitably yet legitimately (Habermas, 1975), and the conflict between liberalism and democracy (Wolfe, 1977). Each of these derived from an underlying theory of the state. Some of these are pluralist, and others are based on capitalist class relations and the state as responsible for developing the ideology and organizing "public" resources to successfully reproduce class inequality.

Weiler's theory of the state is not clear in these works on compensatory and reciprocal legitimacy. But given the typologies of state educational policies he analyzes (juridical, experimentation, and client participation) and his focus on the reciprocity of knowledge and power, it seems that he views the state as the ideological organizer of the reproduction of unequal power relations—close to Habermas's view of the "manipulative" state. Nevertheless, the main point Weiler makes is that whether those at the top of the power hierarchy are largely a political or bureaucratic elite as in Foucault or a hegemonic fraction of the capitalist class (national or global) as in Gramsci or Offe, educational policy and control over the definition of legitimate knowledge are tools of state power to legitimize the state and therefore to reproduce unequal power relations.

It is interesting that Weiler analyzes universities in terms of reciprocal legitimacy between knowledge and power—in other words, in terms of the needs of the state to control the production of knowledge in universities and the needs of knowledge producers to gain legitimacy from the power structure. In the German context of the early twenty-first century, this may be the most relevant analysis to make, but in nation-states or subunits of the nation-state (with jurisdiction over education) going through major expansions of higher education or trying to develop "world-class universities," it may be more relevant to use compensatory legitimation to understand how and why this expansion occurs. For example, in a comparative study of university expansion and change in Brazil, Russia, India, and China (the BRIC countries), we used an Offe-Weiler theoretical framework to understand the complexities of BRICs' national higher education policies in a globalized economy and ideological environment (Carnoy, Loyalka, et al., 2013):

For all their different histories, in today's globalized economy, BRIC states do have in common that they reproduce political power largely by seeking political legitimacy, that they seek this legitimacy at both a domestic and international level, and that they consider their higher education policies as playing a potentially important role in achieving legitimacy.

The main argument is that these states use the expansion of education, including university education, to promote capital accumulation in the hands of the powerful (either private owners of capital or the state itself) with political legitimation in the eyes of workers and employees (Offe, 1973). In this theory, education helps realize the self-interest of the state actors (including the intellectual elites in public universities) to increase state revenue and reproduce state power (Weiler, 1983). Different groups in the state bureaucracy may have different views on how best to reproduce state power—that is, to keep control of the state's revenue and how it is to be used—but ultimately competing bureaucratic groups are situated in a state that must legitimate itself or collapse (Carnoy, Loyalka, et al., 2013, p. 27).

In addition:

The close connection the population perceives between state higher education policy and access to a high-value investment good creates a direct relation between the state's higher education policies and the state's political legitimacy. State higher education strategies can also affect political legitimacy indirectly. State legitimacy is closely related to families' material well-being and employment and to better prospects for their children, which, in turn, depends on economic growth. If the effectiveness of educational policies is related to the rate of economic growth, the state's political legitimacy may be considerably raised or diminished by the quality of its educational strategies. This applies even to such nondemocratic states as China such and quasi-democratic states as Russia. (Carnoy, Loyalka, et al., 2013, p. 21)

Thus, Weiler's concepts of legitimacy can be applied in various contexts and without being specific about the theory of the state underlying the overall analysis. In effect, he is making the case that compensatory and reciprocal legitimation are essential to understanding how and why the modern state uses educational policy. However, this can carry the analysis only so far. Ultimately, in doing "good" comparative education research using compensatory legitimation theory, it is important to have a dynamic theory of the state to identify the roots of the legitimacy crisis that educational policies are being used to "solve." For one, this allows us to analyze whether the state's educational policies are likely to "work" in legitimizing the state, and second, it allows us to better identify possible contradictions in the process of legitimation. The next chapter reviews research that attempts to develop an underlying state theory for their analyses and delves into sources of contradiction in state education policies in the context of these theories.

CHAPTER 8

The 1980s

The State and Comparative Education

I AM NOT SURE when in the 1970s I realized that for me, as an economist, to come up with more complete and nuanced analyses of education, I needed to understand the nexus of a nation's political system—the state—and its economy and society. In almost every country, education is a service supplied by the state. The state spends public revenue to develop a curriculum that instills basic skills and good behavior in youth and to hire teachers to teach that curriculum. Most of these decisions are highly political, and for good reason. Schooling is the designated allocator of income and social roles in capitalist and post-capitalist societies. Even when a significant proportion of students attend private schools, it is the state that defines the meaning of private and public education. In most countries teachers in private schools are paid using public revenues, and because the state is the main supplier of and plays such a dominant role in defining education, the process by which changes take place in education systems is largely shaped by the political relationship of the nation's citizenry to the state and the way that the state has organized the educational system politically.

As I noted years later:

I realize that delving into state theory is a lot of work, but without this framework we will have trouble making sense of why educational systems and practices operate as they do. Without this framework, we also have serious problems in doing coherent comparative analysis, particularly across countries. Without some theory of the state, how does one begin an explanation of why country X puts much more resources into schooling than country Y? Without some theory of the state, how do we define educational access and the distribution of educational quality among members of the society? Indeed, how do we explain the educational system—what is taught, who teaches, and who learns what? Or, for that matter, how do we explain the great variance in teacher practice, or the distribution of teachers and students among schools? (Carnoy, 2006, p. 557)

Once I understood how key political relations were to conceptualizing education, I began to read theories of the state, from Hobbes and Locke and John Stuart Mill to standard pluralist theories to the neo-Marxists, such as Gramsci (1996 edition), Althusser (1976), Poulantzas (1976), and Miliband (1969, 1973). These readings helped me situate my ideas on the investment and reproductive roles of education in a broader political economy that included state theory. Competing theories of the capitalist state include the state acting in the "common good"—a state that acted "to harness men's passions by allowing their interests to overcome those passions" (Carnoy, 1984, p. 13); the pluralist state, in which the common good is defined "as a set of empirical decisions [by elected representatives and a state bureaucracy] that do not necessarily reflect the will of the majority" (Carnoy, 1984, p. 37); and the state as the ideological and repressive apparatuses of the capitalist class.

In 1977, Hank Levin and I began writing a book that ultimately became *Schooling and Work in the Democratic State*. It was not a comparative study. It was about the United States. Nevertheless, our analysis was situated in a broader array of state theories, and it served to motivate researchers worldwide to begin incorporating state theory into comparative and international education analysis. I consciously used the word "ultimately" in describing the publication of the book because it went through two versions. The first was completed in 1978, but we really did not feel satisfied that we had gotten it "right." We had sent it to Michael Apple for consideration in his series at Routledge but withdrew it and made the decision to start all over again. As noted earlier, "delving into state theory is a lot of work." In the meantime, I went to Paris in 1978 on a yearlong sabbatical. This delayed redoing the book, but it also helped both me and Levin to get a better handle on what we really wanted to say.

We had been working closely together on various projects at Stanford since we arrived there from the Brookings Institution about three months apart in the 1968–1969 academic year. Although he was not in SIDEC, he was very interested in international education and participated in many SIDEC activities, including helping the program recruit students in Central America when he traveled there on his consulting trips for international agencies. He also advised many SIDEC students and attended our seminars for MA graduates held in a different Caribbean region site every summer. When Stanford was trying to "remove" me from the faculty in the early 1970s, Levin helped me form a research center off campus, the Center for Economic Studies, and helped us raise money to rent an office and to support a small staff (and eventually to support me if I were to leave Stanford and its School of Education). We channeled most of our consulting through the center and did some very interesting research there with a great group of young researchers on a variety of topics, mainly labor market segmentation (Rumberger and Carnoy, 1980), workplace democracy (Carnoy and Shearer, 1980), and worker cooperatives (Jackall and Levin, 1984). The workplace democracy project gave Levin and me the opportunity to travel through Europe for several weeks in the spring of 1975, studying various experiments in worker control. Among these were the Triumph motorcycle plant in Meriden, England, which had been turned into a cooperative by Triumph workers when Triumph was forced to merge with Norton motorcycles in 1973; the Saab engine plant in Sweden; and the worker cooperatives of Mondragón, in the Basque region of Spain. In 1976, we edited a book, *The Limits of Educational Reform*, that pulled together much of the research that the center had been doing up to that time. That work very much influenced our early thinking in *Schooling and Work in the Democratic State*.

One of my goals in going to Paris was to sit in on some of Nicos Poulantzas's classes on state theory. Poulantzas was a neo-Marxist political philosopher teaching in France; a major intellectual force redefining Marxist thought through his focus on the state. Although he started out as a structuralist, heavily influenced by Althusser, he evolved in the 1970s such that by the time I got to Paris in September 1978, he had just published *State, Power, and Socialism* (Poulantzas, 1978), in which he characterized the capitalist state as a site that generated contradictions in the process of reproducing class relations. Once I got a place to live in Paris with my two sons, I found Poulantzas's name in the telephone book and did the unthinkable—I cold-called him at home and asked where I could attend his classes. Overcoming the initial shock of getting that call, he invited me to come to his biweekly graduate seminar at the Institut des Hautes Études, which I attended for the entire academic year.

When Levin and I met in Paris in December 1978, on one of his visits to the OECD, we decided to rewrite the book. I was getting a more solid conception of the state as a site of contradictions, and he felt that we had not gotten the first version right. That rewrite was a long time in the making. Meanwhile, Derek Shearer and I had published *Economic Democracy* (Carnoy and Shearer, 1980), and I spent two years writing *The State and Political Theory,* which was a review of theories of the state from classical eighteenth-century theories to the neo-corporatist and neo-Marxist reconceptualizations of the 1960s and 1970s. Nevertheless, despite the detours, Levin and I finally finished writing *Schooling and Work in the Democratic State* in 1983–1984, and it was published in 1985.

We were somewhat surprised that in the Reagan era the book received its strongest critiques from the Left. These critiques so misrepresented what we had said in the book that in our answer to them, Levin and I found it necessary to recapitulate our argument in the 1986 article "But Can It Whistle?" responding to these critiques:

The book begins with the paradox that schools are both like the workplace and yet very different from the workplace. Both schools and workplaces tend to be large, bureaucratic, impersonal, hierarchical, and routinized. Both tend to motivate performance with external rewards such as grades and wages, rather than through the value of the activity itself. Both are dominated by expertise and formal authority, regulations, and work schedules. The same racial and social class groups that do poorly in the workplace also do poorly in school.

But schools also differ from the workplace in some very important respects. Although American schools are marked by inequalities, schools do more than any other major social institution to provide equal opportunities for participation and rewards. Enormous differences in status and compensation between men and women in the labor force are not reflected in education, where gender differences are relatively small, continue to diminish, and cut in both directions. Although the top 20% of the United States population in educational attainment receive about twice as much education investment as the bottom 20%, the richest 20% in income have almost 10 times the income and own about 95% of all wealth.

Students and teachers have more constitutional protections than employees in other workplaces. For example, both students and teachers are entitled to considerable freedom of expression without fear of suspension on the part of students or job loss on the part of teachers. These rights and the various egalitarian reforms have been won through mobilization, political action, and use of the courts by social movements that have arisen in the democratic tradition. Though schools are largely organized like workplaces, screening and preparing youth for inequality, they are far more equal and participatory than most offices or factories.

From this analysis, it became clear to us that schools did not just "correspond" to the workplace, reproducing wage labor for capitalist production. Rather, they were also characterized by another dynamic that pushed for participation, equality, and expansion of rights, often in conflict with the unfettered reproduction of wage labor. It is a struggle between these two dynamics that provides a powerful framework for explaining educational change.

Such a struggle is hardly an accident. Schooling is situated within the democratic, capitalist state, the state that has both egalitarian and inegalitarian characteristics associated with popular movements and demands for rights, participation, and equality, on the one hand, and the economic and political power and ideology of capital on the other. These provide a basis for struggle over the power of the state in serving democratic versus capitalist interests, and a similar scenario is played out in the schools.

The heart of the book's analytical framework lies in the development of a theory of the state that demonstrates how the struggle takes place within the state and then shows how it is played out within the schools. The framework is used to understand historically such issues as changing socialization for work and the changing workplace, the historical and contemporary tensions and maneuvering between the democratic and capitalist dynamics, and a detailed future scenario that is used to predict changes in work and in schools.

Our theory of educational change in modern capitalist societies, we argue, necessarily *has* to be situated in a theory of politics—of the state. This is not a minor shift in emphasis from previous critical theory, nor is it simply an adjunct to these previous works. It is a *different* view of why and how educational change occurs

We see the state as the condensation of conflictual class and social relations, the product and shaper of such relations. We argue that, historically, the capitalist state has attempted to displace class and social conflict into the political arena by redefining workers, capitalists, farmers, blacks, and women away from their roles in civil society into individuals who are national citizens with equal political rights and responsibilities. But in so doing, the political arena (the state) has itself become the primary site of social conflict in which the rules are linked to, but different from, the capitalist production sector. By conferring equality on individuals as citizens, the capitalist state allows for the possibility of political configurations which can drastically alter the conditions of capitalist accumulation.

Most important from our standpoint, the existence of a democratic state has allowed for the development of a democratic dynamic that, although certainly linked historically to capitalism, is also inherently in tension with it. The educational system is a crucial element of the state apparatus and is therefore situated in the heart of sociopolitical conflict characterized by this tension between the two dynamics. It is this tension that is fundamental to our understanding of educational change. We contend, finally, that in different periods of history, largely depending on the strength of social movements seeking greater political empowerment, the democratic or reproductive capitalist dynamic dominates, either molding education to meet "democratic" demands (gains for subordinate groups) or reproductive ones for wage labor (gains for the capitalist imperative). Our analysis, therefore, allows for "authentic" gains by subordinate groups—changes in the work process, state, and educational system that are not simply co-optations by a dominant capitalist class, but represent victories for social movements, even to the extent of altering the rules of the game. (Carnoy and Levin, 1986, pp. 529–531)

Thus, the main contributions of *Schooling and Work in the Democratic State* were to show, first, that the main political tension in education is between the major roles it plays in reproducing economic inequality and in opening the door to greater equality; and second, that analyses of educational systems in countries such as the United States can be understood only by situating the struggles that characterize education within the larger economic and political struggles in a democratic, capitalist state.

Levin's and my analysis differed considerably from my earlier, "structuralist" argument in *Education as Cultural Imperialism* or from Bowles and Gintis's analysis in *Schooling in Capitalist America*. *Schooling and*

Work in the Democratic State made the case that change can and does take place in education and other sites of the state, although not necessarily in a linear fashion. These changes in education have repercussions for civil society, again not necessarily linearly. Levin and I did not take the next step to apply our model cross nationally, racially, or gender-wise, but we were sure that our argument had important implications for analyzing education comparatively. To do so meant developing an understanding of the political and social forces that formed the state in each society and how these forces were reflected in the public institution called the educational system. Our application to the US education system of this underlying theory of education as a political-social construct of the state was an example of a more general approach to analyzing education:

Public schools in America are an institution of the State, and like other State institutions are subject to the pull of two conflicting forces over their control, purpose, and operation. On the one hand, schools reproduce the unequal, hierarchical relations of the capitalist workplace; on the other, schooling represents the primary force in the United States for expanding economic opportunity for subordinate groups and the extension of democratic rights.

These forces are in structural opposition, creating contradictions—i.e., conflicts and internal incompatibilities—in education that result in a continuing struggle over direction. Although at any given time one of the forces may appear to dominate and achieve hegemony, the existence of underlying contradiction means that the struggle continues in various latent forms. Contradiction is at the heart of educational change by generating a series of continuing conflicts and accommodations that transform the shape of the schooling process. Changes generated by educational contradictions also induce changes in the workplace.

Schools are characterized by contradiction and conflict through their very function of serving American capitalist expansion and the democratic political system. These democratic and class-reproductive dynamics are conditioned by the larger social conflict outside the schools. To the extent that the democratic dynamic gains ground, the educational system diverges in certain respects from the structural exigencies of reproducing capitalist relations of production and the division of labor. This divergence, in turn, is capable of exacerbating or changing the character of social conflict. It is therefore not only conflict in production that can lead to crises in capitalist development, but also contradictions in reproduction. In the latter case, crisis emerges from the failure of one of the more important institutions of reproduction to reproduce properly the labor skills, the division of labor, and the social relations of production (Carnoy and Levin, 1985, pp. 144–145)

We argued that there are three types of contradictions associated with schooling, all of which result directly or indirectly from the tension that arises between the democratic thrust of schools and their role in reproducing the class and work structure:

The first type of contradiction manifests itself in the political struggle over resources for schooling. Since schooling is "public," it has been the object of social and reform movements committed to increasing the social mobility of subordinate groups. These movements have usually sought to increase the resources going to schooling for school expansion generally and for the education of working-class and minority groups in particular. But such resource demands may reduce the capacity of the State to enhance the profitability of capital, with the result that conflict will occur over school expansion between capital and labor in times of declining of stagnant profits, slow economic growth, and declining real wages—as in the 1970's and early 1980's.[1]

A second type of contradiction is internal to the educational process. The reproductive dynamic creates pressures in schools to produce a labor force with skills, attitudes, and values that fit into the hierarchical division of labor and to reproduce capitalist relations of production. At the same time, the democratic dynamic emphasizes individual liberty and democratic participation as well as equality of opportunity and occupational mobility through education. The student must be prepared to participate in an authoritarian and hierarchical system of work, but also be prepared to benefit from and contribute to a system of egalitarian democratic practices. To a large degree, establishing curriculum, teaching process, and educational structure that support one set of requirements must be done at the expense of the other. As we will show below, one consequence of this type of contradiction is the development of workers who are overeducated for the types of jobs that will be available to them.

A third type of contradiction is imported into the educational process through the fact that the schools correspond with the workplace. Contradictions of this type arise out of the correspondence process itself. As the features of the workplace are embodied in schools, so are the contradictions of the workplace embodied in schooling practices. Especially important is the educational manifestation of the contradiction between capital and labor. (Carnoy and Levin, 1985, pp. 145–146)

The first of these contradictions is fundamental to understanding why, for example, many developing countries (Brazil, Chile, Malaysia, Korea, India, Philippines, just to name a few) allow for such a high fraction of the expansion of postsecondary education to be taken up by private institutions, increasingly by for-profit private institutions. Private higher education has become an important source of capitalist profits in these countries, and the private higher education industry becomes an important lobby group in the state, simultaneously pushing for government subsidies and reduced regulation. It could be argued that expanding higher education by any means possible serves to increase social mobility, and therefore, even if higher education is a profit-making industry, by privatizing higher education the state is helping to "democratize" society. However, there is little evidence that private institutions cater particularly to working-class students, and, if these institutions are lightly regulated, there is little evidence that they contribute effectively to increased social mobility. In the United States, for example, private, for-profit universities have used government student loans to subsidize their expansion and their profits, mainly encumbering middle-class and poor students with personal debt and giving them an inferior education, without providing them better, higher-paying jobs and so forcing many of them to default on loans (see Deming et al., 2012).[2]

For educators, the second contradiction is the most interesting. We argued throughout the book that schools have, as a primary goal, the production of workers with the "appropriate cognitive and vocational skills for existing jobs or on-the-job training and with behaviors, habits, and values predisposing them to the organization of capitalist production . . . [and] it means promoting an ideology among youth that portrays capitalism as the embodiment of individual liberty and democracy and inculcates political loyalty to it as a system" (Carnoy and Levin, 1985, pp. 147–148). Educators have never liked either of these notions, as they seem to degrade the loftier ideals of education and the ideal that educators could produce in schools alternative ideologies that are more collective and altruistic than those reflected in capitalist production and market competition. Levin and I agreed that there was this inherent contradictory strand in capitalist education:

At the same time the schools are charged with producing citizens who know and care about democratic rights and equal opportunity and who are able to participate fully in the economic, social, and political life of society. The result is that schools generate a range of functions that contradict the efficient reproduction of capitalist workers. We have identified five of these functions that support the democratic side of schooling: (1) democratic participation; (2) social equality; (3) social mobility; (4) cultural development; and (5) independence of the educational bureaucracy. Each serves to divert the schools from the preparation of properly socialized workers by inculcating in students' various traits that are in conflict with work requirements. (Carnoy and Levin, 1985, p. 148)

We go on to observe that because schools are expected to serve capitalist labor markets and to fulfill democratic ideals of individual rights and social mobility, education sits at the juncture of major contradictions in democratic capitalist societies:

Attempts to provide greater equality of educational opportunities impart a dynamic to the school quite different from that of the workplace. There is an implicit tension between what schools are expected to do for the poor and discriminated against and what the economy is supposed to do for them. These expectations have been galvanized into the social movements that have challenged educational inequalities associated with race, gender, and family income, as well as other sources of what has been perceived as unequal treatment. These movements have pressured schools to pursue egalitarian outcomes, even when they are not consistent with the priorities of the workplace or of taxpayers. For example, testing and tracking patterns are constantly being challenged in the courts and by parent groups. Federal attempts to provide compensatory resources for low-income children have had to counter the attempts of local educational authorities to use such assistance to replace funding that would have otherwise been provided for the poor out of state and local sources.

Not all these practices have created more equal educational outcomes, but they raised expectations of more nearly evenhanded educational practices. For example, there is evidence of only modest improvements in the relative test scores of children from low-income backgrounds, despite almost two decades of compensatory programs . . . ; this suggests that the schools alone cannot compensate for substantial economic and other disadvantages. The evidence on the effects of school integration is also ambiguous. In fact, the previous chapter suggests that social class-related reproduction is sometimes subtle and independent of resource availability, and that certain forms if reproduction cannot be easily altered by educational policies. But the expectations of greater equality in the schools and the use of social movements and the courts to obtain it have contributed to a dynamic for the schools that undermines the strict preparation of workers. (Carnoy and Levin, 1985, pp. 150–151)

We detail many other characteristics of the schooling process that emanate from its contradictory position in the capitalist reproduction process, including the alienation of students and teachers. For example, the role of teachers as both authorities judging the potential for social mobility of students in their charge and workers in a capitalist organization of production, albeit a public-sector organization, creates a series of contradictions, for schooling and for the larger reproduction process:

In a sense, teachers have little choice, given the lack of alternatives for influencing the educational process and their own working conditions. They have to conduct their struggle for fundamental occupational rights as though they were private-sector workers in basic conflict with their employer. But demands for higher teacher wages create a dilemma for the State. If parents pay higher taxes, the dilemma is solved; but if, as is now the case, there is resistance to paying more, schooling services must be cut, with obvious implications for the capability of the schools to deliver properly prepared and socialized youth to the workplace.

Teacher negotiations and strikes also affect the process of student ideological formation. School administrators take an active role in turning community sentiment—especially parent and pupil sentiment—against negotiating teachers with threats that students will sacrifice learning and potential employment and college eligibility if the strike is prolonged. Anti-teacher sentiments may be further reinforced by an anti-union bias, which has been promoted by business interests and has become more prominent in recent years. Teachers are characterized as selfish and greedy rather than "pulling together" on behalf of the community as workers are supposed to do on behalf of the corporation. Demanding higher wages and striking against the *community* is characterized as "typical union activity." Yet even this antilabor sentiment contains contradictions, for these are the same teachers who are responsible for judging pupil performance and for inculcating pupils with values and skills once the negotiations and strikes are over. How can the teacher be at once selfish and also a source of inspiration for learning and dedication to knowledge? (Carnoy and Levin, 1985, p. 158)

Many other writers in this period emphasized "resistance" in schools as an important potential source of contradiction in the class reproduction process. In the US, Sennett and Cobb (1972), Giroux (1981), and Apple (1982); in England, Willis (1977); and in France, Baudelot and Establet (1971), all discussed, from different perspectives, the school as a place of resistance to class domination by working-class youth. However, Levin and I were not convinced that such resistance engendered in schools because of student and teacher alienation was a primary contradiction of capitalist education.

Sennett and Cobb (1972) and Willis (1977) showed that differential treatment of working-class youth—signaling to lower-class children that they will not do well in school and that expectations for them are minimal—generates responses of overt defiance among some adolescents. "The boys," as Willis called them, seek to gain esteem and leadership among peers by acting out against authority. Doing well in school among lower-class youth may be considered as "giving in" or cooperating, particularly because it is so unusual for them to do well. Good students from this group appear to be selected by the teacher for special consideration. Most adolescents, however, simply "drop out" in the classroom, resisting passively by not listening even though required to be in school until the age of sixteen:

Baudelot and Establet (1971) stress collective resistance. Schools are defaced and youth rebel openly in the classroom, even attacking teachers. The school is just one more dominating institution that has to be overthrown, a continuation of the class struggle in the workplace. Yet Baudelot and Establet stress that the struggle in the school is not the same as in the workplace. Students are not workers; they do not produce, and there is no surplus extraction on the part of schools. Thus, the nature of the struggle is totally different: it is resistance to incorporation into production in a particular way, and resistance to the values and norms being pressed onto working-class youth—values that are alien and designed to dominate. (Carnoy and Levin, 1985, p. 159)

For Sennett and Cobb, Willis, and Baudelot and Establet, resistance is generated by the incorporation of class conflicts and class-consciousness into the schools:

The reproduction of the social structure generates resistance on the part of those who will occupy the lowest rungs in that structure—those designated to fail in school and therefore to fail in life. The fact that many pupils must do poorly (or just not well) in school to fill the ranks of subordinate labor markets creates the possibility of resistance to class-structured education. It is the reproduction of capitalist social relations and of racial divisions, therefore, that is the source of resistance; conflicts inherent in capitalist society, though different in nature from those of the schools, are carried over into the schools. Social conflict is thus also carried over into the educational system, even though its form may be different from that in the workplace and other social institutions.

Giroux (1981) and Apple (1982) call on Gramsci's dialectical concept of hegemony and counter-hegemony in arguing that schools reproduce class but that the practices of schooling—in attempting to expand and deepen capitalist hegemony—are resisted by counterhegemonic tendencies in working-class youth, young women, and minorities. (Carnoy and Levin, 1985, pp. 159–160)

However, counterhegemony, as Gramsci defined it, is necessarily rooted in social and political movements, and in a revolutionary political party, which translates counterhegemonic ideologies into political action. Apple and Giroux never spell out the relation between movements and resistance by these various groups to the hegemonic "hidden curriculum" in schools. Willis's "boys" resist the school's attempts to socialize them into doing well and entering the capitalist rat race, but a lot of good it does them—they end up in the same working-class jobs as their fathers, at the bottom of the hierarchy.

Our argument in *Schooling and Work in the Capitalist State* was that resistance is embedded in social conflict, and it is social conflict outside schools that shapes the way class-structured schooling is resisted in different ways by working-class youth, minorities, and other marginalized groups. We insisted that the most important contradictions to the structure and practice of class-based education are induced as part of class and social conflict inherent in that society:

The constant struggle to expand democratic rights, both political and economic, also takes place within education, expanding the role of schools in the process of social mobility and in the more equitable treatment of subordinate groups. Therefore, social conflict shapes educational change over time. Resistance to ideologically based curricula and other schooling practices has to be set in the context of this conflict. Such resistance is not independent of the struggle going on outside the schools. . . . [W]e consider that resistance to schooling practices is a secondary rather than a primary contradiction. We agree that counter-hegemony is often manifested as indirect resistance by pupils to the ideology imposed upon them by the schools. But we think that more important forms of counter-hegemony inherent in social movements have historically influenced the very ideology that schools imposed. Thus, dominant ideology as reflected in schooling is continually shaped by social conflict both outside and inside the schools. (Carnoy and Levin, 1985, p. 160)

EXTENDING STATE THEORY TO
COMPARATIVE EDUCATION

Schooling and Work in the Democratic State (and Bowles and Gintis's *Democracy and Capitalism*) laid the groundwork for using state theory to understand educational change, but it was left to another work, published four years later, to apply state theory to comparative education analysis. That book, *Education and Social Transition in the Third World* (1989), came out of an academic exchange program in the mid-1980s between

SIDEC and the Institute of International Education (IIE) at the University of Stockholm under the sponsorship of the US State Department. Joel Samoff, an expert on African education policies who had been teaching in SIDEC since 1980, Hans Weiler, and myself were the principal investigators on the SIDEC side, and Ingemar Fagerland, director of the IIE, and Vinayagum Chinapah and Jan-Ingvar Löfstedt, IIE professors, on the Swedish side. We had had a decades-long collaboration with the IIE, mainly because of Torsten Husén, who had been coming to Stanford since the 1960s. But our two institutions' researchers had been going back and forth for about ten years when we landed the State Department grant.

The long, systematic discussions we had during the exchange with the IIE researchers about our experiences in "revolutionary" Third World countries evolved into the idea of putting it all into a book. In *Education and Social Transformation in the Third World*, Joel Samoff and I, and three graduate students—Mary Ann Burris and Carlos Alberto Torres from Stanford and Anton Johnston from IIE—analyzed the role of education in five countries transitioned from dependent capitalism to various forms of socialist economies and governments: China, Cuba, Tanzania, Mozambique, and Nicaragua.

The book developed an analysis of change in these transition societies that focused on the state and politics and the importance of education as a locus of state-led change. We argued that the state, not the production system, is the main source of the dynamic of postcapitalist revolutionary societies, and it is politics, more than the relations of production, that drives their social development. We also claimed that our analysis of how and why these states restructured their educational systems to lead in the transformation process also helped us understand, through comparison and contrast, how and why educational systems in traditional dependent capitalist countries maintained inequality.

Our task in *Education and Social Transformation* was not an easy one. We had the Levin and Carnoy analysis to work with, but it and other efforts to situate education in various versions of state theory had done so in industrialized, politically democratic capitalist economies. As we described in the introduction to *Education and Social Transformation*, the countries we were analyzing had, it was true, overthrown capitalist states through revolution, but the states they overthrew were not advanced capitalist states. Their economies were barely industrialized, mainly agricultural, and their civil societies and social structures were very different from those in advanced economies:

Relative inattention to the struggle on the small scale has regularly jeopardized the transition on the large scale. The new leadership generally assumed that the conquest of the economy, with appropriate revolutionary guidance, would carry with it the transformation of other sectors and the resocialization of the populace. Nowhere did that occur. The conquest of the economy itself was often halting and partial and, with the exception of China and perhaps Cuba, remains incomplete. Having seized the reins of power (or perhaps more accurately, having occupied the offices of authority), the new leadership was initially inclined to focus on production at the expense of mobilization. Although increased output and productivity were, and are, essential for the transition, the preoccupation with production obscured the durability of the old understandings and social relations and undermined the politicization necessary to challenge them. (Carnoy and Samoff, 1989, p. 362)

We found that the states that emerged in the five countries had several other common features. One was that they all had anti- or noncapitalist orientations and therefore immediately came into conflict with the interests of the industrialized countries that supported the previous regime—in most cases, they faced sanctions and military confrontation. Second, they all sought to collectivize production through public ownership, and they oriented this public ownership to the more equal distribution of goods and services, including the most important of these, education and health care. Third, education in these societies differed from education in capitalist states largely because the state in all the countries we studied was committed to building a mass society, in which individual gain is subsumed to national needs and objectives and social transformation is the basis for economic growth and for increased political participation. Another common feature was the dominant role of the state "in all spheres of social transformation and development—and with that role, a fundamental tension between the respective domains of central authority and local democracy" (Carnoy and Samoff, 1989, p. 6). Also:

On the one hand, the new state's legitimacy and its development program depend on its ability to mobilize and incorporate the citizenry. On the other hand, the new state—often permeated by the old state's bureaucrats, structures, methods, and philosophies—not only has a direct economic interest in steering the country's social transformation from the center but is impeded by outside aggression and internal resistance to intensify centralization and authoritarian practice. The result is that these states have always made significant large-scale efforts to develop new organs of popular democracy at various levels of the society, but have simultaneously developed a bureaucratic and authoritarian structure, which manages to undermine and circumvent people's power. The tension between these two forces simultaneously impedes and dynamizes the process of social transformation. (Carnoy and Samoff, 1989, p. 6)

The lessons for comparative education from studying these countries emanate largely from the much less opaque relationship in them between the state, the creation of a new social structure, and education. The educational system is a principal vehicle for the state to move the society in a particular direction, and therefore school personnel are directly responsible to the state for achieving rather well-defined state-set access and equity goals. It is thus impossible to avoid analyzing these educational systems without a well-developed theory of the transition state:

Education is seen in such societies as a route to all things. It is expected to be the primary vehicle for developing and training skills to ensure that the next generation in the society is adequately prepared for the specific tasks that the society expects of it. . . . The schools are expected to have the kind of responsibilities and perhaps even more than in societies where profound social transformation is not on the agenda. (Carnoy and Samoff, 1989, pp. 7–8)

The flip side of the crucial role that public education is supposed to play in transforming these societies is that education is an even more important lens than in capitalist societies through which we can assess social and political change in the transition process:

Studying educational policy is essential to understanding the reality of this transformation. The case studies confirm that education in transition states is viewed, much more than in capitalist countries, as the key to economic and social development. After the takeover of the conditioned state, whether by revolution or independence, there has been a rapid expansion of both formal schooling and non-formal adult education. The expansion has included and especially focused on those segments of the population least empowered in the conditioned political economy.

In addition to the rapid expansion, both to increase skills and to reduce inequalities in access, education in such societies is expected to play a key role in the transformation of social relations. This role is shaped by the ideal of making educated labor the keystone of a more productive, modernized, participative economy, based on a collectivist or socialist ideology. Educational expansion and content are also shaped by the ideal of developing a new, indigenous, and revolutionary sense of national history. Part of that ideal is to give a prominent place in creating history to groups marginalized by conditioned capitalism.

But our case studies show that the reality of revolutionary transition in a world dominated by capitalist financial institutions, transnational manufacturing and service enterprises, core countries' dominance of technological creativity and their conflict with the Soviet Union (which translates into potential conflict with all "socialist" states) has required important compromises with these ideals by the revolutionary leadership, including compromises on educational expansion and content. These compromises have consequences for the transition process.

They may help explain, for example, why educational expansion and reform do not appear to develop, at least in the short term, a new consciousness among those who attend school. Nor do they appear to lead directly to social transformation. In part, slower than expected progress toward these goals is attributable to the demand for traditional skills in order to meet short-term production and organizational needs—needs accentuated by economic sanctions, political subversion ("destabilization"), and military intervention. In part, it also seems to be the result of conscious government decisions regarding education and political participation. Education in transition states, for example, continues to be characterized by formality and hierarchy. In part, this reflects the emphasis on the development of basic skills and the importance of maintaining centralized control in a situation of persisting external threat. In part, it stems from the uncritical adoption of external models, and in part, it is due to the tendency by revolutionary leaders to increase bureaucratization and control. Our analysis suggests that whatever its proximate origins, there seems to be a clear relationship between increased bureaucratization in the transition state and increased reliance on traditional hierarchical formal schooling as the principal means of defining and transferring knowledge. (Carnoy and Samoff, 1989, pp. 362–363)

Samoff and I concluded that these societies focused on enhancing labor rather than capital, and that the single most important educational achievement in these societies was the ability to reach out to adult populations and incorporate them into the newly defined nation through literacy campaigns:

Even though the goals of the literacy campaigns were not solely educational, they showed the powerful relationship between political mobilization and educational outcomes. In every case, the campaigns were intended to bring masses of rural and urban illiterates (usually the most marginalized elements in the pre-revolutionary society) into the revolutionary project and to raise the consciousness of already schooled teachers and students participating in the campaign. Mobilizing the schooled and unschooled in the teaching and learning of reading and writing has been effective in (1) developing a new concept of nation in both groups; (2) creating an identification with the revolutionary or independence movement, even among those who did not participate directly in the country's liberation; and (3) empowering politically, through literacy—an important symbol of political power in conditioned capitalist society—the previously illiterate. (Carnoy and Samoff, 1989, p. 366)

The second important educational achievement in the countries we studied was the relatively rapid development of a mass educational system for children and adults; the third great achievement was the equalization of access to knowledge both among social classes and between genders, and, to some extent, the demystification of expertise (or, put another way, a decrease in the separation between manual and mental work), and the fourth achievement—developed largely through the expansion of the educational system—was the increased capacity for self-government.

But the book also concluded that slow improvement in the material conditions of life in these poor countries and limits on political participation had important implications for the legitimacy of their state leaders (who promised rapid increases in both growth and participation) and largely, except in the case of China, failed to deliver:

Although education moved toward equalized access to knowledge, it failed to create the kind of social and political consensus imagined by the leaders of these transition states. This made vanguard and mass parties face the unpleasant reality that either education had to be made devoid of all critical analysis (and that critical analysis had to be suppressed in general)—severely limiting further social transformation—or political organizations have to be made participative and accountable, and thus potentially threatening to those in power. In other words, increased participation is neither necessarily socialist nor sufficient for social transformation. (Carnoy and Samoff, 1989, p. 364)

The message our study delivered for comparative education analysis was clear: understanding education in any society means starting with understanding the state, in both industrialized democratic and dependent capitalist economies, where the relationship between the state and public education is less direct and runs through the capitalist economy, and in these five countries, where the relationship is more direct because of the centrality of politics. Yet as Levin and I argued in our analysis of US education, even if it appears in a different form, the education system in bureaucratized transition societies is also the site of struggle between a democratic dynamic (mass mobilization and individual rights) and the agencies of the state representing powerful reproductive interests—in the case of these countries, authoritarian bureaucracies.

Education and Social Transition in the Third World was published the same year as the fall of the Iron Curtain and the end of communism in Eastern Europe. Two years later, the Soviet Union dissolved. In the years since, except for Cuba, the transition societies we analyzed in the book reinstated capitalist economic institutions in varying degrees, mainly to attract foreign investment and increase economic growth. Market capitalism, it turns out, is generally a more effective system for accumulating capital than a command economy, and working with foreign capitalists creates greater opportunities for economic growth than having them working to undermine your economy, and economic growth, for both small and large economies, capitalist and noncapitalist, is a crucial element in furthering state legitimacy. Even so, the relation between education systems and the state in all five countries remained much more direct and, in most, more equal than in neighboring, traditionally dependent capitalist societies.

A BRIEF REFLECTION ON STATE THEORY
AND COMPARATIVE EDUCATION

In the 1990s, work on state theory abated, but the need for it in comparative education did not. What I and others learned about using state theory to gain insights into education remains an essential ingredient in my research and teaching. Recently, a postdoctoral student trained at UC Berkeley, Rebecca Tarlau, spent two years at Stanford working on a book and several articles on social movements in Brazil and their impact on educational change (Tarlau, 2018). She used state theory as a core element in her analysis of these movements and of educational reform (e.g., Tarlau, 2017). Others, such as Roger Dale (1997) and Robert Morrow and Carlos Torres (2000), continue to bring state theory into their work on educational change. With economic globalization, state theory has gradually moved to the next stage of expanding the discussion to include the possibly new role of the national state in a globalized environment (see Carnoy and Castells, 2001). Nevertheless, the theory has not kept up with the massive changes taking place in the world and their implication for the process of reproduction and contradictions in education. The next chapter focuses on some of the work that has been done on globalization—it touches on the state, but not nearly enough.

CHAPTER 9

The 1990s

Comparative Education and the
Impact of Globalization

COMPARATIVE AND INTERNATIONAL EDUCATION, by its very nature, has always been "global." True, for pre–World War II comparative educators, "global" meant Europe and the United States. That changed after the war to include the Soviet Union and countries in Africa, Asia, and Latin America. Nation-states were generally the unit of analysis, and the entire world served as the site of study. Yet researchers usually specialized in areas of the world, and that is still largely the case.

The field was also marked by a semantic debate on "comparative" versus "international" education. This debate focused on the difference between research that attempted to situate an educational issue in a comparative framework—for example, how and why the relation of students' social class to student attainment varies across national contexts—and research that focused on educational policy in a country that was not the author's own (a "foreign" country) or on applying educational policies in, say, a developing country. In that sense, most of the work of the World Bank or regional development banks would be classified as international education.[1]

By the early 1990s, there was widespread recognition—at least among economists and sociologists—that a major shift had occurred in the meaning of "the world," particularly in world economic relations. This "globalization" was intimately intertwined with an information revolution that, combined with new forms of communication, allowed for nonstop interactions in real time among individuals, private enterprises, and governments. The meaning of space and time in human thinking had changed. Because of the massive increase in access to information worldwide, cultures that could dominate information spread rapidly, and cultures that had once been isolated and exotic became less so, sometimes to their benefit, and often not. Large transnational companies, already important in world markets, were well positioned to become even more dominant, and nation-states lost significant control over domestic economic policy. Some analysts, such as Manuel Castells (1996) and Anthony Giddens (1999), saw a radical shift in the very conception of the nation-state, both economically and politically.

Which new approaches did comparative education researchers develop to deal with globalization? The nation-state had traditionally been the fundamental unit of analysis in comparative education, even in dependency, world society, and world system theories, all of which saw comparative education in global terms. A significant number of comparative educators went at this problem, as shown by the rich collection of articles compiled and introduced by Nelly Stromquist and Karen Monkman, *Globalization and Education* (2000). We at Stanford were among them. Our location in Silicon Valley, the world's center of new information and communication technology innovations, and in California, linked by trade and culture to the booming economies in Asia, gave us a clear window into this new phenomenon.

In the early 1990s, faculty at Stanford and University of California Berkeley—I, Manuel Castells, Stephen Cohen, and Fernando Cardoso—wrote *The New Global Economy in the Information Age* (1993). We did not discuss education directly, but we did argue that, paradoxically, in a globalized economy, nation-state education policies would play an even more important role than they had in the past:

The world economy has changed profoundly over the past three decades, and with those changes have come new political strategies for national development. Revolutionary transformations in the demand for goods and in the way they are produced have affected long-term national growth possibilities, how governments relate to their national economies, and how national economies relate to each other. The world economy is becoming more competitive, more global, and increasingly dominated by information and communications technology.

Nation-states still have a crucial role in influencing the course of their economic development. They also a range of policy choices framed by political forces. This is evidenced by the variation in macro- economic and social policies even among highly industrialized Western capitalist nations. But the "informatization" of the world economy changes the conditions of possibilities for national policies. . . . National politics in such a view is subordinated to economics. The nation-state functions mainly as a supplier of human capital to complement multinational investments in machines and technology. (Carnoy, Castells, et al., 1993, pp. 1–3)

In 1996, Manuel Castells published the first volume, *The Rise of the Network Society,* of his famous trilogy on the information age—*The Information Age: Economy, Society, and Culture.* The trilogy helped many of us see the importance of addressing how globalization was affecting national educational systems, and Castells urged me to articulate into a book many of the ideas he and I had discussed about the impact of globalization on national labor markets and educational reforms. This I did, first as a pamphlet for the International Institute of Educational Planning, *Globalization and Educational Reform: What Planners Need to Know* (2000a), which focused on education, then a second piece, also called "Globalization and Educational Reform" (2000b), which went into Stromquist and Monkman's (2000) book, and, finally, a much more ambitious work, *Sustaining the New Economy* (2000c), which described how globalization had affected work, family, and community in developed nations.

Although now almost twenty years old, the analyses in the IIEP pamphlet and the piece in the Stromquist and Monkman book, which focus directly on education, are as relevant today as they were then. In them, I make the case for why globalization is different from the previous period of educational "internationalization," and why it was already clear by the 1990s that economic globalization would put increasing pressure on nation-states to focus on education to enhance their economic and social position in this new information-driven global environment:

A global economy is not a world economy. That has existed since at least the sixteenth century. Neither is it an economy where trade, investment, and resource exploitation take place worldwide. It is not even an economy where the external sector is dominant. For example, neither the United States nor the bloc of western European countries (taken as a whole unit) show foreign trade as a major part of their economic activity. A global economy is one whose strategic, core activities, including innovation, finance, and corporate management, function on a planetary scale on real time. And this globality became possible only recently because of the technological infrastructure provided by telecommunications, information systems, microelectronics machinery, and computer-based transportation. Today, as distinct from even a generation ago, capital, technology, management, information, and core markets are globalized. (Carnoy, 2000b, p. 43)

These writings presented my main ideas on how globalization shapes national educational policy. I argued that globalization is having a profound effect on education at many different levels, and will have even greater effect in the future, as nations, regions, and localities fully comprehend the role educational institutions have in transmitting skills needed in the global economy, but, even more important, in reintegrating individuals into new communities built around information and knowledge:

Two of the main bases of globalization are information and innovation, and they, in turn, are highly knowledge intensive. Internationalized and fast-growing information industries produce knowledge goods and services. Today's massive movements of capital depend on information, communication, and knowledge in global markets, and because knowledge is highly portable, it lends itself easily to globalization. If knowledge is fundamental to globalization, globalization should also have a profound impact on the transmission of knowledge. (Carnoy, 2000b, p. 43)

I also argued, as we did in *The New Global Economy in the Information Age* (1993), that even as the world economy becomes increasingly globalized, the nation-state will remain as the crucial political structure where educational policy is played out, though under increased pressure from global forces at two levels: first, forces that impinge on the underlying politics of the nation-state, such as regional divisions exacerbated by uneven economic development in the global economy, and the increasing use of information technology at the global level to define nation-state politics; and second, global organizations that explicitly attempt to shift policy making from the nation-state to the global level. This is not the overarching ideological conception of the modern nation-state discussed in world society theory that converges nations' thinking about education, human rights, and the importance of science. Rather it is an explicit attempt by international organizations to apply uniform educational policies to all nation-states. Even so, I argued that nation-states retain considerable control over how they choose to finance and reform educational systems:

Ultimately national states still greatly influence the territorial and temporal space in which most people acquire their capacity to operate globally and where capital has to invest. National states are largely responsible for the political climate in which businesses conduct their activities and individuals organize their social lives. Some analysts have called this underlying context for social and economic interaction, "social capital" (Coleman, 1988). Others have focused on "trust" (Fukuyama, 1995). National public policy has an enormous influence on social capital and trust. Even the World Bank, supposedly a global institution, has "rediscovered" the national state as crucial to national economic and social development (World Bank, 1997). It makes a huge difference to a nation's economic possibilities when the national state is capable of formulating coherent economic and social policies and carrying them out. It makes a huge difference if the national state can reduce corruption and establish trust, and it is difficult to imagine achieving greater social capital in most places without a well-organized state. (Carnoy, 2000b, p. 46)

Subsequent papers I wrote as recently as 2016 have elaborated these ideas, but they have not changed in any fundamental way. Essentially, I claim that the main effect of globalization on national education has been through increasing payoffs to higher educated labor because of new technology and the organization of work. This, in turn, has contributed to a tendency for income distribution to become more unequal, particularly in the developed countries, where in the postwar period, economic growth had been sustained in the context of relatively equal income distribution. In addition, competition for capital among nation-states has reduced the capacity for nation-states to raise tax revenues, hence reducing the funds available for education. This has shifted the cost of education to private individuals and to the privatization of educational delivery:

- In financial terms, most governments are under pressure to reduce the growth of public spending on education and to find other sources of funding for the expected expansion of their educational systems.

- In labor market terms, the payoff to higher levels of education is rising worldwide as a result of the shifts of economic production to knowledge intensive products and processes. Governments are also under increased pressure to attract foreign capital, and this means a ready supply of highly skilled labor. This, in turn, places increased pressure on governments to expand their higher education and, correspondingly, to increase the number of secondary school graduates ready to attend postsecondary institutions. In countries that were previously resistant to providing equal access to education for young women, the need for more highly educated low-cost labor tends to expand women's educational opportunities.

- In educational terms, the quality of national educational systems is increasingly being compared internationally. This has placed increased emphasis on math and science curricula, standards, testing, and on meeting standards by changing the way education is delivered. (Carnoy, 2000b, p. 44)

My central argument is that globalization has had its main impact on education through the relative reduction in public funding for education even as it expands to bring increased numbers of students into higher levels of schooling. Because of the higher cost of university education, this is where the cost shifting is greatest. I call these finance-driven reforms, and they have manifested themselves not only in the reduction of public spending per university student in most countries of the world but also in the increased decentralization of public school systems, which in their extreme version have led to privatization reforms at the primary and secondary levels:

With financially driven decentralization, lower-income regions often end up having to lower the cost of schooling more and to put their already more at-risk school population in a worse situation than higher income regions. . . . But lower-income regions are not only faced by lower levels of physical resources that they can bring to bear on educational delivery. They also lack the human resources for managing educational systems. So in the name of the persuasive argument that bringing educational delivery closer to the clients makes education more relevant and responsive to local needs, financially driven decentralization reform is likely to reduce access and quality of education in those regions with the least resources.

Financially driven decentralization reform is also likely to put increased pressure on teacher salaries, especially in the lowest-income regions, hence to create resistance among the very educational actors needed to improve the quality of education. Especially because teachers continue to work largely unsupervised behind the closed doors of classrooms, focusing so heavily on top-down cost-saving deflects attention from a second fundamental reality: if nations hope to increase the cognitive skills of their young populations through schooling they will have to rely on autonomous, motivated, and skilled professional teachers. How these teachers regard themselves, how well they are prepared to do their job, and how committed they are made to fed to their pupils' academic success are keys to producing both basic and advanced learning in any society. This requires a heavy dose of public sector involvement, and not just at the basic education level. Teacher recruitment, education, and technical assistance through in-service training are almost universally public sector-financed and managed. If they are to be improved, it is the public sector that will be responsible.

Since globalization is articulated in the form of finance-driven decentralization reforms, its main effect on the educational systems of many developing countries is to increase inequality of access and quality. It also puts enormous pressure on regions and municipalities to go after teacher salaries in order to reduce costs, creating conflict with the very group needed to produce favorable educational change. Many of the reforms implicit in structural adjustment are actually needed, but their form of implementation results in a series of negative impacts that could be avoided by more coherent focus on school improvement rather than on simple financial objectives. This requires national state interpretations of how to improve educational process and practice within the context of globalization rather than on globalization's financial imperatives themselves. (Carnoy, 2000b, pp. 50–51)

GLOBALIZATION AND THE ROLE OF INTERNATIONAL INSTITUTIONS

One important element of the globalization phenomenon and the way it has influenced comparative and international education in the past three or four decades is the rise of international institutions as major players in shaping national education policies. This is crucially important for comparative education theory. As I described in the first chapter, international and comparative educators were aware of the key role that UNESCO played in organizing comparative education and international testing in the 1950s and 1960s, of the USAID influence of international development education in the 1960s and 1970s, and of the dominance of the World Bank in educational research in the 1980s and early 1990s. However, no one had captured how these institutions and others, such as the OECD, with its expert-led education missions around the world, had taken on added clout in a globalized economy.

This is precisely what Karen Mundy researched when she came to Stanford in 1996, fresh from her doctoral work at the University of Toronto under comparative education scholars Dr. Ruth Hayhoe and Dr. Joseph Farrell, and also from three years as a teacher in rural Zimbabwe. Mundy describes her research on global governance:

My primary focus was on the evolution of the global architecture for international educational development. At Stanford, I established a line of research around the theme of "global governance and educational change," and my work evolved to include consideration of the roles played by international organizations and transnational civil society in shaping global educational norms and policies.

I spent a lot of time studying the major international organizations and how each interacted with national educational systems and tried to influence their development. However, my research went beyond case studies of individual international organizations and how each shaped education in the post–World War II period. I argued that education had emerged as part of the "embedded liberalism" of the post–World War II world order, and became a driver in the globalization of public policies. In the emergent international architecture, the right to education spread as an international liberal norm, and education became an increasingly important domain for international action—be this in the form of the creation of standards, international development projects, or advocacy campaigns to extend the "right to education." Educational policies and practices that had once been the putative domain of the nation state, were increasingly shaped by global institutions and interactions. This was particularly true for low-income developing countries, whose capacity to develop national policies was low and financial resources to expand enrollment lacking. The international organizations quickly filled these gaps with well- defined ideas about educational structures, curriculum, and evaluation.

My first publications on this theme provide a careful history of the evolution of the international education architecture, focused primarily on the way in which international organizations, including UNESCO, the World Bank and UNICEF became increasingly active in shaping global education norms [Mundy, 1998]. I drew out contrasts among these three organizations, showing how the World Bank gradually became not only the largest source of multilateral financing for education in the developing world, but also a critical player in the spread of market based education policy prescriptions that were in tension with the focus on universality and rights advocated within UN organizations (Mundy and Verger, 2015). I also documented the fragmented role played by OECD countries and their bilateral aid agencies.

In subsequent research at Stanford and at the Ontario Institute of Educational Studies at the University of Toronto, where I returned in 2002 as the Canada Research Chair, I documented the dramatic shifts in the international aid regime during the 2000s and its impact on education. After the adoption of the Millennium Development Goals, there was a move towards sector based aid programs that, for the first time, addressed the largest barriers to expanding access, including recurrent costs like teachers' salaries and provision of funding directly to schools in the form of school capitation grants (Mundy, 2010). National and transnational civil society actors emerged as critical partners in the rising focus on system reform—providing a counter balance to the neo-liberal prescriptions offered by the World Bank at the global level and bringing new forms of citizen accountability at the country level [Mundy and Murphy, 2001].

Today, the international architecture for promoting universal education continues to suffer from having a small base of significant donors. In addition, there has been significant volatility among these donors since 2010. The group remains highly fragmented with many partners engaged in some countries and too few in others (Rose et al., 2013). This contrasts with the health sector, where global funding rose much more rapidly and continuously during the 2000s and where a much more significant level of new funding was put in place for global health funds (e.g., GAVI and the Global Fund).

Education aid also remains poorly targeted to the countries and populations most in need. Throughout my career as a critical scholar of global governance in education, I have retained a strong belief in the importance of global institutions in shaping the normative direction of educational systems [Mundy, 2016]. Like many comparative education scholars, my work has included substantial engagement with international organizations themselves. In 2014, I took on the role of chief technical officer for the Global Partnership for Education (GPE), which is a multi-stakeholder fund devoted uniquely to the achievement of Education for All (EFA) in low-income countries and lower-middle-income countries affected by conflict and fragility. GPE was among the most important new institutions born after the Dakar World Education Forum and the Millennium Development Summit. (Personal communication from Karen Mundy, April 15, 2017)

Mundy's initial globalization piece in 1998 focused on the post–World War II history of these international organizations and "became increasingly active in shaping global education norms." This did not happen all at once. Mundy's contribution to understanding this important role of the multilateral agencies in organizing worldwide education policies—especially in developing countries—in the current globalized economic environment was to show both how globalization was associated with a "new" economic philosophy that emerged in the developed countries in the1980s and how multilateral agencies increased their role in defining educational policies as part of the globalized environment. Her underlying argument is that postwar multilateralism and these multilateral institutions "provided a distinctive political space, through which an 'imagined' world order was negotiated, constructed, and (at times) contested" (Mundy, 1998, p. 452). This space—in Mundy's conception—formed part of what Gramsci called the hegemonic project, an ideological framework organized by a fraction of the capitalist class able to gain dominance over other fractions to reproduce class power. Gramsci wrote about hegemony in national terms, but Mundy applied the concept of hegemony to international relations, and cast the international organizations created after

World War II as part and parcel of the hegemonic project of developed countries' ruling elites on a world scale. She chronicles how this political space—hence the hegemonic project, the conception of world order, and the role of the multilateral agencies as mediating institutions in that world order—changed as the world economy globalized and the international economic and political conditions shifted in the last two decades of the twentieth century. Importantly, education played a key role from the very beginning of the hegemonic project organized after World War II, but this role changed with the change in hegemony in the new globalized environment.

Mundy shows how international institutions created in the postwar period to develop a new multilateralism became institutionalized in the context of the dominant postwar Keynesian economic model. She argues that in terms of educational policy, this produced what she calls redistributive multilateralism, in which the developed countries became convinced that the Third World held the key to both the expansion of a liberal world economy and the containment of communism, and funding for international development became the center of attempts to integrate postcolonial nations into the Western world order.

Agencies such as UNESCO and the World Bank—especially UNESCO in this early period—shaped education policies that fit into a larger economic development ideology based on Keynesian welfare-state societal compromise that dominated advanced capitalist countries. In the first chapter of this book, I discussed UNESCO's important role in developing these education policies in the 1950s and 1960s through regular education conferences with "experts," which ultimately also shifted the intellectual underpinning of these policies to the social sciences. As Mundy writes, the driving philosophy of UNESCO and other bilateral and multilateral agencies at this time was embedded in the "ideals of a rights-based redistributive multilateralism inscribed in the UN charter and the mandates of its specialized agencies" (1998, p. 457). It was also imbedded in a US-dominated hegemony that included the "decolonization" of European colonies in Africa and Asia, increasing US influence in those former colonies, and the growing conflict in developing countries between US interests and those of the Soviet Union.

By the end of the 1960s, Mundy shows, this hegemonic project began to unravel. The Vietnam War, the world oil crisis, increasing inflation (especially in the United States), and increasing competition to US-European manufacturing dominance from Japan, as well as the continuing threat of anticapitalist revolutions in developing countries, delegitimized Keynesianism and the concept of redistributive multilateralism. This created the conditions for a new hegemonic project in the developed countries, and that came in the form of Thatcherism in England and Reaganism in the United States. Although not all developed country elites agreed with this new hegemony, the combined influence of the US and the UK, especially financially and politically, dominated, which in turn affected multilateral organizations:

Changes in international political economy had major repercussions for postwar multilateral organizations. Central decision making about the world economy became more firmly entrenched during the 1970s in institutions that excluded both developing countries and popular non-state actors-the Group of Seven, the OECD, and the IMF. Within these predominantly Northern institutions a new vision of world order was born and steadily spread among OECD countries, one that argued for limited state intervention and saw an unencumbered global market as the most efficient arbiter of resources and guarantor of growth. This ideology was further strengthened by the collapse of the Soviet Union, which marked both the end of viable alternatives to Western, capitalist development and the erosion of a central argument for development assistance spending. The decline of the postwar era's limited redistributive multilateralism intensified after 1989, while new defensive and disciplinary forms of multilateralism took center stage among OECD countries. These broader shifts in international political economy and multilateralism precipitated major changes in international educational cooperation. (Mundy, 1998, pp. 468–469)

As advanced capitalist countries slowed their support for the redistributive forms of multilateralism embodied in UN institutions during the 1980s, they also began to heighten their involvement in other forms that shut out developing countries. Examples of this include the OECD, which increasingly became a forum for Northern countries to discuss the expansion of regional economic multilateralism to help a bloc of advanced capitalist countries adjust to a new world economy (e.g., NAFTA and the EU). These forms of multilateralism can be described as "defensive," insofar as they equipped advanced capitalist countries with educational defenses suitable for heightened competition in the context of economic globalization. They are "disciplinary" in that they helped diffuse neoliberal approaches to public policies developed in the United States and Britain, placing particular emphasis on the use of cross-national comparison to show the relative efficiencies of downsizing the state and reorganizing the public institutions in which the rights and entitlements of the social welfare compromise were forged. (Mundy, 1998, p. 471)

This is where Mundy's work and mine join. My entry point into globalization's impact on education is the increased worldwide competition facilitated by information technology and new communication systems combined with the concomitant rise of new economic actors on the world economic stage. I argue that these forces decreased the capacity of nation-states to finance education and other social services—multinational corporations' ability to move among nation-states reduce any single nation-state to tax their profit and, simultaneously, decrease nation-states' willingness to enable workers' incomes to rise, and hence raise income-tax revenues.[2] At the same time, globalization increases pressure on nation-states to expand higher, more expensive levels of schooling, namely university education, to compete more effectively in the world economy and to satisfy increasing demand based on relatively high and increasing payoffs to postsecondary degrees. I focus on the impact of these forces on nation-state policies—after all, the nation-state is generally the political arena in which broad education policies are worked out as part of national hegemonic projects. This has resulted in increased privatization, especially of postsecondary education—both turning over educational management to private organizations and cost sharing in educational finance, mainly through tuition fees. It has also resulted in attempts to reduce costs at all levels of schooling by applying educational technology for distance learning and in an increased emphasis on testing and accountability as part of a general emphasis on increasing "efficiency" in educational management and public finance.

Mundy approaches the same issue from the standpoint of the new hegemony as it reveals itself through international organizations. She shows how these organizations are both the product of the new hegemonic project of the developed country capitalist classes (led by those in the US and England) as they confronted the realities of a globalizing economy, and the legitimizers, even shapers, of that project, particularly in developing nation-states. This is critically important, especially because in an increasingly globalized economy, it is logical that economic and political power is increasingly dispersed among competing nation-states, and that international organizations take on a greater role than, for example, the US did in the past in representing and legitimizing educational policies on a world scale. Mundy identifies, for example, the OECD as having taken the lead role in defining such policies, and it has been able to do so because it has been able to take international testing to a new level of meaning at a global level. I discuss this in a later chapter, but here it is important to understand Mundy's larger point: international organizations such as the OECD are the political carriers of developed country hegemony in the globalized economy—of neoliberal ideology and its finance-based reforms shaping education as education becomes ever an ever more crucial legitimizer of this hegemonic project:

Among these new types of multilateralism, the OECD provides perhaps the clearest example of a shift toward defensive and disciplinary forms. The OECD has displaced UNESCO as the central forum for educational policy coordination among advanced capitalist countries and is now the main multilateral provider of cross-national educational statistics and research in the North. The OECD's central focus in education for almost two decades has been how to adjust education to changing economic requirements in the context of stagnating budgets. In recent years, its work has been profoundly shaped by the U.S. emphasis on privatization, choice, standards, and cross national testing-issues that reflect a much broader reordering of domestic politics in that country. (Mundy, 1998, p. 472)

Mundy also shows how the World Bank, which, unlike the OECD, is a major financer of education projects in developing countries, had to adjust the educational policies it pushed in those countries in the face of the new hegemony. She argues that the World Bank implemented "structural adjustment" policies in borrowing nation-states that forced cuts in educational spending in the 1980s, only to see those cuts negatively affect educational expansion and educational quality. This, and declines in donors' appetite for expanding overall assistance to developing countries, forced the bank to revise its approach to education in the 1990s. Nevertheless, it managed to shape that approach to conform to the ideology of efficiency inherent in the "defensive" multilateralism of the globalization era:

> How far has the Bank's new approach gone toward embedding educational multilateralism in the neoliberal hegemony of the late twentieth-century world order? The Bank's recent educational prescriptions, in line with its renewed interest in poverty alleviation, echo the marriage of populist and modernization arguments forged in 1970s World Bank discourse: education enhances individual productivity and overall economic growth, and it ensures political stability through greater equality. At the same time, these new strategies are remarkably close to the defensive and disciplinary approaches to educational reform being debated among advanced capitalist countries. They emphasize the more efficient use of inputs (teachers, texts, and tests), the introduction of privatization and choice to increase efficiency, greater reliance on cost recovery through parent and community participation, and a shift of resources from higher to primary education. Perhaps even more important, the [World] Bank's educational prescriptions have been implemented through new, disciplinary modalities of educational multilateralism: programs of sector-wide educational financing and adjustment and the strategic use of policy- and conditionality-based lending. In a sense, this shift completes the historical displacement of grant-based forms of development cooperation delivered through multilateral organizations democratically accountable to sovereign member nations. (Mundy, 1998, pp. 474–475)

Mundy's research was taken up extensively across the field of comparative education. The most logical explanation for this is that, as in the other theoretical contributions reviewed in this book, her research provided a coherent, broad framework for understanding phenomena that comparative education analysts had observed in their own work in developing countries. As with those other theories, it resonated with and contributed new insights into the experiences of researchers in the field.

In the introductory chapters to this book, we discussed the historical context for the growth of international development education programs in the late 1950s and early 1960s, including Stanford's SIDEC program. In the first twenty years after World War II, the dominant ideological context for international education was that expanding education that pushed democratic values and individual rights was key to combatting authoritarian (read: fascist and communist) regimes. Free markets were also an important component of this "norm set," but it was not until later— the late 1970s and 1980s, to be precise—that fully blown neoliberalist approaches to economics and education (e.g., privatization, competition, teacher incentives) took hold. As Mundy shows, these approaches were led by the World Bank and International Monetary Fund, and they succeeded because of those institutions' financial capacity and resulting dominance in norm setting, and, as she also points out, this ideological approach was greatly influenced by shifts to the right in political configurations in the United States and the United Kingdom, two key players in the financing and agenda setting of international organizations. Ultimately, the OECD also became a key international player in the "defensive multilateralism" associated with the developed countries' use of international organizations post-1980.

Mundy's work and my own on globalization and education do not fit neatly either with world society or world culture theory or with world systems theory. World culture theory situates educational and other change in national societies in the institutionalization of modernization and the meaning given to modernization by historical forces outside the control of any nation in some vague but international ideological space. Mundy's theoretical framework suggests that after World War II and well before globalization, at least part of the locus of defining world order and educational ideology had shifted out of any single or combination of developed country nation-states (the US and former colonial powers or the dominant Cold War powers) to international organizations. But she claims that the ideology that defined educational policies was based on the hegemonic project that in turn was largely defined by the United States. Thus, the new locus did not "push" a broadly accepted conception of modernity, as world culture theory posits. Rather, the "push" came from a set of well-defined institutions set up by the victorious Western democracies at the end of World War II. These dominant Western developed nations' "surrogate" institutions were the carriers and shapers of global educational policies, watched closely (and financed) and ideologically influenced by political currents in the same Western democracies that created them. When the economic and political currents and the hegemonic projects changed in the 1970s and early 1980s, the conception of educational expansion as expressed internationally also changed. Mundy's argument suggests, convincingly, that for developing countries the international organizations set the agenda within this broader context. Yet Mundy contends—consistent with world systems theory (Wallerstein, 1974)—that this agenda derives from an economic world order that originates in the dominant developed countries and which the hegemonic faction in those countries believes best serves them.

Going back to the role of the (developed and developing) nation-state in all this, let me reiterate that, in my view, although international institutions are important in defining the shape of education in developing countries, so are nation-states, both through their national histories and their current national political economics, and within larger, federal countries, such as Brazil, India, Russia, Argentina, Mexico, and South Africa, there is even considerable variance of policies and policy effectiveness among states or provinces. It is fair to argue that the broad ideology of expanding or "improving" education as "necessary" for economic and social development and meeting the requisites of a modern nation strongly influences the context for national educational policy, but the ultimate arbiter of educational policies is the nation-state (or the subnational juridical entity responsible for delivering education to its population):

All of these effects of globalization on education are passed through the policy structures of national states, so it is these states that ultimately decide how globalization affects national education. There is much more political and even financial space for the national state to condition the way globalization is brought into education than is usually admitted. Testing and standards are a good example of this space, and ICT [information and communications technology] is another. States can provide schooling access more equally, improve the quality of education for the poor, and produce knowledge more effectively and more equally for all within a globalized economy. . . .

Despite the dominant global elite drive for greater efficiency and privatization in education, there are increasing examples of national efforts to shift resources to the poor and of making public educational systems more effective for everyone, even if this may appear to be less efficient. . . . Although it is difficult to counter strong, worldwide ideological trends and, indeed, the objective reality of financial globalization, states can and do choose to emphasize more productive, more equal, and more effective public education even in the highly competitive global economic environment, if it is politically functional for them to do so . . . national educational policies are politically contested within the nation-state, and educational policy is the result of how that political contest evolves at the national and local level. (Carnoy, 2016, pp. 39–40)

What does this new focus on globalization mean for comparative educators? First, it means that they need to pay close attention to the economic and social stresses of globalization on developed and developing societies. How do these, in turn, affect competing dominant factions in the developed countries and the role they fashion for education as they attempt to gain hegemony? Second, comparative educators need to pay attention to key international organizations and how they translate global economic, social, and political conflicts into the educational policies they push in developing and developed countries. Third, comparative educators should reflect on the possible contradictions between the educational policies being pushed in the context of this hegemonic project and emerging social movements that create new demands on educational policies in direct conflict with the current set of "efficiency reforms." Finally, it is important for comparative educators to carefully analyze the measures of educational effectiveness being used by the international organizations and to develop alternatives. I explore both possibilities in the chapters that follow.

CHAPTER 10

The 2000s

Impact Evaluation and Comparative Education

JUST A REMINDER: a main theme of this book is to review major theoretical influences on comparative and international education over the past five decades and to understand the way they continue to influence the field. I have discussed how, during this half century of transformation, researchers at Stanford and other universities developed new underlying conceptions of comparative education based on theories of institutional functionalism, structuralist reproduction, institutional theory, post-Marxist state theory, and theories of globalization. All these—to one degree or another—have recast comparative and international analyses of education.

As I noted in my brief historical introduction, and will discuss in the next chapter on international testing, a dominant conceptualization of comparative education (and of education more generally) since the 1960s has been an empirical functionalist approach that views education as "producing" outcomes, primarily student academic achievement, but also affective skills, citizenship, and moral norms in ways that interact and are consistent with (functional with) other institutions in strengthening a society's social fabric. The push by comparative educators (and UNESCO) in the late 1950s and 1960s to bring "social science" into comparative and international education, and the founding of the IEA to gather the data needed for empirical estimates of educational outcomes across countries, were the main manifestations of this approach (Noah, 1973; Husén, 1983). It has had major "staying power" in comparative education analyses even when confronted by the innovative challenges to the functionalist view described in earlier chapters.

Faculty and students in SIDEC and later ICE have made many contributions to empirical work in this social scientific functionalist approach to international and comparative education beginning in the 1960s and continuing to the present day. You can learn a lot about education in different countries using the functionalist approach, and we have. It assumes one view of why education is the way it is and what the relationship is between an individual and the educational system. It allows us to estimate some relations within the education system or between the system and other institutional structures of society. For example, about one-third of the MA and PhD students currently at Stanford doing international and comparative education do some form of impact evaluation or econometric analysis of educational reforms, teacher labor markets, or other educational issues in developing countries for their MA theses and doctoral dissertations. This is probably a higher proportion than at other institutions, but many students at the institutions in our field are attracted to empirical studies of educational production.

One way to view this approach is that by estimating these empirical relationships, researchers hope to better describe how educational systems function—that is, how school inputs and student characteristics relate to each other or how educational systems are designed (e.g., teacher incentives, vouchers) in, for example, one country or in different country contexts. It is fair to say that Stanford's ICE faculty and students consider this empirical work mainly in this way—that is, serving as a gateway to developing new theoretical insights into education within and across countries. The greatly expanded availability of education data worldwide and the pressure to focus on using data has changed the comparative and international education research environment. Yet the overarching goal of doing research in education should continue to focus on developing new understandings of education and its relation to society. To accomplish that goal requires new models, including those that challenge functionalism—in earlier chapters, I reviewed some of those challenges and the insights they have provided.

Nevertheless, another way that (most) researchers view estimating these relationships using functionalist models is that different parts of the educational system or the educational systems across countries are differentially "efficient" because they are not optimal. Empirical estimates therefore help "improve" education. In this sense, James Coleman's research attempting to estimate the impact of students' social class background and of school inputs on student achievement in the United States (Coleman, 1966; Coleman and Hoffer, 1987) may have had as much or more influence on comparative and international education as any of the institutional, structural reproduction, world society, or state theories discussed in the previous chapters. Although many interpreted Coleman's work as showing that students' family background was more important than school factors in determining student academic outcomes, his research also led to an enormous literature on school "production functions" beginning in the late 1960s. To a large extent, the work of the IEA—especially the initial results from the First International Mathematics Survey (FIMS) showing the importance of students' family background in explaining variation in mathematics achievement (Medrich and Griffith, 1992)— was an outgrowth of the empirical model used by Coleman in *Equality of Educational Opportunity* (known popularly as the Coleman report). But like Coleman's research, the FIMS study was intent on trying to draw relationships between school practices and student test scores.

At Stanford, both Henry Levin and I were quickly swept up in the rush to estimate the impact of school inputs on student outcomes. Levin focused on the United States. Even before coming to Stanford, he and Samuel Bowles had published an important critique of the Coleman report and engaged in an exchange with Coleman in the pages of *Journal of Human Resources* (Bowles and Levin, 1968). The study Hans Thias and I did in 1968 on rates of return to schooling in Kenya (see Chapter 3) also attempted to estimate crude production functions for schooling (Carnoy and Thias, 1972). A year later, Thias and I convinced the World Bank to send us to Tunisia to estimate production functions for Tunisian secondary schools (seventh through eleventh grade). With Richard Sack, at that time a student at Stanford, we interviewed almost four thousand students in all sixteen of Tunisia's secondary schools. We obtained their grades and initial sixth-grade entrance exam scores, and we estimated the effects of some teacher characteristics on "value added" in Tunisian high schools (Carnoy, Sack, and Thias, 1977).

Growing availability of student achievement data, including from longitudinal surveys, greatly helped school production function analysis to explode in the 1980s in the United States and, to a lesser extent, worldwide (because of fewer data) (Hanushek, 1986, 1995; Harbison and Hanushek, 1992; Levin, 1995). Parallel to school production analysis, many studies tried to measure the impact of specific interventions, such as educational television, or of more general characteristics of educational institutions, such as private schools, or school decentralization, or "effective schools" on student achievement. In Chapter 1, I mentioned that the World Bank became the main producer of research in international and comparative education in the 1980s, surpassing all universities' comparative education centers. The World Bank's staff research focused on school production function analyses and impact evaluation, mainly because staff had access to government surveys in developing countries and/or had the financial resources to gather their own data in developing countries on student outcomes and school inputs.

Three serious problems have plagued such analyses. These are important enough that I repeat them in the next chapter on international testing. First, school production functions have generally not been grounded in a theory of student learning that explains the process by which school and family inputs are converted into achievement outcomes. This lack of theory extends to whether the student or family, classroom, school, district or municipality, state, or nation is the appropriate decision-making level for educational resource allocation (Levin, 1980). Second, these analyses usually specify only a single output of schools—academic achievement. The education system, including the family, classroom, school, and so forth, produces more than just student academic achievement, and the various outputs produced may vary considerably across families, schools, districts, and even states and nations. If only one output (e.g., test scores) is used to define education production unit effectiveness, units that focus on other outputs (e.g., music or art or discipline) could be incorrectly identified as "inefficient" is using school resources (Carnoy, 1995b). Researchers could use multiple outputs in their estimates, but it is rarely the case that they do. Third, separating (identifying) the effects of school inputs on student outcomes from the characteristics of students and their families is difficult because students are usually not randomly assigned to schools and teachers and teachers and other inputs often are not randomly assigned to schools and students. Selection bias was recognized to be an important issue in the original Coleman report (1966) and was a major topic of discussion in Coleman and Hoffer's (1987) research on the differences between private (mainly Catholic) and public schools.

It is the third problem that has received most attention. By the 1990s, economists and sociologists had begun to conduct educational experiments and apply research methods developed by statisticians to approach causal inference using nonexperimental data (Rubin, 1974; Rosenbaum and Rubin, 1983; for a summary of these methodologies, see Schneider et al., 2007; Murnane and Willett, 2010). Experiments had been regularly used in psychology and in medical research to test the effects of drugs and other treatments and to test theories of human behavior, but seldom in education. Nevertheless, two famous experiments had been conducted in education well before the 1990s—one, the Perry preschool study in 1962–1967, in which about 58 of 123 low-achievement, low-income African American three- and four-year-old children were randomly assigned to one to two years of high-quality preschool and all 123 (both treatment and control groups) followed into adulthood, and a second—the large-scale class-size experiment in Tennessee begun in 1985, in which more than 6,000 students and more than 300 teachers were randomly assigned to normal size (25 students per teacher) and small (15 students per teacher) classes and tested annually from first to fourth grade. The students were ultimately followed into the labor force.

In the early 2000s, the newly created Institute of Educational Sciences within the US Department of Education set norms for educational research, declaring educational experiments as the "gold standard" for estimating the effects of educational interventions on student outcomes (US Congress, 2002). Quasi-experimental approaches to causal inference were also accepted for inclusion in the IES's "What Works Clearinghouse" (for a description, see Schoenfeld, 2006), and these turned out to be the great majority of validated studies published by IES. The use of experiments to estimate the impact of educational interventions spread to other countries, notably by MIT's Abdul Latif Jameel Poverty Action Lab (J-PAL), a network of 145 affiliated professors from forty-nine universities, including researchers at Stanford and other US, European, and some Latin American and Asian universities (for a recent review of such studies, see McEwan, 2015). Empirical studies of education using nonexperimental data and employing statistical methods that approach causal inference also exploded in the past two decades. Scholars worldwide, including in Latin America (Brazil, Chile, Colombia, Mexico, Peru), South Africa, and Asia (India, China), now regularly make estimates of effects on student outcomes of educational inputs and policy reforms approaching causal inference.

All this research can be classified as educational impact evaluation, and it represents the new, more methodologically sophisticated version of the research done in the 1970s and 1980s to estimate relationships between educational inputs and outputs, including the IEA studies in the 1960s, 1970s, 1980s, and even 1990s. There have been several excellent recent reviews of impact evaluation studies—specifically randomized control trials (RCTs)—for understanding the kinds of studies that have been done and what they show about the effects of various interventions intended to improve schooling outcomes (Glewwe and Muralidharan, 2015; Deaton and Cartwright, 2017; Loyalka, in press). According to an interview in May 2017 with my colleague in the international and comparative education program at Stanford, Prashant Loyalka, who has done dozens of impact evaluations in China and Russia and is the author of one of those reviews:

Among different methods used today, impact evaluation tries to answer questions about causality, tries to see what works in education and why it works. It is valuable because of its potential rigor. Well-designed and executed impact evaluation studies can be expected to estimate unbiased causal effects. Conducting impact evaluations of programs and policies, in different countries and contexts, can enable researchers and policymakers to amass evidence about what works in education and why.

In a meta-analysis of impact evaluations—specifically, randomized trials—that met methodological quality standards, Wellesley economic professor and ICE graduate Patrick McEwan argues that the vast nonexperimental literature that analyzes student outcomes in primary schools in developing countries has made many contributions to our understanding of educational processes, but it also faced two major challenges:

First, regression analysis with nonexperimental data could not always distinguish between the causal effects of schools and the confounding effects of the children and families that happen to attend those schools. Second, many empirical studies used proxies of school quality, such as teacher credentials and pupil-teacher ratios, that did not encompass the wider menu of investment choices available to policymakers. A growing number of randomized, controlled experiments have addressed both challenges. Random assignment of students or schools to school-based treatments improves the internal validity of causal. Moreover, researchers have evaluated policy-relevant treatments that encompass (a) instructional interventions that incorporate teacher training, textbooks, computers and technology, and/or changes in the size and composition of classes; (b) school-based health and nutrition interventions, such as deworming, school meals, and micronutrient supplementation; and (c) interventions that modify stakeholder incentives to improve learning, such as information dissemination, student or teacher performance incentives, flexible teacher contracts, and reforms that affect school management and supervision. (McEwan, 2015, pp. 353–354)

McEwan finds surprisingly small effect sizes (the increase in student performance measured in standard deviations of test score) for school-based nutrition treatments, student deworming, treatments that provide information to parents or students, and treatments that improve school management and supervision. But he found much larger average effect sizes for other school interventions: "The largest average effect sizes are observed for treatments that incorporate instructional materials (0.08); computers or instructional technology (0.15); teacher training (0.12); smaller classes, smaller learning groups within classes, or ability grouping (0.12); contract or volunteer teachers (0.10); and student and teacher performance incentives (0.09)" (McEwan, 2015, p. 354).

The good news from McEwan's meta-analysis is that some important commonsense educational interventions related to teaching, like teacher training and classroom reorganization, have significant, positive effects of student test performance. The bad news—and perhaps bad policy advice—coming out of the analysis is that interventions such as better nutrition for students or deworming, which surely make children healthier and happier regardless of their test scores, are shown to have nonsignificant effects on test scores. This raises questions about the objective of some of these studies, or, at worst, whether they are matching the correct output measure with the intervention being studied, or whether the right nutrition input had been studied. Improved teacher training and classroom reorganization are probably implemented mainly to improve students' learning of the material being taught. It is much less clear that nutritional interventions or even administrative interventions have as their primary objective to increase student learning in the short term or at all.[1]

In addition to randomized trials, many researchers use other quasi-experimental methods, such as regression discontinuities and difference-in-difference-in-differences (DDD) with longitudinal data. These methods approach randomization (Schneider et al., 2007) to identify the effects of school and out-of-school educational interventions. Regardless of the methodology, as I discussed earlier, the underlying assumption of any impact evaluation is that it can provide reliable (meaning that if the treatment is applied to a randomly selected group of students or to a randomly selected classroom or school it will likely produce the estimated effect on student academic performance) information to policy makers to help them make better decisions regarding educational systems.

In the rest of this chapter, I focus on three impact evaluation studies recently completed by Loyalka and his colleagues at the Rural Education Action Program (REAP) at Stanford and in China. Two are randomized trials and the other uses a strong identification strategy to relate treatments to student outcomes. All three studies were conducted in China in collaboration with Chinese researchers, and all three address very important questions in Chinese education. The first study uses nonexperimental data to approach unbiased estimates of the impact of vocational education in China on the outcomes of students in computing majors. The second study uses an experimental design to test the effect on teacher practice and student mathematics achievement of a two-part teacher professional development program (PD), consisting of in-person PD (a fifteen-day training at a centralized location) and supplemental online PD, given to teachers in one central province of China. The third study conducted a randomized trial to estimate the effects of several different designs of teacher pay incentives on teacher teaching strategies and student outcomes.

The study of vocational education assessed the impact of attending vocational versus academic high school on the dropout rates, math achievement, and computing skills of the average student attending academic and vocational high schools in China. It drew on longitudinal survey data on ten thousand students collected over an academic year (2011–2012) by the authors in the most populous prefectures of two provinces, Shaanxi and Zhejiang. Because the students attending academic high schools differ substantially in terms of baseline characteristics, the main issue in assessing whether the vocational students had significantly different dropout rates and test score gains from academic high school students in the year covered by the before and after tests was selection bias. The authors used an instrumental variable based on test score cutoffs on the ninth-grade examinations and a matching procedure to reduce selection bias. The study found that vocational school students acquired fewer computer skills than students in academic high schools and suffered losses in mathematics skills while in vocational school:

Taken together, our findings demonstrate that attending vocational high school actually hurts students relative to attending academic high school. First, vocational high school encourages drop out (or at least does not encourage students to stay in school). Second, vocational high schools are failing to equip students with computing skills even relative to academic high schools (which spend little class time teaching computing). Third, attending vocational versus academic high school results in the loss of math skills. (Loyalka et al., 2015, p. 160)

Because a typical justification for channeling lower-ability students from lower social classes into vocational schools is to help less academically inclined students complete high school and pick up useful skills for the labor market, the authors tested whether lower-scoring and lower-social-class students do better completing and gaining these skills in vocational schools than in academic schools:

The findings indicate that attending vocational high school may hurt disadvantaged (low-income and low-ability) students even more than their advantaged counterparts. Low-income and low-ability students who attend vocational (rather than academic) high school drop out more than the higher income and ability students. There is also some evidence to indicate that low-income and low-ability students are even less likely to gain computing skills than higher income and higher ability students and at least as likely to see a reduction in their general skills compared to higher income and higher ability students. These findings are true even though vocational schools are (by design) supposed to benefit such students. For this reason, according to our results, we conclude that low-income and low-ability students would have fared better in academic high schools. (Loyalka et al., 2015, p. 164)

The authors recommend that the Chinese government consider reducing its investment in vocational education in China. This is a serious indictment of the Chinese education system, considering that more than 40 percent of Chinese high school students attend vocational schools. Although policy makers are unlikely to consider reducing enrollment quotas in vocational high school, substantial reforms should be considered before further financial and political resources are diverted to vocational high school. One approach would be to reduce the enrollment quotas in vocational high schools and allow for higher enrollment quotas in the more effective approach to human capital development—academic high school:

Furthermore, the results of this study should give pause to policymakers seeking to promote VET in other developing countries. Our results show that, at the margin, students in the most popular major in vocational school in two Chinese provinces lose general skills without any apparent gain in technical skills . . . [The consistency of our results with those from other developing countries] suggests that other developing countries with substantial investments in vocational secondary education may also fail to enjoy significant returns on their investment. By diverting resources away from academic high school, developing countries may be reducing the number of students who can access a human-capital enhancing opportunity to attend academic high school. (Loyalka et al., 2015, p. 169)

In the second study, Loyalka and his colleagues conducted a large randomized evaluation of China's flagship national teacher professional development program and two accompanying post-training interventions that are believed to strengthen the impact of teacher PD. They collected survey data on 600 teachers and 33,492 students in three hundred rural junior high schools in one province in central China, as well as extensive observational and interview data from a large number of teachers and their classrooms. In the first stage, the three hundred schools were randomized into three different blocks (one hundred schools to a block), to one of three treatment conditions: "no teacher PD" (control group), "teacher PD only," and "teacher PD plus follow-up." In the second-stage randomization, half the schools in the two treatment groups (PD only and PD plus follow-up) were randomized to receive a post-training evaluation or not. The PD program applied to teachers in the treated schools focused on improving mathematics teaching in junior high schools. The in-person PD was a fifteen-day training at a centralized location. The content of the session largely followed guidelines set by the Ministry of Education, After finishing the in-person PD, trainees were able to access the online PD program and were asked to turn in three short essay assignments through the online platform, including an overall reflection on the PD online program. For the sample of trainees to be treated with a follow-up, they received mobile text messages and phone calls, which alerted them to the existence of new, supplementary materials and assignments on the online platform and provided progress reports about how much trainees were using the online platform, as well as further encouragement to use it. For those trainees who were in the sample receiving the post-training evaluation, they were informed right after finishing the in-person training that they would have to participate in an evaluation to be conducted at their school two months hence and would have to prepare and give a twenty- to thirty-minute lesson plan about how they would teach student a particular math topic of their choice according to what they had learned in the in-person PD.

Overall, none of the PD treatments combinations had a significant impact on student achievement. There was also no significant effect of individual program components. Further, the study found that PD and post-training components had no impacts on student dropout, math anxiety, intrinsic or instrumental motivation for math, or amount of time students spent on math inside and outside the classroom. Neither was there significant impact of PD on student-reported teaching behaviors in the classroom—teacher practice, care, management, and communication—or on teacher knowledge, attitudes, and beliefs. However, the findings do suggest some heterogeneous effects, with PD and its post-training components having significant, positive effects on the achievement of students taught by less-qualified teachers and larger negative effects on the achievement of students of more qualified teachers.

What are the possible reasons professional development has so little impact even on teachers' behavior, not to speak of student outcomes? The researchers suggest several reasons based on their interviews with teachers. First, the content of the PD curriculum was not "particularly accessible or relevant . . . [almost half] of the material [was] 'extremely theoretical' with little application to the real world" (Loyalka, Popova, et al., 2018, p. 18). Second, the PD content was also delivered in a passive and rote manner, and there was little time for dialogue or interaction with trainers. Finally, "teachers reported being constrained in trying to apply the practical applications they did learn from PD in their classrooms. . . . [T]he heavy and fast-paced curricula of junior high schools left little room for new types of teaching practices or classroom management styles" (Loyalka, Popova, et al., 2018, p. 18).

Loyalka and his colleagues conclude that, although their findings are not necessarily generalizable to other countries and contexts,

this study again serves as a cautionary tale for policymakers interested in improving the quality of their teacher labor force. Given the huge emphasis and government expenditures on teacher PD, policymakers and other developing countries—with often fewer resources and organizational capacity in China—may wish to reconsider their current PD programs. . . . In particular, they may wish to examine the impact of low-cost but potentially ineffective PD components, such as those that exploit technology as a substitute for human trainers. Second given the billions of dollars spent each year on PD in China alone, policymakers may wish to consider investing in other types of PD programs that find more support in education theory and practice. Finally, if the costs involved in building capacity to implement other types of PD programs are prohibitive . . . policymakers may wish to divert resources to other possible ways of improving the quality of the teaching force. (Loyalka, Popova, et al., 2018, p. 20)

These articles by Loyalka and his colleagues are typical of impact evaluation research in that they estimate the effects of a specific policy in one country. Even though most, if not all, of them relate their analyses to studies done elsewhere, their "localness" (e.g., certain provinces, rural schools) raises two major issues about such analyses. It is possible the assumption implicit in these evaluations is correct that policy makers want to do the most "educationally effective" thing but do not have the information that what they are doing actually does not work. It is also possible that the unbiased information provided by the evaluation's analysis reveals something to the authorities that they may or may not have known, but in either case, they would not change the policy because it is driven mainly by political, not educational, objectives. In the vocational education study, the political objective is likely keeping down academic secondary-school enrollment in order to decrease pressure to expand higher education. In a PD study, the overriding political factor may be the need to support the large bureaucracy around professional development.

Even if policy makers are not motivated to act on new information, the impact evaluations in these two studies provide an important description of the Chinese educational system, and analysts could use the results to try to understand why the Chinese government continues to "store" so many young Chinese in vocational schools or spend billions of dollars on professional development that has virtually no impact on anything. However, Loyalka, along with most researchers doing impact evaluation, feels that bringing the results of convincing estimates to policy makers will encourage them to make changes, either (in these cases) to improve the quality of vocational schooling and reduce the proportion of students assigned to vocational education, or to improve professional development and reduce the resources allocated to professional development.

Loyalka's work on teacher performance pay takes on another concern with impact evaluation. Many evaluations do not adequately develop the theoretical connection between the design of the intervention and the effect the intervention should have on student performance. In this case, Loyalka and his colleagues designed the intervention to test whether the design of performance pay matters for changing teacher behavior and student scores and whether the design matters not only for the average student but also for the different students a teacher has in the classroom (Loyalka et al., forthcoming):

Another subject that has been examined extensively is the impact of teacher performance pay on student achievement. The underlying assumption of teacher performance pay programs is that teacher effort is low or misaligned with improving student learning. There is some evidence suggesting that teacher effort is low in developing countries, as teachers often do not show up to school and even when they do, they may not engage in teaching [see Chaudhury et al., 2006; Carnoy, Chisholm, and Chilisa, 2013]. As such, providing teachers with pay incentives based on student outcomes could improve these outcomes.

There are a number of impact evaluation studies, in a wide variety of countries, which have tested the effect of teacher performance pay. In the United States, there have been several randomized trials testing the effect of teacher performance pay. The first two, one in Tennessee and one in New York, did not find significant effects on student performance [Springer et al., 2011; Fryer, 2013]. But the second two, one in Chicago and one in Washington DC, did show positive effects [Fryer et al., 2012; Dee and Wyckhoff, 2015] Studies from Israel and India have also shown positive effects of teacher performance pay [Lavy 2002, 2009; Muralidharan and Sundararaman, 2011]. But teacher performance pay had few if any effects in Kenya [Glewwe et al., 2010], Mexico [Behrman et al., 2015], and Pakistan [Barrera-Osorio and Raju, 2015]. There are thus wide disparities in the effects of teacher performance pay among various experiments.

We explored one major reason why there may have been disparities across different performance pay studies: namely that the design of the performance pay treatment may have been different. The way in which performance pay incentives were designed in different studies may not have been optimal.

Barlevy and Neal (2012) created a new kind of teacher performance pay incentive scheme that, at least in theory, could maximize teacher effort and student learning. The authors also argued that their "pay for percentile" scheme would reduce triage, where teachers focus on one group of students to the exclusion of others.

Based on Barlevy and Neal's theory, we conducted an experiment in China to test whether pay for percentile incentives were more effective at improving student math achievement than "levels" or "gains" incentives used in other programs. We found that only students in the "pay for percentile" classrooms increased their math scores over the course of a year—about 0.15 standard deviations in test score, roughly equivalent to a semester. We also found, in alignment with theory, that teachers in those classrooms improved student achievement at all parts of the within-class distribution.

We also tried to understand why the pay-for-percentile scheme was effective. We asked a long series of questions to students about teacher behavior. We found that, similar to what Muralidharan and Sundararaman (2011) found in India and what Glewwe and his colleagues (2010) found in Kenya, there was no change in teacher classroom management or teaching practices. But unlike those other studies, we asked about curriculum coverage, and the students reported that they had been exposed to more curricula and more difficult curricula. The exposure to more difficult curricula was mirrored by students performing better on the more difficult test items. (Interview with Prashant Loyalka, May 2017)

Loyalka's results in this case double down on an important finding of the professional development study, namely, they suggest that many experiments do not produce the expected outcomes, whether for an intervention that "logically" should produce modifications of teacher behavior (PD) or for incentives that, according to labor-market theory, should increase effort, because they do not account for the overall conditions under which teachers teach in schools and are not actually based on well-grounded theories of what changes teacher behavior and which options teachers have for trying to improve student outcomes. The pay-incentive experiment is especially telling because student outcomes are affected by increased teacher "effort," but mainly by an increase in how much the math teacher teaches mathematics and what happens to the difficulty of the content as the time spent on the subject increases. This finding about curriculum coverage is consistent with other results estimating the effect of classroom time that teachers devote to a subject on student achievement (Rosa et al., 2018; Lavy, 2015; Rivkin and Schiman, 2015), except that none of those studies tests teacher pay incentives, but rather curriculum quality and time taught on subject. Thus, the policy implications of both the teacher PD and teacher pay-incentive experiments may be that interventions that do not focus on increased time on subject matter and the difficulty of the subject matter taught are likely not to have much impact.

A third issue is whether and how impact evaluation contributes to comparative and international education. Because impact evaluation has become so important in international research, what is its potential to influence comparative education? Can it lay the groundwork for new theoretical insights? I raised this with Loyalka. He discussed some possibilities and limitations:

Results from experiments or quasi-experiments, while potentially internally valid, are not necessarily externally valid or representative. A fairly large number of impact evaluation studies rely on non-representative samples. It is therefore difficult to generalize the results from these studies to a well-defined population or subpopulation.

There have been some efforts to address this limitation of generalizability in the last several years. For instance, there has been some effort on the part of researchers to randomly sample experimental participants from a well-defined population [e.g., Muralidharan and Sundararaman, 2015]. There are also attempts, as in medical research, to do systematic reviews and meta-analyses to try to summarize research results across different situations and countries. There are even efforts underway to support experimental studies that use the same design and same measurement instruments in multiple countries simultaneously. For example, researchers may receive support to look at the impact of a specific intervention in three different countries at the same time, say one from South Asia, one from Africa, and one from Latin America. Researchers are asked to use the same intervention, the same research design, as well as similar measurement and survey instruments. Once having done that, researchers further examine the policy context and see why interventions were more effective in one region or another.

There are questions whether the effort to do the same experiments across countries will go forward because it is expensive to support such studies. Systematic reviews and meta-analyses also rely on non-innocuous assumptions about how to summarize results from different contexts and disparate interventions. In the end, I believe we need a much greater number of studies that replicate interventions across different contexts. (Interview with Prashant Loyalka, May 2017)

It is the case that impact evaluations have been used in the past comparatively to draw insights into educational policy and even broader theoretical considerations about education's role in society. The best case I can think of is the impact evaluation studies of Chilean vouchers in the 1990s and early 2000s and the insights they provided into the discussion about education and markets (Parry, 1996; McEwan and Carnoy, 2000). Voucher impact studies in the United States (see Carnoy, 2017, for a recent summary) and India (Muralidharan and Sundararaman, 2015) have generally shown similar results to Chile and potentially provide the basis for a better understanding of the role of private and public education worldwide.

Young Lives, a research project on childhood poverty begun in 2000 in Ethiopia, Peru, Vietnam, and Andhra Pradesh, India, coordinated by the University of Oxford's Department of International Development, is another example of an international study in the broad genre of impact evaluation that has provided comparative results on various inputs into the educational process. There have been hundreds of papers published from the Young Lives longitudinal data, and some of them examine the same variables in the four countries studied. It would be worth assessing whether some educational processes are universal across countries and what the possible implications of the results are for variation across systems.

Loyalka has a somewhat more stringent condition for using these impact evaluations comparatively:

I agree that we can gain insights from these comparative impact studies, so long as they are methodologically (that is, internally, and hopefully also externally) valid. The most productive direction of this kind of comparative work, I think, is to evaluate the same intervention in different contexts. Interpreting the results from difference contexts would then require more quantitative and qualitative analyses (how social and educational context affects the outcomes of, say, a teacher training intervention). I think in the end, we need many studies to understand why the same intervention produced different results in different contexts. We should also pay more attention to the interplay between theory and empirical results, especially in trying to understand how results can vary across contexts.

For example, two experimental studies gave information to students about the value payoffs to taking higher levels of schooling—one in the Dominican Republic [Jensen, 2010] and one in Madagascar [Nguyen, 2008]. In both cases, this information had the effect of reducing dropout and increasing student attainment. I did the same experiment in China [Loyalka et al., 2013], and it had absolutely no effect. We also found that if we gave even more information to the students about how to navigate their school, it had a negative effect because it overwhelmed them, seeming to dampen their aspirations. Thus, the context is important, and it would be very useful to understand why a similar intervention in different contexts can produce different results. (Interview with Prashant Loyalka, May 2017)

Whether these types of insights will emerge from comparative impact evaluation remains to be seen, but the potential is certainly there, as has been true of earlier evaluations. The advantage of the current brand of impact evaluations is its potential for internal validity. Thus, similarities and differences in the causal effects of interventions and reforms across contexts, should they be comparable, could tell us a lot about the effect of contextual differences, which in turn might help us develop new conceptualizations and theories about the role of education in various sociopolitical contexts, and possibly about whether this role is converging globally or driven by national or even subnational economic, political, and social conditions.

CHAPTER 11

The 2000s

International Tests and Comparative Education

THE MOST INFLUENTIAL "movement" in comparative and international education in the past fifteen to twenty years has been large-scale international tests. As I described at the beginning of this book, international testing was initiated by comparative education researchers in the 1960s to provide better information for making comparisons among educational systems. It was never expected or intended to substitute for deeper analysis of differences among educational delivery systems and explanations for how and why these differences exist. Yet because of increased international economic competition and the increased influence of international institutions, both associated with globalization (discussed in Chapter 9), and because international testing—unlike most impact evaluation, for example—is by its very nature internationally comparative, it has become the dominant force in shaping comparative education research.

We comparative educators have always been of two minds about international tests. One part of us loves them. The data that tests and accompanying surveys produce have created great opportunities to undertake interesting international educational comparisons and, more recently, to estimate and compare relatively unbiased school effects across countries (e.g., Lavy, 2015; Rivkin and Schiman, 2015; Khavenson and Carnoy, 2016; Carnoy et al., 2016; Zakharov et al., 2016). They have also helped us gain insights into national educational systems and to draw comparison between them. This would not have been possible without such data.

A good example of how international test scores enabled me to achieve a better comparative analysis is the 2007 book *Cuba's Academic Advantage*, which I wrote with two Stanford PhD students, Amber Gove and Jeffery Marshall. We started our analysis by using UNESCO's 1997 Latin American Laboratory for Assessment of the Quality of Education (LLECE) results for Latin American third and fourth graders to show that Cuban students' outcomes on the LLECE test adjusted for both individual- and school-level social-class variables were much higher than in other Latin American countries on both the math and the reading test, even taking into account these other factors. We spent the rest of the book using more typical comparative qualitative analysis to try to explain why. We compared three countries in much more detail—Cuba, Brazil, and Chile. We visited teacher preparation programs in universities, interviewed teachers and policy makers, and videotaped and analyzed classroom teaching. These more micro-level analyses were made much more convincing by prefacing them with the LLECE test data showing how Cuban children fared in an international test compared to their counterparts in the rest of Latin America, including Brazil and Chile.

Our other mind on international testing is that we are deeply disturbed by the way international test results are being used, particularly by the OECD's Programme for International Student Evaluation (PISA) program, to push educational policies based on correlations between a "treatment" and student outcomes, or, even worse, not based on any direct empirical evidence—only the fact that a country has high or increasing student test scores and has done one thing or another in education that seems like good educational policy. These policies may or may not be effective, but exemplifying high-scoring countries can produce perverse incentives, such as the promotion, implicitly, of prioritizing test results as the be-all and end-all of education; teaching to the test (Khavenson and Carnoy, 2016); and strongly suggesting that educational practices and structures can be easily transferred from country to country—an argument that years of comparative education research have shown to be largely false (e.g., Phillips and Ochs, 2003). Richard Rothstein and I have summarized these concerns in a long piece (Carnoy and Rothstein, 2013). A group of us in Russia and the United States did a more formal empirical critique using longitudinal data for a sample of Russian eighth graders who took the Trends in International Math and Science Study (TIMSS) test in 2011 and were given the 2012 PISA test at the end of ninth grade (Carnoy et al., 2016). I also did a short policy brief on these issues (Carnoy, 2015), which I discuss further in this chapter. In it, I lay out the key problems that various critics have raised about international testing. The Carnoy and Rothstein paper and the Russia paper are easily accessible on the websites of the Economic Policy Institute and the *American Educational Research Journal*.

In Chapter 1 of this book, I described the beginning of international testing in the 1960s and the findings of those early studies. The IEA, created in 1962, was a concerted effort promoted by UNESCO and funded by the US Office of Education to gather data on student achievement and student family background across national systems of education. As part of bringing the social-scientific method and empirical testing to comparative education, the IEA's tests and surveys for the First International Mathematics Study (FIMS) in 1964, the Second International Mathematics Study (SIMS) in the early 1980s, and the Third International Mathematics and Science Study (TIMSS) in 1995 were designed to establish through international comparisons why students in some educational systems could learn more mathematics and science than students in other countries. The designers of the tests never intended them to be used in ranking how much students in one country were learning in mathematics and science compared to how much students were math and science students were learning in another country (Medrich and Griffith, 1992).

In terms of the IEA's objectives, the first thirty years of tests and surveys (1964–1995) were only partially successful. The IEA did show that, at great expense, it was possible to test students across multiple countries with different educational systems and to collect extensive information about students, teachers, and schools in different grades. They also provided a great deal of descriptive material about how educational systems in different countries differed—much more detail than the simple descriptive data in pre–World War II comparative education studies. There were also some interesting findings about relationships between student achievement and other variables, although these were largely correlational. For example, the various surveys consistently showed the important relation between students' socioeconomic background and their math and science achievement, even in higher grades. Research was also able to show that the effect of tracking on student achievement did not definitively have either a positive or negative effect on students in lower and higher tracks (Medrich and Griffith, 1992). Finally, the surveys showed that one school input, greater opportunity to learn—specifically, more extensive coverage of the subject matter tested—had a consistently positive effect on student performance (Schmidt et al., 1997; Schmidt et al., 2001).

Beyond these results, initially important as they might have been, the extensive data collected—especially beginning in 1995 with the first TIMSS—did not provide further convincing insights into the differences between educational systems that might produce greater student learning. The "theory" behind using student achievement data to understand the workings of educational systems in different countries—if there were any theory at all—can best be described as "national production functions" for education, in which a set of observable educational inputs "produce" the latent academic skills measured by an international test. As Henry Levin (1980) pointed out in the early days of production function analysis, this so-called theory of educational production is highly problematic. The theory has difficulty identifying the production unit in which each set of resource allocation decisions is made—such as which characteristics of teachers should be determinant in hiring teachers, class size, which curriculum to use, which classroom supplies to buy, and so forth (do these allocative decisions take place at the classroom, school, district or municipality, state, or national level?).

Thus, identifying causal factors in the educational system that might influence student outcomes across countries using international test scores as the measure of performance was problematic to begin with because the theory underlying such national comparisons was weak.

As I discuss further below, national comparisons inherently assumed that the nation is the decision-making unit that develops and implements the most relevant policies regarding the educational system. This clearly varies from country to country. Also, even assuming that the model connecting educational inputs and student test scores was correctly specified, identifying causal relations was difficult because IEA surveys were cross sectional, and, although the 1995 survey tested both seventh and eighth graders in the same school, these were not the same individual students. Data on the seventh-grade cohort provided a control only at the school level. The results were therefore correlational, fraught with issues of selection bias in how students were assigned to schools and to teachers, as well as how teachers might choose or be chosen by schools.[1]

Despite the difficulty that repeated international surveys had in moving beyond "better curriculum" in identifying the factors that improve student learning in schools and national systems, international testing began exploding in the late 1990s and became extremely influential in comparative educational analysis. In addition to the early IEA tests and surveys, which evolved into the *Trends in International Mathematics and Science Survey* (TIMSS) in 1999, 2003, 2007, 2011, and 2015, applied in most years to both fourth graders and eighth graders, and the *Progress in International Reading Literacy Study* (PIRLS), applied to fourth graders in 2001, 2006, 2011 and 2016, UNESCO in Santiago began to test third and fourth graders in a number of Latin American countries, first in 1997 (LLECE, now called Primer Estudio Regional Comparativo y Educativo, or PERCE), then third and sixth graders in 2006 (Segundo Estudio Regional Comparativo y Educativo, or SERCE) and 2013 (Tercer Estudio Regional Comparativo y Educativo, or TERCE), UNESCO in Paris began testing second and fifth graders in French-speaking countries in Africa and, more recently, French-speaking Southeast Asia, with the Programme d'Analyse des Systèmes Éducatifs de la CONFEMEN (PASEC) test in various years beginning in 1993–1994 and sixth graders in Southern and Eastern Africa, with the Southern and Eastern Africa Consortium for Monitoring Educational Quality (SACMEQ) test in 1995, then in 2000 and again in 2007. The PASEC is unusual because in some countries, students took a pretest and then later in the year a posttest. Thus, depending on the country, it is possible using the PASEC to test whether teacher characteristics are related to a "value added" measure of achievement gain. The SACMEQ is unusual because it tests sixth-grade teachers in the subject that they teach, and teachers can be linked to individual students. This makes it particularly valuable for estimating teacher knowledge effects on student achievement across countries (Zakharov et al., 2016).

By the late 1990s, the OECD began its Programme on International Student Assessment (PISA) among OECD member countries and some non–member countries. Unlike the other international tests, PISA chose to evaluate fifteen-year-olds in randomly selected schools (students surveyed could be in different grades) in each participating country and focused on collecting survey data on students and schools (through a principal questionnaire); it did not collect data from teachers. All data on teaching and curriculum coverage in PISA continue to come from student questionnaires, although it is likely that in 2018, PISA will add a teacher questionnaire. PISA tests students every three years in reading, mathematics, and science, focusing on one of those subjects each time it repeats the test and survey—reading in 2000 and 2009, math in 2003 and 2012, and science in 2006 and 2015. PISA has also developed a test that can be administered to fifteen-year-olds in a single school, so the average results of its students can be "compared" with the average performance of students in different countries.

Furthermore, whereas the TIMSS and the UNESCO Latin America and Africa tests essentially report only test results and descriptive tables related to some student characteristics, the PISA does extensive correlational analyses and makes policy prescriptions regarding which inputs and educational system organizations allegedly make students in high-performing countries achieve higher results. PISA also features analyses on what educational policies have been behind large average gains over time in certain countries (e.g., OECD, 2016).

Yet like all the other international tests going back to the FIMS, PISA is a cross-sectional survey, so its analyses are rife with issues of selection bias—even more so because students surveyed and tested in the PISA are usually not in the same grade. Many, if not most, of PISA's policy recommendations are therefore not justified by the analyses. From the answers to questions about teachers and teaching asked to students in the PISA survey, some analyses have been able to identify, to varying degrees, the causal effect on achievement of opportunity to learn (Lavy, 2015; Rivkin and Schiman, 2015). Beyond that, other estimates featured in PISA reports, such as the impact of school autonomy and computers on student achievement (e.g., Fuchs and Woessman, 2004a, 2004b; OECD 2016) are correlational but not causal. Thus, they are potentially biased estimates and could mislead policy makers.

The discussion about comparative education research in the late 1950s that led to the creation of the IEA could never have imagined the current boom in international testing. The IEA founders would surely have considered it a complete aberration of their original intent. Yet they would still probably be torn, as I am, about the value of this flood of testing, because all these tests and surveys have indeed produced a mountain of data used by researchers worldwide. From a descriptive standpoint, more is known than ever before about students', teachers', and schools' characteristics in dozens of educational systems. We have always understood that the organization of education in some countries differs greatly from the organization in other countries, but we have much more detail about those differences—for example, that the training and pay of teachers varies widely, that the concentration of students in schools from poor and higher-socioeconomic-status families also varies greatly across countries, and that girls' and boys' scores on these tests are rather equal in some countries and very unequal in others. The data have also allowed researchers to do a multitude of comparisons across countries that suggest how such variations may relate to alternative student learning or, viewed alternatively, how they may reflect differences in how societies with different values organize and invest in their children's education.

These could be regarded as the positive contributions of international testing to comparative education research. All the publicity given to student achievement worldwide and to the comparisons between countries could also be seen as having greatly increased the status of comparative education as a field of study. As I pointed out earlier, with economic globalization came an increased focus on international competition and on the role of education as an important input into a nation's capacity to compete in a global economy. In this globalized, interdependent environment, trade issues and industrial policy until recently seemed to have been taken away from national governments and relegated to international regulators. Thus, labor force skills and productivity took on new urgency as one of the major elements of policy that were largely in control of the nation-state. Comparative education researchers' capacity to tell policy makers at home what they could learn from other countries' "high performing" educational systems assigned the field growing importance in the academic pantheon. Membership in comparative education professional associations and meetings increased rapidly in the 2000s, and so did publications in journals focusing on international education and international development.

On the downside, besides the already mentioned difficulties in providing real answers from international test data for the vexing problems that test scores have indicated exist in national education systems, most politicians and policy makers never look past the average national test scores and national rankings. The announcements of international test results in December of the year after the test is administered are promoted by the testing agencies as part of a worldwide sales campaign, particularly by the OECD, to sell more countries, and now even schools, on buying into the test. The media fanfare in each country around these announcements emphasizes the average national score, how it compares to other nations' scores, and how the nation's score has changed from the previous round, three or four years earlier. Based on such comparisons, judgments are made about the quality of a nation's educational system, not only by the media and the politicians, but, surprisingly, also by the testing agencies. No effort is made in these pronouncements to discuss scores adjusted for the many differences in the background of the students among countries, the other investments parents and nations may be making in students outside of school (e.g., tutoring, cram courses, preschool or day care), and whether a particular test is taken seriously in a country or is simply administered with little monitoring on a certain day near the end of an academic year. These are all factors that could greatly affect average scores even from one period to the next in the same country (Carnoy and Rothstein, 2013). The IEA founders clearly warned against all this, as have subsequent analyses, but to little avail.

Richard Rothstein and I became so concerned about these downsides—especially that presenting average national test scores not adjusted for differences in the family background of the young people tested was a fair representation of the quality of schooling in one country compared to another—that we wrote a long critique showing how international test scores comparisons would be different if the scores were adjusted not only for differences between countries but also adjusted for changes from test year to test year in the socio-economic background of students sampled in each country (Carnoy and Rothstein, 2013). The critique drew a detailed response in the press from the PISA staff, and we responded to them in turn. We thought and still think we were right that average international test scores should be presented to the public as a measure of student achievement only after adjusting them for students' level of family academic resources, such as books in the home or mother's education or the PISA student socioeconomic index. This would represent somewhat more accurately the quality of a country's educational system, at least partially excluding the role of family factors in a student's academic achievement:

Extensive educational research in the United States has demonstrated that students' family and community characteristics powerfully influence their school performance. Children whose parents read to them at home, whose health is good and can attend school regularly, who do not live in fear of crime and violence, who enjoy stable housing and continuous school attendance, whose parents' regular employment creates security, who are exposed to museums, libraries, music and art lessons, who travel outside their immediate neighborhoods, and who are surrounded by adults who model high educational achievement and attainment will, on average, achieve at higher levels than children without these educationally relevant advantages. Much less is known about the extent to which similar factors affect achievement in other countries, but we should assume, in the absence of evidence to the contrary, that they do. (Carnoy and Rothstein, 2013, pp. 7–8)

I have heard two defenses by the testing agencies (and by agencies such as the World Bank supporting the spread of testing) that such "raw score" comparisons are not as bad as they seem. The first defense is that competing in such "league tables" motivates countries to make educational reforms when they may not have done so in the absence of being "exposed" every few years to the harsh light of national educational accountability. The oft-cited case of German shock at its PISA results in 2000, the immediate moves to implement reforms, and the subsequent hefty improvement of average scores, is the example commonly used to back this "league table defense." More recently, Poland's rapidly rising PISA scores have served as another example of response to the competition.

The second defense I have heard, and this from the technical team at UNESCO Santiago in referring to the TERCE results, is that although there are vast differences in poverty levels of Latin American countries taking the TERCE test, the unadjusted average scores reflect the "social reality" that a nation's educational system faces in improving student performance. In other words, even though the unadjusted score lumps together family factors that schools inherit when the student begins school at six or seven years old, and although the average family background is much different in Honduras or Guatemala from that in Chile, we should not let the Honduran educational system believe that it is actually doing a better job with its sixth graders relative to Chile than is characterized by average unadjusted TERCE results because, after all, Honduran schools need to face up to the fact that their students are simply less prepared academically than Chilean students when they enter first grade.

These defenses are not without merit. It is important to draw attention to inadequate schooling and how to improve it. It is also important to motivate politicians and the public to want to improve schooling, particularly for those that are getting the most inadequate versions of it. But here is the main problem with ranking countries using unadjusted test scores. If the testing agencies intend to have politicians and the public at large interpret the differences in these unadjusted average scores as reflecting differences in what students should be learning at school, and therefore differences in learning that educational system improvement should be able to overcome, they are misleading everyone about what even the best thought out schooling policies can achieve on their own. We know that much learning takes place outside schools, at home, and at sites of other academic investments parents make in their children during summers and after school. Misleading politicians and the public that policies meant to increase student learning in lower-income countries and lower-income communities should focus largely on K–12 school improvement increases the chances that student learning will improve only in modest increments, if at all. Policy makers will tend to ignore child health care, early childhood exposure to academically rich environments, early child nutrition, the social conditions in the communities where children live, and exposure to academically richer environments outside of school hours. All these factors contribute significantly to high academic performance in countries where students do well on international tests.

The other problem with the rankings is that, although highly ranked Country A may, indeed, have an education system that is more effective in delivering, say, mathematics education to students than schools in lower ranked countries, it is not possible to convincingly identify the reasons why that is the case from the data in student and other surveys given with the test. I commented earlier that this has been an issue with international testing since its launch in the 1960s. In some countries, such as the US, UK, Finland, and Russia, students perform very differently on the TIMSS mathematics test and on the PISA mathematics test. In the US and Russia, for example, where students have taken both TIMSS and PISA tests in all years, the average scores in the TIMSS adjusted for students' family academic background rose substantially in the 2000s, but average PISA scores stayed relatively flat during this same period, although in Russia they did increase in 2012 and 2015.

It is even difficult to ascertain why test scores go up and down over time—in some countries, these changes are large. For example, PISA scores have declined substantially in Australia since the early 2000s, but no one can provide an adequate explanation why (Morsy et al., 2017). Some have argued that PISA scores have risen substantially in Poland because of a reform that eliminated vocational schooling in the ninth grade. A study that tested this claim found significant but small effects of the reform on PISA scores for ninth graders, which disappeared once students entered the vocational track in tenth grade (Jakubowski et al., 2010). The large increases in German PISA scores have been estimated to be primarily the result of gains by students of Slavic origin, and these do not seem connected to any specific educational reform (Stanat et al., 2010).

Because they have become such a powerful shaper of thinking in comparative education, there have been many critiques of international tests. I summarized these in a 2015 policy paper, grouping critiques into categories. Some I have already mentioned, but it is worth discussing several of the others. I call one of them "PISA politics and the Shanghai case":

In 2009, China participated for the first time in the PISA (Hong Kong has participated since 2000 and has taken the TIMSS from 1995 [to] 2011). Although students in a number of provinces took the test, the OECD only reported—or was allowed to report—the Shanghai (highest) scores. These turned out to be by far the top of the PISA rankings. Students in Shanghai outscored students in Singapore and Hong Kong (other "Chinese" cities) by about 0.5 standard deviations in mathematics and 0.3 standard deviations in reading. Thanks to these results and the publicity given them by the OECD's media team, Shanghai students' performance quickly became a benchmark for how well students worldwide should be able to achieve academically. Shanghai scores also became conflated with China's *national* performance. (Carnoy, 2015, pp. 4–5)

Tom Loveless (2013) of the Brookings Institution and James Harvey (2015) of National Superintendents' Roundtable both claimed that the Shanghai sample had excluded important parts of the fifteen-year-old population in Shanghai, greatly biasing the scores upward. Loveless also critiqued the OECD's decision to publish the Shanghai scores as if they were Chinese national scores without publishing student scores in the other Chinese provinces that had taken PISA in 2009 and 2012, all with lower scores, some much lower, not to speak of the 66 percent of China's students living in rural areas who had not participated in the PISA test:

The controversies over the validity of international tests as measures of students' knowledge and the representativeness of (PISA) samples reveal an important aspect of these tests. Not surprisingly, the agencies producing (and selling) them have a vested interest in defending them against all critiques, even when those critiques prove to be correct. The OECD in particular has consistently pulled out all stops in defending even the most indefensible uses of "national" test score rankings, such as publishing and touting the results for an unrepresentative sample from one Chinese city when the test was also applied in many other Chinese provinces but not published. If the validity of these tests comes into question, what is the reason for nations to pay dearly to participate in them and to know their results? As critics have learned, transparency beyond rather opaque technical appendices to reports is not in a testing agencies' interest. (Carnoy, 2015, p. 5)

Another critique I discuss in the policy paper is an extension of the argument Rothstein and I made regarding the OECD's use of country average test score rankings to draw conclusions about the quality of their educational systems. Even when we adjust the average test scores for individual student socioeconomic differences, several Asian countries top the rankings (by far) and thus, in the OECD's view, should serve as exemplars of "good" educational policies. I draw on Mark Bray's (2006) research to argue that this OECD view downplays the enormous investment that families in Asia make in out of school tutoring and in cram schools:

More generally, the main line coming out of international comparisons is to "copy" the policies of higher scoring countries. Because students in East Asian countries, such as Korea, Japan, Singapore, and, most recently, Shanghai [and Vietnam] achieve such high levels of test scores, the OECD and the media consistently feature these countries as having exemplary educational systems. Some reasons given for educational quality in East Asia are the high level of teacher skills, particularly in mathematics, high teacher pay, and, in some countries, such as Korea, rather equal distribution of students from different social class backgrounds across schools. Others have similarly argued that test scores tend to be higher, on average, in countries with more equal income distribution. Again, these "reasons" are at best correlational and are not based on causal analysis. Even more suspect is the notion that the higher test scores are the result mainly of school quality rather than the massive amount of out-of-school tutoring and test-prep taken by East Asian students.

Families in some cultures are more likely to put great emphasis on academic achievement, particularly on achievement as measured by tests. They act on this emphasis by investing heavily in their children's out-of-school academic activities, including in "cram courses," which focus on test preparation [Bray, 2006; Ripley, 2013]. In a world that puts high value on test scores, perhaps such intensive focus on children's academic achievement should be applauded. However, whether it is a good choice for middle and high schoolers to spend most of their waking hours studying how to do math and science problems, and whether it is likely that families in other societies would buy into this choice for their children, are highly controversial issues and certainly only somewhat related to the quality of schooling taken by students in a particular society. (Carnoy, 2015, p. 9)

A third issue I discuss in the policy paper is the relationship between economic growth and national test scores. This relationship is a driving "motivator" behind the appeal of international rankings of student performance on these tests. (Who would care about national student test scores unless they meant something for national economic development or military power, or something with political importance?). The underlying argument is that average national mathematics test scores are the single best predictor of national economic growth in the period 1960–2010 (Hanushek et al., 2013). There are many issues I cover in the review concerning the magnitude of this test score–economic growth connection, but let me focus on two of them: the US as an "anomaly" in the argument and, in the best of cases, given empirical estimates of the test score–productivity relationship, the likely small impact that large increases in test scores would have on productivity.

Hanushek and colleagues (2013) themselves consider the US an exception to the test score–growth rate "rule." Diane Ravitch (2013) goes further to argue that US students have always scored relatively lower than many developed countries on international tests, and despite dire predictions going back to the early 1980s that this would lead to economic disaster, the US is still the world's leading economy, with the world's most vibrant pop culture, and a highly productive workforce. As a counterexample, Ravitch could also have cited the dismal performance of the Japanese economy over the past twenty years despite its students' top-five ranking in the PISA and TIMSS league tables since 1999–2000.

A more general point is that the empirical work that exists on the earnings–math score relation, while statistically significant and positive, is surprisingly small. In the most cited study, by Murnane and colleagues (1995) a math score one standard deviation higher in the early 1990s was associated with a 9 percent higher wage. More recent research, by Castex and Dechter (2014) uses data from the 1980s and 2000s to show that during those two decades, the return to cognitive ability declined by between 30 percent and 50 percent for men and women, and that returns to years of education increased. They argue that the decline in returns to ability can be attributed to differences in the growth rate of technology between the 1980s and 2000s:

To put this in perspective, if average U.S. PISA math scores in 2012 (481) were to equal Finland's (519), and if earnings were a good proxy for productivity, productivity/earnings in the U.S. would increase by about 3% if we assume the

1980s returns to higher ability, but only about 2% or less if we assume the lower estimates for the 2000s. If Korean math scores were the target, productivity/ earnings in the U.S. would go up by 6% or 3%–4%, depending on the assumed returns. These are not mind-boggling gains. Moreover, the U.S. 8th grade math scores on the Long-Term Trends (LTT) survey of the National Assessment of Education Progress (NAEP) . . . increased about 0.6 of a standard deviation in the past 34 years (1978–2012), perhaps playing a role in greatly increased worker productivity in this period—but not resulting in any significant increase in average real wages or weekly earnings. Meanwhile, [corporate] profit rates have skyrocketed. If this is what the math score–economic growth proponents have in mind, then our main objective as a nation in increasing mathematics scores is to increase company profits . . . but not necessarily worker wages. Only a deep cynicism would make that a convincing case for educational reforms targeting increased math scores. (Carnoy, 2015, p. 8)

The most recent critique I have made of the international test rankings is that they almost always draw comparisons between "national educational systems." Some of the systems are indeed national, administered by a central government with decision-making power over a national curriculum and national teacher labor markets, teacher training, and teacher remuneration policies. But other nations are federal systems, in which education decision making is juridically controlled by subnational units such as states or provinces. The United States, for example, does not have a national educational system but rather fifty-one state systems (including the District of Columbia), and in some of them, very large urban school districts that have more students than entire smaller states. The federal government has relatively little to say about what states and these large school districts do about organizing their education. The average international test scores in US states range from some of the highest among developed countries to some of the lowest. There are many federal countries— Argentina, Brazil, Canada, India, Russia, Australia, Germany, Mexico, and Switzerland, among them. They tend to be large and have considerable variation in average student achievement among their juridical entities.

I and my colleagues have argued that, where possible, it is often more useful and theoretically more justifiable to compare and analyze student performance and educational policies over time between states within these federal countries than comparing their average national performance with other countries. Students and families in states within the same country generally share similar educational culture and educational practices outside schools. Teacher labor markets and remuneration vary among states, but teacher-training regimes generally are quite similar. This all makes it easier to identify administrative and instructional reasons students in some states make significantly larger gains over time than do students in other states.

We have made such state comparisons in three countries—the United States (Carnoy et al., 2015), Brazil (Carnoy et al., 2017), and Australia (Morsy et al., 2017). In the first two, we use national test data over a fifteen-year period, and in the third, PISA data from 2000 to 2015. In the US and Brazil, we analyze differences in student gains over time in similar, usually neighboring states, and in Australia, we try to explain why PISA scores declined at different rates in different states, and why PISA scores in Australia have declined so steadily for so long:

The case for looking inward, across states, within the United States, is compelling. On international tests, student performance and performance gains in, say, mathematics vary greatly among U.S. states. Nine states took the 2011 TIMSS and three states took the 2012 PISA. In some of these states, such as Massachusetts and Connecticut on the PISA, and in seven of nine states that took the TIMSS, higher socioeconomic class students scored as high or higher in mathematics and much higher on the PISA reading test than similarly advantaged students from European countries and Canada. Based on NAEP data and the link between the 2011 NAEP and the 2011 TIMSS [NCES, 2013], if students in Texas, Vermont, and North Carolina had taken the PISA in 2012, they, too, probably would have scored very high. In other states, such as Florida on the PISA and California and Alabama on the TIMSS, higher socioeconomic class students scored far below similarly advantaged students in higher scoring states and other countries. (Carnoy, 2015, pp. 12–13)

One interesting result of examining the individual US state data is that students who identified themselves as of Asian origin in the Massachusetts PISA sample scored 569 in the 2012 PISA mathematics test, significantly higher than the average in Korea (554), and about the same as students in Singapore (573). Asian students in Massachusetts came from a lower socioeconomic background than average students in Singapore or Korea and went to Massachusetts schools. Using OECD logic, this suggests that Massachusetts's schools are at least as good as schools in Singapore and better than those in Korea (here we compare students with similar cultural background attending schools in different educational systems), so if European-origin students from Massachusetts attended English-medium schools in Singapore, they would perform about the same as in they do Massachusetts—that is, they would score lower than the Asian-origin students in both systems. It also suggests that the Asian-origin students may be doing something academically outside of school in Massachusetts (and in Singapore and Korea) that the non-Asian students are not, such as working with tutors and enrolling math camps and cram schools.

The Brazil study is especially interesting because it provides the theoretical justification for doing intranational comparisons over international comparisons:[2]

Is comparative and international education research correct in focusing so heavily on the nation-state as the relevant unit for analyzing education comparatively? Generally, yes. In most countries, major aspects of formal education are defined by nation-state economic and political histories. Educational change is typically played out in national political structures, and understanding how those changes occur typically requires a theory of the nation-state. It therefore usually makes sense to regard educational systems as "products" of nation-state political, economic, and social structures.

[However] . . . the degree to which the national governments influence "national" education does vary from country to country, largely due to the way that nation-states define themselves politically and the role that this political definition has on shaping educational delivery. The most important instance of the nation-state that raises theoretical questions about focusing so heavily on national educational comparisons is the federal state. Federalism is the name given to a system of government in which sovereignty is shared between a central governing authority and constituent political units, such as states or provinces (Watts, 1992). These political units are generally bound together by a constitution that spells out the rights and obligations of the constituent members. A typical reason that nation-states are federal is that historically regions found it in their interest to join together as a larger nation-state, but agreed to do so under the condition that they retain considerable autonomy.

In every federal nation-state, primary and secondary schooling is the juridical responsibility of the constituent states, not the federal government, although the federal government is often the main source of revenue for education in the states, and in some countries, it legislates education reforms that are subsequently implemented by the states. Yet, even in federal countries with mainly central government financing, and even considering differences in economic development levels among states, federal countries are marked by considerable variation across constituent states in teacher labor markets, curriculum, evolution of access to schooling, and the politics and ideology of state bureaucracies. Thus, in terms of comparative education analysis, there is persuasive support in political theory to consider sub-national state comparisons in federalist nations. (Carnoy et al., 2017, pp. 727–728)

For better or worse, international tests will continue to dominate comparative and international education in the foreseeable future. Besides the apparent (and increasing) fetishism in hypercompetitive modern society with rankings and ratings, testing has become a big business and test makers such as the OECD, the IEA, and their subcontractors (e.g., the giant textbook publisher Pearson Education, which now produces the PISA tests) have a self-interest in spreading the use of testing and evaluation. In addition, some social scientists are eager to convince the world that if countries improve their education systems in ways that increase their students' performance on international tests, future economic output will increase significantly more rapidly (Hanushek and Woessmann, 2015)—this despite evidence that national labor productivity and productivity increases depend on a great many market, institutional, and organizational factors that are more important than test scores, and that countries should probably devote as much or more energy to those factors as to increasing student achievement on a particular test. As I pointed out earlier, the United States is just one important counterexample of a country with consistently "low" PISA and TIMSS mathematics scores but high and, at least until the early 2000s, relatively rapidly increasing productivity. In addition, over the past thirty years, the United States has had reasonably high economic growth rates—higher than its higher-PISA-scoring European counterparts. Japan is a good example of a country with high mathematics test scores, productivity somewhat lower than that of the US, and low growth rates. Thus, nations would be foolish to believe that simply or primarily increasing student test scores will lead to higher worker productivity and higher economic growth rates.

However, it is worth improving schools and student learning for their own sake and probably for the sake of the conceivable political and social externalities of developing a more learned population, and, indeed, a more learned population can contribute to higher economic growth under the right conditions. If improving learning is modern societies' goal, it is likely that comparative educators will learn more about what improves student learning from following the same students and measuring their achievement as they progress through the grades of national and state education systems in various social contexts rather than from "benchmark" tests such as TIMSS or PISA. Longitudinal surveys and student test scores over time will be especially useful where specific cohorts of students are subject to educational reforms or outside-school activities, and others are not. In the meantime, the hype surrounding education in high-scoring countries on PISA and TIMSS will continue to provide a great excuse for educators, politicians, policy makers, and journalists to travel to those countries and to bring back recommendations that have little or no chance of being implemented in their home educational and political contexts.

International test-score rankings and the research that emanates from the test surveys will also continue to dominate the field of international comparative education, for better or worse. The ability of comparative education researchers to critique the worst practices of international agencies and national and international educational policy makers, journalists, and politicians in "interpreting" and using these results to influence educational policies is crucial for the legitimacy of the field. In the next chapter, I touch on some changes that could take place in the design and use of international tests that could also contribute to a better understanding of educational systems comparatively. In the meantime, academic comparative educators have an important role to play in trying to do causal analysis with the international test data and in keeping everyone honest about what international rankings really can tell us about how good or bad educational systems are.

CHAPTER 12

Where Is Theory Headed in International and Comparative Education?

AFTER FIFTY YEARS of innovations in how we study education comparatively and internationally, what will be the new ideas that shape comparative education for the next generation? I know that some of you may have interpreted the discussions of impact evaluation and international testing in Chapters 10 and 11 as suggesting that functionalism has won out and will dominate well into the future. Yet other interpretations of that discussion might suggest that both impact evaluation and testing could generate interesting new ways to frame comparative education that are not necessarily functionalist. We should also not sell short the possibility of developments in state theory and world society or culture theory that would provide significant new insights into educational systems and educational change. Furthermore, even though the theoretical approaches described as influential in explaining the how and why of educational expansion and organization have emerged over the past five decades primarily from sociology, economics, political science, and political economy, current work in cultural studies and learning theory may in the future increasingly influence international and comparative education.

In this chapter, we speculate about these possible directions for comparative and international education theory. We begin with what may emanate from impact evaluation and international testing. That leads quite naturally into the new directions state theory and world society theory could take as the influence of globalization and information technology on political economy and ideological norms (including individual identity) intensifies. We also make a foray into how other theoretical conceptions of educational issues might have an impact on comparative education over the next generation. An important disclaimer: no matter how prescient our insights in these speculations, it is highly likely that we will largely miss the boat. Today, somewhere, young academics are thinking about comparative and international education in ways that do not fit past thinking. In that case, our futurology could be completely off the mark.

THEORETICAL INNOVATIONS EMERGING FROM IMPACT EVALUATION AND INTERNATIONAL TESTING

To start with, recall Loyalka's comment mentioned in Chapter 10 of this book on the possibilities for impact evaluations to inform comparative education theory:

We can gain insights from these comparative impact studies, so long as they are methodologically valid internally and to some extent externally. The most productive direction of this kind of comparative work, I think, is to evaluate the same intervention in different contexts. Interpreting the results from difference contexts would then require more quantitative and qualitative analyses (how social and educational context affects the outcomes, say, of a teacher training intervention). I think in the end, we need many studies to understand why the same intervention produced different results in different countries. We should also be more thoughtful about how, for example, different theories might explain variation in results across contexts.

Existing theories may not be able to explain these contextual differences, and this could lead to the same kind of questioning that Levin, Samoff, and I went through in applying state theory to US education and education in socialist countries, or that Meyer, Ramirez, and their colleagues undertook in developing world society theory. Internally and even somewhat externally valid impact evaluations in different contexts would provide comparative educators with varying causal effects of the same (or a very similar) intervention in across observably different contexts. As Loyalka observes, in the absence of numerous impact evaluation cases of the same intervention with varying results needed for valid quantitative testing of contextual differences, explaining such differences would involve qualitative analysis. This should not deter comparative education analysts, just as it did not deter Meyer, Ramirez, and colleagues in the 1970s from using a limited number of national cases to "test" their institutional explanation of school expansion in the post–World War II era. Nor has state theory ever relied on empirically valid tests to make the case for certain state theories "explaining" educational change within and across nation-states.

A good example of internally valid impact evaluation results across contexts waiting for a theory to explain them is the difficulty analysts have had to find large positive competitive effects from school choice schemes, whether choice is based on school vouchers or, in the United States, also on access to privately run charter schools. Neoclassical economic theory, a reasonable theoretical framework for explaining many facets of economic behavior, posits that competition among producers extracts greater effort from firm owners and workers. Why, then, are positive effects from competition so small (Carnoy, Adamson, et al., 2007; Muralidharan and Sundararaman, 2015; Epple et al., 2017)? Why don't students in public schools show reasonably large test-score gains when schools and teachers in those schools are threatened by the loss of their students to nearby voucher or charter schools? One reason might be that voucher and charter schools "cream" the best students with the most motivated parents away from public schools, and this dampens any measured gains made by public schools exerting more effort, therefore underestimating competition effects.[1] Yet most studies of competition effects cannot find evidence that creaming the students with the most motivated parents is important enough to offset the overall conclusion that competition effects may be positive but are very small (Belfield and Levin, 2002; Epple et al., 2017). Even most private schools have difficulty doing better than public schools with similar students (CREDO, 2013; Carnoy, 2017). Until now, none of those who uses neoclassical economic arguments—or, for that matter, Weberian bureaucratic theory (Chubb and Moe, 1990)—has come up with a compelling theoretical explanation for why schools do not behave like other economic units, or, alternatively, what it is about even private-run schools, allegedly unencumbered by government regulations and bureaucratic politics, that usually make them different from typical economic production units.

The mass of student test data and student, teacher, and school survey data collected within countries and cross-nationally could also produce new theories for why students in some national or subnational entities are making greater learning gains than in others. Even the observed results we already have from analyzing student performance on international, national, and state tests provide clues to new conceptualizations in comparative education. For example, we mentioned in Chapter 11 that intranational comparisons in countries with federal systems are not only justified in terms of the juridical locus of decision making in federal countries but also that such comparisons are set in a more homogeneous political and cultural context than typically found in comparisons between nation-states. This is an advantage when we want to isolate "administrative-political" factors influencing the effectiveness of the educational system, but it is a disadvantage when we are seeking to test theories of political-educational culture at the level of the nation-state (Khavenson and Carnoy, 2016).

We argued in Chapter 11 that the current analysis of international test data has been cast into a functionalist mold. This mold assumes that formal education policies play a crucial role in how much students learn at the national level, that every nation-state can and wants to implement policies that improve student learning for all students because schools are allegedly functional to improving the social fabric of the nation-state, and that functionalist models using the international test data in their current form can reveal the optimal policies for nation-states to increase their students' test scores.

As we discussed, these assumptions are highly suspect. This is likely an important reason the IEA's and many comparative educators' dream that more data alone would unravel the mysteries of student learning differences (Noah and Eckstein, 1969) never materialized (Medrich and Griffith, 1992). It suggests that the functionalist models behind the original and current international testing enterprise are inadequate to the task. We need other theories to explain why, for example, student performance on the PISA and TIMSS is so much higher in certain Asian countries than in the rest of the world, or why student performance on the PISA has risen in some countries such as Germany, Poland, and, in an earlier period, Finland, and declined significantly in Australia, Finland (since 2009), the Netherlands, Hungary, Slovak Republic, and the Netherlands (Morsy et al., 2017). Coming up with new theories of comparing student learning across nation-states requires looking beyond formal educational systems themselves and traditional measures of socioeconomic background toward expanded conceptualizations of social capital, culture, and where and how children engage (or are engaged) to acquire the knowledge that the international surveys test. One example of such an attempt was a book of mine comparing education in Cuba, Brazil and Chile (Carnoy, Gove, and Marshall, 2007), which used data from the UNESCO Latin American 1997 LLECE test to suggest that much of the difference between Cuban and other Latin American primary school pupils' mathematic performance could be explained by Cuba's state-generated social capital in the form of successfully minimizing school violence, children's work outside the home, and other factors associated with extreme poverty.

NEW DIRECTIONS FOR WORLD SOCIETY AND STATE THEORIES?

In addition to what the most recent trends in international educational research might generate in new ways of deepening our understanding of student learning and the trajectories of educational systems, we cannot underestimate the capacity of established theories such as world society and world culture and theories of the state to reinvent themselves using the new data on education across so many different societies. I asked Patricia Bromley, a former student and now professor in the International Comparative Education program at Stanford, to reflect on where institutional theory in comparative education may be headed. She wrote:

The success of world society theory within comparative education stems from its explanatory power. The perspective afforded greater insight into empirical trends that were only partially accounted for or generally overlooked. Looking to the future, new work in this vein will likely stay true to two core features of the early studies: First, the tradition is characterized by a strong orientation towards explaining trends that emerge from the empirical world and, second, the work draws attention to culturally and socially constructed facets of empirical phenomena. Within the continuity of this general framework, several new directions are emerging.

To begin, there is a growing backlash against the liberal and neoliberal cultural and social ideologies that have dominated the globe since the 1980s; that is, a reaction to the values and institutions that are tied to Western-based world culture. On economic fronts, critiques of free-market, privatization, and de-regulation policies are on the rise, especially since the financial crisis of 2008. Even mainstream economists at the International Monetary Fund now report that the benefits of neoliberalism have been "oversold" and may contribute to increasing inequality. On political fronts, we see a decline in liberal democracy; for instance, Freedom House reports that more countries have experienced losses than gains in freedoms since 2005. Just as there is a groundswell of opposition against dominant global economic and political ideologies, there is rising resistance to the social dimensions of a world culture rooted in Western liberalism. For example, there is a striking increase in legal restrictions on foreign funding to non-governmental organizations, which are adopted in more than 50 countries over the period 1994–2015. International non-governmental organizations are central carriers of world culture, and growing numbers of formal restrictions on this process indicate a dramatic break from prior practice.

A core arena for future research is likely to be related to arenas of contradiction, contestation, resistance and possible decline of the post-WWII cultural framework. At its core, world society theory is premised on the idea that many observable features of countries around the world stem from their linkage to a world culture characterized by liberal and neoliberal beliefs. Thus, as the dominant themes in world culture unravel or change, features of countries and education systems should change as well. Perhaps a new global order will emerge; perhaps polarization will increase with both resistance and expansion continuing; or perhaps we will move towards a less global, more fragmented world order. Regardless, an exciting direction for future research is to consider not only innovations that diffuse similarly around the world, but also to look for areas of dissent, decline, stagnation and fragmentation [e.g., Bromley, 2014; Bromley & Cole, 2017].

An additional promising direction of research is at the intersection of world society theory and the broader tradition of sociological neo-institutionalism in which it is embedded. Neo-institutionalism has long been used by constructivist scholars in international relations to explain global organizations, and especially since the 1990s a global organizational and policy architecture has emerged in education [Bromley, 2010; Mundy et al 2016]. New directions in the sociology of organizations can offer much insight into comparative education trends, particularly for considering why organization expands worldwide both in number and internal complexity, and for explaining the inconsistencies and contradictions that are built into contemporary organizations [Bromley & Powell, 2012; Bromley & Meyer, 2015]. (Personal communication from Patricia Bromley, June 2017)

State theory in comparative education is also likely to respond to massive changes since its last incarnations in the 1980s. It needs to incorporate globalization of the world economy, major changes in the way individuals relate to one another and acquire knowledge, the feminization of world labor markets and its impact on family organization, greatly increased inequality of income and wealth and its implications for national and regional politics, and major changes in education and communications technology (Carnoy, 2000c; Castells, 1996, 2009, 2012). Karen Mundy and I and others (e.g., Dale, 1997) have made modest attempts to do that, but most analysts are stuck on criticizing neoliberalism or relying on 1970s theoretical frameworks. There are great opportunities to move beyond that using everything from good quantitative data to political ethnographies to school observations to case studies (Tarlau, 2017).

OTHER NEW DIRECTIONS IN COMPARATIVE EDUCATION THEORY

Other than world society or world culture theory and the way it considers the changing views toward women's role in society as an important "new" element in conceptions of modernity, we have not discussed the past contributions of feminist theory or cultural theory in more general terms. As Francisco Ramirez noted in Chapter 6, "The gender focus allows us to see how scientific authority and human rights emphases can be aligned. The former is utilized to lament the underutilization of female human capital due to lack of access to scientific and technical education and to barriers to their success therein. The latter is rooted in equity frames and leads to the contention that it is unfair to deprive women of their right to these fields of study, especially since these are gateways to higher paying jobs" (personal communication with Francisco Ramirez, April 2017).

Christine Min Wotipka, an ICE faculty member who writes on gender in the framework of world culture theory (Ramirez and Min Wotipka,

2001), singles out the early contributions of Gail Kelly and Carolyn Elliot, Nelly Stromquist, and Elaine Unterhalter. Kelly and Elliot highlighted the role of education in the growing scholarship on women in the labor force, politics, and economic development (Kelly and Elliot, 1982). Stromquist (1995, 2016)—like Min Wotipka, a SIDEC graduate—and Unterhalter (Unterhalter 2007, 2009, 2014) advanced critical gender perspectives in comparative education.

Min Wotipka argues that these studies and the work of the gender and education committee in the Comparative and International Education Society did much to make gender a more important issue in comparative and international education. She also points out that gender research has evolved far beyond focusing on increasing educational access for girls and the positive effects of girls' education on society:

Gender scholars in comparative education continue to call for the need to look beyond parity and consider issues of quality education (Baily and Holmarsdottir, 2015). This includes considering how educational experiences are gendered, such as through their experiences with sexual violence and harassment (Leach et al., 2014; Parkes, 2015), and how gender and education intersects with poverty, social class, race and other forms of power (Unterhalter, 2012). . . . [Other] areas that can be expected to develop further in gender and education are those related to the education of refugees and migrants (Altinyelken, 2009; Bartlett and Ghaffar-Kucher, 2013) and gender and conflict (Burde and Linden, 2014; Russell, 2016). More research has looked at men and masculinities (Shirazi, 2015) and the role of men and boys in changing gender norms (Baric, 2013; Kato-Wallace, 2014). At the same time, scholars caution against further essentializing the sexes with research that focuses solely or girls and women versus boys and men (Cornwall and Rivas, 2015). Finally, new methods and methodologies in gender research in comparative education encourage researchers to acknowledge the importance of reflexivity and the role of the researcher (Baily et al., 2016). Some examples of research in gender and education that does this has been undertaken through the use of *photovoice*, a photo elicitation methodology (Shah, 2014), as well as analyzing student writings (Khoja-Moolji, 2016) and stories and drawings (DeJaeghere and Lee 2011). (Private communication with Min Wotipka, June 2017)

Feminist theory therefore has the potential to alter many aspects of how we compare education internationally and especially may alter our own assumptions concerning the organization of education, the definition of educational goals, and the evaluation of educational processes. Two fundamental questions are whether the comparisons we choose to make in comparative and international research would change if we internalize a feminist perspective and whether the methods we use to make those comparisons would also change. Thus far, the research that focuses on women and women's issues in comparative education may have shifted the research agenda, but it largely uses the same theory and methodology to study these issues—for example, standard world society theory or standard state theory—to estimate its results and come to its conclusions. Some changes are appearing, but will these innovations continue and where will they take comparative education?

Current learning theory also has enormous potential for changing the way we think about education comparatively. It can do so in several important ways. First, it can completely change the way we use international tests such as the PISA or TIMSS to gauge whether students are "learning more" or whether education is more "effective" in one country than in another. The international tests now measure something about learning—TIMSS, allegedly whether students are learning an internationally agreed upon set of math and science concepts "typically" taught in schools, and PISA, allegedly a set of "problem solving" skills associated with success in the twenty-first-century world of work. However, these may not be the only, or even the most important, aspects of learning that we want to measure comparatively as indicators of national educational systems' goals in advancing individual and social progress. Second, current learning theory may help us find new ways to better understand what education systems actually do in different societies rather than comparing educational systems' "effectiveness" in doing the one or two things we choose to measure about them.

One direction learning theorists are headed is to broaden the notion of learning we measure. Thus, rather than focusing on subject area skills, these broader notions of learning measure a single "underlying" skill such as critical thinking. Tests of critical thinking have been developed and applied to university students in the United States (Arum and Roksa, 2012) and computer science students in the United States, China, and Russia (Loyalka, Liu, et al., 2018). Another example is the OECD's measure of "creative problem solving" skills, derived from analyzing the open-ended 2012 PISA problems (OECD, 2013). As in measures of "creative problem solving skills," critical-thinking skills are highly correlated with student outcomes on today's PISA and TIMSS tests, although there is some differentiation. In Arum and Roksa's (2012) research on university outcomes using a critical-thinking test, for example, business and engineering students had lower learning gains in their college years than did social science students. Was this because they were learning less in their programs or because the skills they were learning were not being measured by the items on the test, which were oriented toward comprehending complex text. Nevertheless, those who support this "broadening" of learning measures argue that they are getting at the kind of knowledge that predicts capacity to learn and, more generally, labor market and social success.

Another group of learning theorists are moving in the opposite direction: they are focusing on being able to break down these more broadly defined skills, on measuring a finer set of learning outcomes that students develop in family, school, and other learning environments, and linking those learning outcomes to a variety of tasks and decisions required for success in work and other aspects of adult life.[2] This goes beyond assessing, say, algebra and geometry in math, or subskills in reading. These new measurements could cover persistence, discipline, willingness to postpone gratification, engagement with tasks, and innovativeness, all possibly good predictors of aspects of learning and possibly better predictors of future life chances. Indeed, an extensive literature has developed on the importance of individual socioemotional skills' relationship to both learning and economic and social outcomes (e.g., Zins et al., 2004; Murnane and Levy, 1996; Duckworth, 2016; Dweck, 2006).[3] One implication for comparative education of breaking down learning skills is that rather than ranking countries on measures of skills in a limited set of subject areas or on a more general ability test (critical thinking), comparisons could vary across different measures much more than they do between, say, math and reading and science. Multiple measures could also raise many more questions about where learning takes place other than family, school, and after school tutoring, and how this varies across societies.

There is yet another important dimension to learning theory that could shape the way we think in the future about education comparatively is the notion that most of our learning, work, and social activities take place in groups, not on our own, as individuals. Some learning theorists, such as James Greeno (1998), argued that individuals may learn and solve problems differently (and more or less effectively) depending on their environment, including the individuals around them, and the interactions between individuals. Currently, we evaluate students as isolated individuals and evaluate the learning effectiveness of different societies on the basis of those individual evaluations. But it is possible that in doing so, we miss how different societies or even different ethnic or social class groups within societies might perform were students tested in teams (Schwartz et al., 2016—see "B for Belonging"). If team work is an important component of work productivity and social progress, then comparing societies by their results on team tests is likely to give us new insights into why some societies with similar individual scores function better than others and may have more effective educational systems.

Many of these new approaches are pushing us ever further as comparativists to examine the context of education, to broaden our notion of education, and to use increasingly sophisticated insights into learning itself to examine what education is in different societies and how the different types of knowledge gained are associated with social and economic well-being. Once we develop these insights, our analyses will still have to account for why certain kinds of teaching and learning are emphasized in societies when they may not be very effective in producing the kinds of knowledge we find to be most valuable in maximizing social outcomes. This is where I think that these new contributions of learning theory and the measurements they produce need to be situated in comparative political economic (state), institutional, or cultural theories to explain why formal education is organized in certain ways, and whether or not those ways are converging.

Notes

CHAPTER I

1. I hope that the reader will also be tolerant of my conflating the term "comparative and international education" with the shorter "comparative education." It is possible to think of comparative education studies that are not international and of many studies of international education that are not comparative. When I use the term "comparative education," it should be taken to mean comparative education studies that are done in the broader international context, outside one's home country—thus, comparative and international education. Then the question is, what do we do about research on "other" countries that is not comparative? Historically, the comparative and international education field, which includes the Comparative and International Education Society (CIES), has been welcoming to such research, and so am I in this book. When researchers use international sites outside their home societies for studies of educational systems or processes, I like to view this as "implicit comparison." For a much more complete discussion of the issue of the "conflation of names," please read the excellent recent article by Erwin Epstein (2016).

2. The term "functionalism" will appear throughout the book. Functionalism is one sociological theory of society originating with Herbert Spencer and Émile Durkheim and, in much later writings, further developed by Talcott Parsons and Robert Merton. Functionalism considers society as a system of interconnected parts working harmoniously to maintain a state of balance and social equilibrium for society as a whole. Thus, according to functionalism, society is composed of institutions, including schools, business organizations, and governmental structures (including legal systems) that function to produce a set of outcomes that are consistent with the reproduction of relations in that society—that are "good" for its functioning in certain ways. There are many versions of functionalism, and there are other theories of society—some based on conflict and others on a strong ideological framework. I discuss these differences when they are relevant to understanding how some of the theories discussed take on functionalism as an underlying framework for understanding the nature of the educational system and of educational change.

3. There is not universal agreement that pre-war comparative education was entirely descriptive. For example, Epstein (2008) argues that as early as the nineteenth century, at least some comparative education studies focused on sociocultural context and the role of "national character" in shaping education and educational systems. According to Epstein, this gave early comparative education much more of an analytical bent than it gets credit for.

4. This recalls Campbell's law: "The more any quantitative social indicator is used for social decision making, the more subjective it will be to corruption pressures, and the more apt it will be to distort and corrupt the social processes it is intended to monitor."

CHAPTER 2

1. Including, unfortunately, being one of the developers of the controversial (and failed) strategic hamlet program in the early days of the Vietnam War.

2. As was Hanna, Staley and Platt were engaged in what they considered "good" international development work, trying to expand economic opportunities through better education. They were simply caught up in a political juncture that made them appear to some people to be furthering a new kind of imperialism. Platt moved to Paris to work for UNESCO, and Staley went to work for the Ford Foundation New Delhi office, where he remained until the mid-1970s. Frank Moore became a consultant, moved to northern Virginia, and spent many years working mainly on Africa development issues. Hanna and his wife, Jean, kept up social relations with all three men and their wives throughout the 1970s. Parkyn, too, continued to work as an education consultant after leaving Stanford.

3. Robert Arnove, a SIDEC graduate, filled in for Weiler for part of 1972–1973, then took a position at Indiana University, where he led the comparative education program for the rest of his career.

4. In 1978, because of shifting interests, Alex Inkeles moved to Stanford's Hoover Institution to engage in full-time research. He did, however, retain his one-third position in the sociology department. SIDEC hired Edmundo Fuenzalida, a Chilean political sociologist who wrote on dependency and development, to replace Inkeles in the sociology billet.

5. IIS is now the Freeman-Spogli Institute.

6. Min Wotipka developed her own line of research, focusing on the increasing attention paid internationally to girls' education and to women's rights. She collaborated in this research with Francisco Ramirez and an increasing number of PhD students interested in gender issues and their expression in comparative and international education.

CHAPTER 3

1. As in neoclassical economics more generally, the notion of human capital rests on a functionalist view of education as an institution. The underlying assumption of the human capital model is that an important function of education is to make students more economically productive, and that this function, in turn, increases society's capacity in increase economic output. The mechanism through which education does this is to increase human capital.

2. Manpower planning, or manpower forecasting, is the estimation of the prospective demand of government and industry for highly qualified manpower: "Once manpower needs have been more or less accurately forecast, there remains the still controversial question of translating these manpower demands into the desired supply of educational output" (Blaug, 1978, p. 194). Many countries still use manpower planning to assess how to expand the educational system, particularly to produce certain kinds of graduates—for example, computer scientists, engineers, teachers, and doctors—even though there is considerable evidence that for many such occupations, the relation between getting a degree in that field and working, say, as a programmer (for computer scientists) or teaching (for an education graduate) depends on many factors related to wages, conditions of work, and so on.

3. Very belatedly (and without reference to my earlier work), Colclough and colleagues (2010) "discovered" the relative rise in the rate of return to higher education. They did not, however, discuss what this new reality implied for the theory of the declining rate of return to capital that had been the bedrock of earlier work by Psacharopoulos (1985) and Psacharopoulos and Patrinos (2004). They also incorrectly continue to view the changing pattern of rates as prescriptive of a change in educational investment policies rather than as a reflection of a politically "usual" pattern of past public-sector educational investments

in response to a politically "usual" pattern of private demand for successively higher levels of schooling.

4. As recently as 2013, in my coauthored book *University Expansion in a Changing Global Economy*, we used estimated rates of return to university and secondary education to situate a broader political economic analysis of university enrollment expansion in BRIC countries. We learned that the rates of return to university completion are surprising resistant to decline despite rapid expansion of enrollment apparently because of downward substitution of university trained labor for secondary educated labor.

CHAPTER 4

1. Inkeles was a key faculty member in SIDEC until 1978, when he moved to two-thirds time into research at Stanford's Hoover Institute, retaining his one-third position in the sociology department. He continued to be a productive scholar at Hoover until his death.

2. The coauthor of *Becoming Modern*, David H. Smith, had a distinguished academic career, writing extensively about volunteer and grassroots organizations. He is emeritus professor of sociology at Boston College.

3. Note that in this section, Smith's narrative is enclosed in quotation marks, and the quotes from the book are shown as indented quotes.

4. More recent versions of modernity center on "developmental idealism," a concept introduced by Arland Thornton (2005): "Among the central values of this cultural model, Thornton posited, was the desirability of a modern society, modern family behavior, and freedom and equality. A central tenet of DI was the belief that modern social structures and modern family behaviors have reciprocal causal influences" (Thornton et al., 2015, p. 277).

CHAPTER 6

1. This neo-institutionalism, as it is called, is a theory that studies the way that institutions interact and are shaped by their institutional environment, defined by rules that function as "myths" that govern interactions in a society. The main goal of institutions in their environment is to establish their legitimacy and their legitimacy rests on bringing their structures into isomorphism with the myths of the environment (see, e.g., Meyer and Rowan, 1977).

2. "That power and knowledge directly imply one another; that there is no power relation without the correlative constitution of the field of knowledge, nor any knowledge that does not presuppose and constitute at the same time power relations" (Foucault, 1977, p. 27).

3. This is part of a broader critique of world society theory by anthropologists who focus on highly localized phenomena, including the varying experiences of children from different social classes and cultures undergoing allegedly similar schooling in different nation-states or even in the same nation-state. For a discussion of this critique and the debate between anthropologists of education and world society theorists, see Anderson-Leavitt (2003).

CHAPTER 7

1. In that sense, they were progressive educators in the Dewey mold, as were many of the postwar social scientists writing on education.

2. [Adapted from original note: A case in point is the use of "symbols" as a means of legitimation, a subject on which Murray Edelman (1964, 1971, 1977) has made a highly significant contribution.]

CHAPTER 8

1. We could not foresee this in the early 1980s, when we were writing the book, but much later, in the years after the economic crisis of 2008–2009, when profits were rising rapidly, about thirty-one states spent less per student in 2015 than before the recession. Even by 2017 with soaring profits, twenty-five states were spending less per pupil on K–12 than they did in 2008. This also occurred in state reductions for public institutions of higher education. In effect, many states were unwilling to raise revenues for education by taxing profits even as those profits were increasing rapidly. This suggests that the fight over resources is increasingly biased in favor of capital. See the website of the Center on Budget and Policy Priorities (https: //www.cbpp.org/research/state-budget-and-tax/a-punishing -decade-for-school-funding) and https: //www.scribd.com/document/357039049/2017 -Center-on-Budget-and-Policy-Priorities-higher-ed-funding-report.

2. For default rates, see the website Inside Higher Ed (https://www.insidehighered .com/news/2015/09/11/study-finds-profit-colleges-drove-spike-student-loan-defaults).

CHAPTER 9

1. As discussed earlier, from the standpoint of universities and schools of education in the United States, the fine points of these differences were not very important. Those who studied education in other countries were considered interested in "international issues," often seen as more closely related to area studies programs than to faculty in schools of education who studied US domestic education issues.

2. Developed countries were also weighted down with aging populations and their associated pension and health-care costs, which had been negotiated in an earlier era of expanding social benefits.

CHAPTER 10

1. Yet even then, certain nutrition supplements may work to raise student achievement in school and others don't. For example, the "one egg per day" policy in China was found not to improve student performance, but multivitamin supplements did.

CHAPTER 11

1. Schmidt and colleagues (2001) did use structural modeling to reduce selection bias in their findings on curriculum. Later studies did even better by exploiting the feature that the same students were tested in two subjects (science and math), and in eighth grade, had different teachers in those subjects. Thus, a student fixed-effects approach could test whether different amounts of coverage of the subject matter by each teacher would have an impact on student performance (Rivkin and Schiman, 2015). But such studies are limited in scope with the PISA data because the information available to compare teaching differences among teachers teaching the same student is itself limited. The possibilities for student fixed effect estimates are greater using TIMSS data.

2. The US study has the advantage of comparing national test results (National Assessment of Education Progress, NAEP) across states, with TIMSS and PISA results in several states. We have also done this elsewhere for Brazil in an unpublished paper, but the state PISA samples in Brazil are less reliable than in the US.

CHAPTER 12

1. Conversely, however, voucher and private schools might attract students making relatively low gains in public schools. This would mean that measured competition effects are overestimated.

2. In turn, it is now possible to amass big micro-level learning data from online courses about how students approach and solve problems, and this could lead to more refined and customized methods of teaching problem solving skills in subjects derived from analyzing the approaches students take to learning.

3. Indirectly, this harkens back to Inkeles and Smith's concept of modernity and the role it plays in individual and societal change.

References

Adams, Don, and Robert M. Bjork. 1969. *Education in Developing Areas.* New York: David McKay.

Almond, Gabriel, and Sidney Verba. 1963. *The Civic Culture.* Princeton, NJ: Princeton University Press.

Altbach, Philip, and Gail P. Kelly. 1986. *New Approaches to Comparative Education.* Chicago: University of Chicago Press.

Althusser, Louis. 1976. *Essays on Ideology.* London: Verso.

Altinyelken, H. K. 2009. "Educational Challenges of Internal Migrant Girls: A Case Study among Primary School Children in Turkey." *Research in Comparative and International Education* 4, no. 2: 211–228.

Amin, Samir. 1957. *Les effets structurels de l'intégration internationale des economies précapitalistes: Une étude théorique du mécanisme qui a engendré les economies dites sous-développées.* Paris: Université de Paris.

Amin, Samir. 1974. "Accumulation and Development: A Theoretical Model." *Review of African Political Economy* 1, no. 1: 9–26.

Anderson, C. Arnold. 1961a. "A Skeptical Note on the Relation of Vertical Mobility to Education." *American Journal of Sociology* 66, no. 6: 560–570.

Anderson, C. Arnold. 1961b. "Methodology of Comparative Education." *International Education Review* 7, no. 1: 1–23.

Anderson, C. Arnold. 1966. "The University of Chicago Program in Comparative Education." *International Review of Education* 12, no. 1: 80–91.

Anderson-Leavitt, Kathryn, ed. 2003. *Local Meanings, Global Schooling.* New York: Palgrave Macmillan.

Anyon, Jean. 1980. "Social Class and the Hidden Curriculum of Work." *Journal of Education* 162: 67–92.

Apple, Michael, ed. 1982. *Cultural and Economic Reproduction in Education: Essays on Class, Ideology and the State.* London: Routledge & Kegan Paul.

Arnove, Robert F., Phillip Altbach, and Gail Kelly, eds. 1992. *Emergent Issues in Education: A Comparative Perspective.* Albany: State University of New York Press.

Arnove, Robert F., Carlos A. Torres, and Stephen Franz, eds. 2013. *Comparative Education: The Dialectic of the Global and the Local.* Lanham, MD: Rowman & Littlefield.

Arum, Richard, and Josipa Roksa. 2011. *Academically Adrift: Limited Learning on College Campuses.* Chicago: University of Chicago Press.

Baily, Supriya, and Halla Holmarsdottir. 2015. "The Quality of Equity? Reframing Gender, Development and Education in the Post-2020 Landscape." *Gender and Education* 27, no. 7: 828–845.

Baily, Supriya, Payal Shah, and Meagan Call-Cummings. 2016. "Reframing the Center: New Directions in Qualitative Methodology in International Comparative Education."

In *Annual Review of Comparative and International Education 2015*, 139–164. Bingley, England: Emerald Group.

Baran, Paul A. 1957. *Political Economy of Growth*. New York: Monthly Review Press.

Baric, Stephanie. 2013. "Where the Boys Are: Engaging Young Adolescent Boys in Support of Girls' Education and Leadership." *Gender & Development* 21, no. 1: 147–160.

Barlevy, Gadi, and Derek Neal. 2012. "Pay for Percentile." *American Economic Review* 102, no. 5: 1805–1831.

Barnet, Richard J. 1968. *Intervention and Revolution*. Cleveland, OH: World Publishing.

Barrera-Osorio, Felipe, and Dhushyanth Raju. 2015. "Teacher Performance Pay: Experimental Evidence from Pakistan." Impact Evaluation Series, Policy Research Working Paper No. 7307, World Bank Group, Washington, DC.

Bartlett, Lesley, and Ameena Ghaffar-Kucher. 2013. *Refugees, Immigrants, and Education in the Global South: Lives in Motion*. London: Routledge.

Baudelot, Christian, and Roget Establet. 1971. *L'école capitaliste en France*. Paris: François Maspero.

Becker, Gary S. 1964. *Human Capital Theory*. New York: Columbia University Press.

Behrman, Jere R., Susan W. Parker, Petra E. Todd, and Kenneth I. Wolpin. 2015. "Aligning Learning Incentives of Students and Teachers: Results from a Social Experiment in Mexican High Schools." *Journal of Political Economy* 123, no. 2: 325–364.

Belfield, Clive, and Henry M. Levin. 2002. *The Effects of Competition on Educational Outcomes: A Review of U.S. Evidence*. New York: Teachers College, Columbia University, National Center for the Study of Privatization in Education.

Bennell, Paul. 1996a. "Rates of Return to Education: Does the Conventional Pattern Prevail in Sub-Saharan Africa?" *World Development* 24, no. 1: 183–199.

Bennell, Paul. 1996b. "Using and Abusing Rates of Return: A Critique of the World Bank's 1995 Education Sector Review." *International Journal of Educational Development* 16, no. 3: 235–248.

Bereday, George Z. F. 1957. "Some Discussion of Methods in Comparative Education." *Comparative Education Review* 1, no. 1: 13–15.

Bereday, George Z. F. 1967. "Reflections on Comparative Methodology in Education, 1964–1966." *Comparative Education* 3, no. 3: 169–187.

Blaug, Mark. 1970. *An Introduction to the Economics of Education*. London: Allen Lane.

Blaug, Mark. 1978. *Economics of Education: A Selected Annotated Bibliography*. 3rd ed. Oxford, UK: Pergamon.

Bloom, Benjamin S., ed. 1956. *Taxonomy of Educational Objectives: The Classification of Educational Goals. Handbook 1: Cognitive Domain*. New York: David McKay.

Boli-Bennett, John, and John W. Meyer. 1978. "The Ideology of Childhood and the State: Rules Distinguishing Children in National Constitutions, 1870–1970." *American Sociological Review*, 43, no. 6: 797–812.

Boli-Bennett, John, Francisco O. Ramirez, and John W. Meyer. 1985. "Explaining the Origins and Expansion of Mass Education." *Comparative Education Review* 29, no. 2: 145–170.

Bowles, Samuel, and Herbert Gintis. 1975. *Schooling in Capitalist America*. New York: Basic Books.

Bowles, Samuel, and Herbert Gintis. 1986. *Democracy and Capitalism*. New York: Basic Books.

Bowles, Samuel, and Henry M. Levin. 1968. "The Determination of Scholastic Achievement: An Appraisal of Some Recent Evidence." *Journal of Human Resources* 3: 3–24.

Bowman, Mary Jean. 1964. "Schultz, Denison, and the Contribution of 'Eds' to National Income Growth." *Journal of Political Economy* 72, no. 5: 450–464.

Bray, Mark. 2006. "Private Supplementary Tutoring: Comparative Perspectives on Patterns and Implications." *Compare* 36, no. 4: 515–530.

Bromley, Patricia. 2010. "The Rationalization of Educational Development: Scientific Activity among International Nongovernmental Organizations." *Comparative Education Review* 54, no. 4: 577–601.

Bromley, Patricia. 2014. "Comparing Minority and Human Rights Discourse in Social Science Textbooks: Cross-National Patterns, 1970–2008." *Canadian Journal of Sociology* 39, no. 1: 1–44.

Bromley, Patricia, and Wade Cole. 2017. "A Tale of Two Worlds: The Interstate System and World Society in Social Science Textbooks, 1950–2011." *Globalisation, Societies and Education* 15, no. 4: 1–23.

Bromley, Patricia, and John W. Meyer. 2015. *Hyper-organization: Global Organizational Expansion*. Oxford: Oxford University Press.

Bromley, Patricia, John W. Meyer, and Francisco O. Ramirez. 2011a. "The Worldwide Spread of Environmental Discourse in Social Studies, History, and Civics Textbooks, 1970–2008." *Comparative Education Review* 55, no. 4: 517–545.

Bromley, Patricia, John W. Meyer, and Francisco O. Ramirez. 2011b. "Student Centeredness in Social Science Text-books, 1970–2010." *Social Forces* 90: 1–24.

Bromley, Patricia, and Walter W. Powell. 2012. "From Smoke and Mirrors to Walking the Talk: Decoupling in the Contemporary World." *Academy of Management Annals* 6, no. 1: 483–530.

Bronner, Ethan. 1997. "End of Chicago's Education School Stirs Debate." *New York Times*, September 17, A27.

Burde, Dana, and Leigh L. Linden. 2013. "Bringing Education to Afghan Girls: A Randomized Controlled Trial of Village-Based Schools." *American Economic Journal: Applied Economics* 5, no. 3: 27–40.

Cardoso, Fernando H., and Enzo Faletto. 1979. *Dependency and Development in Latin América*. First published in Spanish in 1971 as *Dependencia y desarrollo en América latina*. Berkeley: University of California Press.

Carnoy, Martin. 1972a. "The Political Economy of Education." In Thomas LaBelle, ed., *Education and Development in Latin America and the Caribbean*, 177–215. Los Angeles: UCLA Latin American Center.

Carnoy, M., ed. 1972b. *Schooling in a Corporate Society*. New York: David McKay.

Carnoy, Martin. 1972c. "The Rate of Return to Schooling and the Increase in Human Resources in Puerto Rico." *Comparative Education Review* 16, no. 1: 68–86.

Carnoy, Martin 1974. *Education as Cultural Imperialism*. New York: David McKay.

Carnoy, Martin. 1984. *The State and Political Theory*. Princeton, NJ: Princeton University Press.

Carnoy, Martin. 1995a. "Rates of Return in Education." In Martin Carnoy, ed., *International Encyclopedia of Economics of Education*, 2nd ed., 364–369. London: Elsevier Science/Pergamon.

Carnoy, Martin. 1995b. "Political Economy of School Production." In Martin Carnoy, ed., *International Encyclopedia of Economics of Education*, 291–296. Oxford, UK: Elsevier Science.

Carnoy, Martin. 2000a. *Globalization and Educational Reform: What Planners Need to Know*. Paris: International Institute of Educational Planning, UNESCO.

Carnoy, Martin. 2000b. "Globalization and Educational Reform." In Nelly Stromquist and Karen Monkman, eds., *Globalization and Education*, 43-62. Lanham, MD: Rowman and Littlefield.

Carnoy, Martin. 2000c. *Sustaining the New Economy*. Cambridge, MA: Harvard University Press.

Carnoy, Martin. 2006. "Rethinking the Comparative—and the International." *Comparative Education Review* 50, no. 4: 551–570.

Carnoy, Martin. 2015. *International Test Score Comparisons and Educational Policy*. Boulder, CO: National Education Policy Center.

Carnoy, Martin. 2016. "Education Policies in the Face of Globalization: Whither the Nation-State?" In Andy Green and Karen Mundy, eds., *The Handbook of Global Education Policy*, 27–42. London: John Wiley & Sons.

Carnoy, Martin. 2017. *School Vouchers Are Not a Proven Strategy for Improving Student Achievement*. Washington, DC: Economic Policy Institute.

Carnoy, Martin, Frank Adamson, Amita Chudgar, Thomas Luschei, and John Witte. 2007. *Vouchers and Public School Performance: A Case Study of the Milwaukee Parental School Choice Program*. Washington, DC: Economic Policy Institute.

Carnoy, Martin, and Manuel Castells. 2001. "Globalization, the Knowledge Society, and the Network State: Poulantzas at the Millennium." *Global Networks* 1, no. 1: 1–18.

Carnoy, Martin, Manuel Castells, Stephen S. Cohen, and Fernando H. Cardoso. 1993. *The New Global Economy in the Information Age*. College Station, PA: Penn State University Press.

Carnoy, Martin, Linda Chisholm, and Bagele Chilisa. 2013. *The Low Achievement Trap*. Pretoria, South Africa: HSRC Press.

Carnoy, Martin, Emma Garcia, and Tatiana Khavenson. 2015. *Bringing It Back Home*. Washington, DC: Economic Policy Institute.

Carnoy, Martin, Amber Gove, and Jeffrey Marshall. 2007. *Cuba's Academic Advantage*. Stanford, CA: Stanford University Press.

Carnoy, Martin, Tatiana Khavenson, Prashant Loyalka, William Schmidt, and Andrey Zakharov. 2016. "Revisiting the Relationship Between International Assessment Outcomes and Educational Production: Evidence from a Longitudinal PISA-TIMSS Sample." *American Educational Research Journal* 53, no. 4: 1054–1085.

Carnoy, Martin, and Henry M. Levin. 1976. *The Limits of Educational Reform*. New York: Longmans.

Carnoy, Martin, and Henry M. Levin. 1985. *Schooling and Work in the Democratic State*. Stanford, CA: Stanford University Press.

Carnoy, Martin, and Henry M. Levin. 1986. "But Can It Whistle?" *Educational Studies* 73, no. 1: 528–541.

Carnoy, Martin, Prashant Loyalka, Maria Dobryakova, Rafiq Dossani, Isak Froumin, J. Tilak, and Rong Wang. 2013. *University Expansion in a Global Economy: Triumph of the BRICs?* Stanford, CA: Stanford University Press.

Carnoy, Martin, Luana Marotta, Paula Louzano, Tatiana Khavenson, Filipe Recch França de Guimarães, and Fernando Carnauba, F. 2017. "Intra-national Comparative Education: What State Differences in Student Achievement Can Teach Us About Improving Education—The Case of Brazil." *Comparative Education Review* 61, no. 4: 726–759.

Carnoy, Martin, and Richard Rothstein. 2013. *What Do International Tests Really Show About American Student Performance?* Washington, DC: Economic Policy Institute.

Carnoy, Martin, Richard Sack, and Hans H. Thias. 1977. *The Payoff to Better Schooling: A Case Study of Tunisian Schools.* Washington, DC: World Bank.

Carnoy, Martin, and Joel Samoff. 1989. *Education and Social Transformation in the Third World.* Princeton, NJ: Princeton University Press.

Carnoy, Martin, and Derek Shearer. 1980. *Economic Democracy.* Armonk, NY: M. E. Sharpe.

Carnoy, Martin, and Hans H. Thias. 1972. *Cost-Benefit Analysis in Education: A Case Study of Kenya.* Washington, DC: Johns Hopkins University and World Bank.

Castells, Manuel. 1996. *The Rise of the Network Society.* Vol. 1 of *The Information Age: Economy, Society, and Culture.* London: Blackwell.

Castells, Manuel. 2009. *Communication Power.* Oxford: Oxford University Press.

Castells, Manuel. 2012. *Networks of Outrage and Hope.* Cambridge, UK: Polity Press.

Castex, Gonzalo, and Evgenia Kogan Dechter. 2014. "The Changing Roles of Education and Ability in Wage Determination." *Journal of Labor Economics* 32, no. 4: 685–710.

Center for Research on Education Outcomes (CREDO). 2013. *National Charter School Study.* Stanford, CA: CREDO.

Chaudhury, Nazmul, Jeffrey Hammer, Michael Kremer, Karthik Muralidharan, and F. Halsey Rogers. 2006. "Missing in Action: Teacher and Health Worker Absence in Developing Countries." *Journal of Economic Perspectives* 20, no. 1: 91–116.

Chinapah, Vina, Jan-Ingvar Löfstedt, and Hans Weiler. 1989. Integrated Development of Human Resources and Educational Planning. *Prospects* 19, no. 1: 11–32.

Chubb, John E., and Terry Moe. 1990. *Politics, Markets, and America's Schools.* Washington, DC: Brookings Institution Press.

Clignet, Remi P., and Philip Foster. 1964. "French and British Colonial Education in Africa." *Comparative Education Review* 8, no. 2: 191–198.

Colclough, Christopher, Geeta Kingdon, and Harry Patrinos. 2010. "The Changing Pattern of Wage Returns to Education and Its Implications." *Development Policy Review* 28, no. 6: 733–747.

Coleman, James S. 1966. *Equality of Educational Opportunity.* Washington, DC: US Government Printing Office.

Coleman, James S. 1988. "Social Capital in the Creation of Human Capital." *American Journal of Sociology* 94: S95–S120.

Coleman, James S., and Thomas Hoffer. 1987. *Public and Private High Schools.* New York: Basic Books.

Cornwall, Andrea, and Althea-Maria Rivas. 2015. "From 'Gender Equality' and 'Women's Empowerment' to Global Justice: Reclaiming a Transformative Agenda for Gender and Development." *Third World Quarterly* 36, no. 2: 396–415.

Counts, George. 1932. *Dare the School Build a New Social Order?* London: Arcturus Books.

Crossley, Michael, Patricia Broadfoot, and Michele Schweisfurth, eds. 2007. *Changing Educational Contexts, Issues and Identities: 40 Years of Comparative Education.* New York: Routledge.

Cunha, Flavio, and James Heckman. 2008. "Formulating, Identifying and Estimating the Technology of Cognitive and Noncognitive Skill Formation." *Journal of Human Resources* 43, no. 4: 738–782.

Dale, Roger. 1997. "The State and the Governance of Education: An Analysis of the Restructuring of the State-Education Relationship." In Albert Halsey, Hugh Lauder, Phillip Brown, and Amy Stuart Wells, eds., *Education: Culture, Economy and Society*, 273–282. Oxford: Oxford University Press.

Deaton, Angus, and Nancy Cartwright. 2017. "Understanding and Misunderstanding Randomized Control Trials." Working Paper No. 22595. Cambridge, MA: National Bureau of Economic Research.

Dee, Thomas S., and James Wyckoff. 2015. "Incentives, Selection, and Teacher Performance: Evidence from IMPACT." *Journal of Policy Analysis and Management* 34, no. 2: 267–297.

DeJaeghere, Joan, and Soo Kyoung Lee. 2011. "What Matters for Marginalized Girls and Boys in Bangladesh: A Capabilities Approach for Understanding Educational Well-Being and Empowerment." *Research in Comparative and International Education* 6, no. 1: 27–42.

Deming, David, Claudia Goldin, and Lawrence F. Katz. 2012. "The For-Profit Postsecondary School Sector: Nimble Critters or Agile Predators." *Journal of Economic Perspectives* 26, no. 1: 139–164.

Denison, Edward F. 1967. *European Economic Growth and the US Postwar Record: Highlights of Why Growth Rates Differ: Postwar Experience in Nine Western Countries.* Edited by J. P. Poullier. Washington, DC: Brookings Institution.

Dos Santos, Theotonio. 1970. "The Structure of Dependence." *American Economic Review* 60, no. 2: 231–236.

Dreeben, Robert. 1968; *On What Is Learned in School.* Reading, MA: Addison-Wesley.

Drori, Gili, John W. Meyer, Francisco O. Ramirez, and Evan Schofer. 2003. *Science in the Modern World Polity: Institutionalization and Globalization.* Stanford, CA: Stanford University Press.

Duckworth, Angela. 2016. *Grit.* New York: Scribner's.

Dweck, Carol S. 2006. *Mindset: The New Psychology of Success.* New York: Random House.

Edelman, Murray. 1964. *The Symbolic Uses of Politics.* Urbana: University of Illinois Press.

Edelman, Murray. 1971. *Politics as Symbolic Action.* New York: Academic Press.

Edelman, Murray. 1977. *Political Language: Words That Succeed and Policies That Fail.* New York: Academic Press.

Eliason, Leslie C., Ingemar Fagerland, R. Merritt, Hans N. Weiler. 1987. "Education, Social Science, and Public Policy: A Critique of Comparative Research." In Meinhof Dierkes, Hans Weiler, and Ariane Berthoin Antal, eds., *Comparative Policy Research: Learning from Experience*, 244–261. Aldershot, England: Gower.

Epple, Dennis, Richard Romano, and Miguel Urquiola. 2017. "School Vouchers: A Survey of the Economic Literature." *Journal of Economic Literature* 55, no. 2: 441–492.

Epstein, Erwin H. 2008. "Setting the Normative Boundaries: Crucial Epistemological Benchmarks in Comparative Education," *Comparative Education* 44, no. 4: 373–386.

Epstein, Erwin H. 2016. "Why Comparative and International Education? Reflections on the Conflation of Names." In Patricia K. Kubow and A. H. Blosser, eds., *Teaching Comparative Education: Trends and Issues Informing Practice*, 57–73. Oxford, UK: Symposium Books.

Fanon, F. 1963. *The Wretched of the Earth*. New York: Grove Press.

Foster, Phillip J. 1965. "The Vocational School Fallacy in Development Planning." *Education and Economic Development* 7: 19–78.

Foucault, Michel. 1977. *Discipline and Punish*. New York: Pantheon.

Foucault, Michel. 2006. *Psychiatric Power*. New York: Palgrave MacMillan.

Frank, Andre G. 1967. *Capitalism and Underdevelopment in Latin America*. New York: Monthly Review Press.

Fryer, Roland G. 2013. "Teacher Incentives and Student Achievement: Evidence from New York City Public Schools." *Journal of Labor Economics* 31, no. 2: 373–407.

Fryer, Roland G., Jr., Steven D. Levitt, John List, and Sally Sadoff. 2012. "Enhancing the Efficacy of Teacher Incentives Through Loss Aversion: A Field Experiment." Working Paper No. 18237, National Bureau of Economic Research, Cambridge, MA.

Fuchs, Thomas, and Ludgar Woessman. 2004a. "Computers and Student Learning." Working Paper No. 1321, CESifo Group, Munich.

Fuchs, Thomas, and Ludgar Woessmann. 2004b. "What Accounts for International Differences in Student Performance? A Reexamination Using PISA Data." Working Paper No. 1235, CESinfo Group, Munich.

Fukuyama, Francis. 1995. *Trust*. New York: Free Press.

Giddens, Anthony. 1999. *Runaway World*. London: Profile Books.

Giroux, Henry A. 1981. Hegemony, resistance, and the paradox of educational reform. *Interchange* 12, no. 2: 3–26.

Glewwe, Paul, Nauman Ilias, and Michael Kremer. 2010. "Teacher Incentives." *American Economic Journal: Applied Economics* 2, no. 3: 205–227.

Glewwe, Paul, and Karthik Muralidharan. 2015. "Improving School Education Outcomes in Developing Countries: Evidence, Knowledge Gaps, and Policy Implications." In *Handbook of the Economics of Education*, 653–743. Rotterdam: Elsevier.

Gordon, Leah. 2015. *From Power to Prejudice*. Chicago: University of Chicago Press.

Gramsci, Antonio. 1996. *Prison Notebooks*. New York: Columbia University Press.

Greeno, J. G. 1998. "The Situativity of Knowing, Learning, and Research." *American Psychologist* 53, no. 1: 5.

Habermas, Jürgen. 1975. *Legitimation Crisis*. Boston: Beacon.

Hanna, Paul R. 1967. "Research in International Development Education Done at Stanford, 1957–1966." Memo (mimeo). Stanford, CA: Stanford University School of Education.

Hanushek, Eric. 1986. "The Economics of Schooling: Production and Effectiveness in Public Schools." *Journal of Economic Literature* 24: 1141–1171.

Hanushek, Eric. 1995. "Education Production Functions" In Martin Carnoy, ed., *International Encyclopedia of Economics of Education*. Oxford, UK: Elsevier Science.

Hanushek, Eric A., Paul E. Peterson, and Ludgar Woessmann. 2013. *Endangering Prosperity: A Global View of the American School*. Washington, DC: Brookings Institution Press.

Hanushek, Eric, and Ludgar Woessmann. 2015. *The Knowledge Capital of Nations: Education and the Economics of Growth*. Cambridge, MA: CESifo/MIT Press.

Harbison, Ralph, and Eric Hanushek. 1992. *Educational Performance of the Poor: Lessons from Rural Northeast Brazil*. New York: Oxford University Press.

Harvey, James. 2015. "Ten Things You Need to Know About International Assessments." *Washington Post*, February 3. https://www.washingtonpost.com/news/answer-sheet/wp/2015/02/03/ten-things-you-need-to-know-about-international-assessments/?utm_term=.89d3712e78b4.

Heckman, James, Jora Stixrud, and Sergio Urzua. 2006. "The Effects and Cognitive and Noncognitive Abilities and Labor Market Outcomes and Social Behavior." *Journal of Labor Economics* 24, no. 3: 411–482.

Hofstede, Geert, and Robert R. McCrae. 2004. "Personality and Culture Revisited: Linking Traits and Dimensions of Culture." *Cross-Cultural Research* 38, no. 1: 52–88.

Hulbert, A. 2007. "Re-education." *New York Times Magazine*, April 1.

Husén, Torsten, ed. 1967. *International Study of Achievement in Mathematics: A Comparison of Twelve Countries* (Vols. 1–2). Stockholm: Almqvist & Wiksell.

Husén, Torsten. 1968. "Ability, Opportunity, and Career." *Educational Researcher* 10, no. 3: 170–184.

Husén, Torsten. 1983. *An Incurable Academic.* Oxford, UK: Pergamon.

Inkeles, Alex. 1960. "Industrial Man: The Relation of Status to Experience, Perception, and Value." *American Journal of Sociology* 66, no. 1: 1–31.

Inkeles, Alex. 1966. "Social Structure and the Socialization of Competence." *Harvard Educational Review* 36, no. 3: 265–283.

Inkeles, Alex, and Daniel Levinson. 1954. "National Character: The Study of Modal Personality and Sociocultural Systems." *Handbook of Social Psychology* 2: 977–1020.

Inkeles, Alex, and Daniel Levinson. 1969. "National Character: The Study of Modal Personality and Sociocultural Systems." *Handbook of Social Psychology* 4: 418–506.

Inkeles, Alex, and David H. Smith. 1974. *Becoming Modern.* Cambridge, MA: Harvard University Press.

Inkeles, Alex, and Larry Sirowy. 1983. "Convergent and Divergent Trends in National Educational Systems. *Social Forces*, 62, no. 2: 303–333.

Jackall, Robert, and Henry M. Levin, eds. 1984. *Worker Cooperatives in America.* Berkeley: University of California Press.

Jakubowski, Maciej, Harry A. Patrinos, Emilio Ernesto Porta, and Jerzy Wisniewski. 2010. "The Impact of the 1999 Education Reform in Poland." Policy Research Working Paper No. 5263, World Bank, Washington, DC.

Jensen, Robert. 2010. "The (Perceived) Returns to Education and the Demand for Schooling." *Quarterly Journal of Economics* 125, no. 2: 515–548.

Kato-Wallace, Jane, Gary Barker, Marci Eads, and Ruti Levtov. 2014. "Global Pathways to Men's Caregiving: Mixed Methods Findings from the International Men and Gender Equality Survey and the Men Who Care Study." *Global Public Health* 9, no. 6: 706–722.

Kelly, Gail P., and Catherine Elliott. 1982. *Women's Education in the Third World: Comparative Perspectives.* Albany, NY: SUNY Press.

Khavenson, Tatiana, and Martin Carnoy. 2016. "The Unintended and Intended Academic Consequences of Educational Reforms: The Cases of Post-Soviet Estonia, Latvia, and Russia." *Oxford Review of Education* 42, no. 2: 178–199.

Khoja-Moolji, Shenila. 2016. "Doing the 'Work of Hearing': Girls' Voices in Transnational Educational Development Campaigns." *Compare: A Journal of Comparative and International Education* 46, no. 5: 745–763.

Klees, Steven J. 2008. "A Quarter Century of Neoliberal Thinking in Education: Misleading Analyses and Failed Policies." *Globalisation, Societies and Education*, 6, no. 4: 311–348.

Klees, Steven J. 2016. "Human Capital and Rates of Return: Brilliant Ideas or Ideological Dead Ends?" *Comparative Education Review* 60, no. 4: 644–672.

Kubow, Patricia K., and Paul R. Fossum. 2007. *Comparative Education: Exploring Issues in International Context.* Upper Saddle River, NJ: Pearson/Merrill/Prentice Hall.

LaBelle, Thomas, ed. 1972. *Education and Development in Latin America and the Caribbean.* Los Angeles: UCLA Latin American Center.

Lavy, Victor. 2002. "Evaluating the Effect of Teachers' Group Performance Incentives on Pupil Achievement." *Journal of Political Economy* 110, no. 6: 1286–1317.

Lavy, Victor. 2009. "Performance Pay and Teachers' Effort, Productivity, and Grading Ethics." *American Economic Review* 99, no. 5: 1979–2011.

Lavy, Victor. 2015. "Do Differences in Schools' Instruction Time Explain International Achievement Gaps? Evidence from Developed and Developing Countries." *Economic Journal* 125: F397–F424.

Leach, Fiona, Máiréad Dunne, and Francesca Salvi. 2014. "School-Related Gender-Based Violence: A Global Review of Current Issues and Approaches in Policy, Programming and Implementation Responses to School-Related Gender-Based Violence (SRGBV) for the Education Sector." Background research paper prepared for UNESCO, New York. http://www.ungei.org/resources/files/SRGBV_UNESCO_ Global_Review_Jan_2014.pdf.

Levin, Henry M. 1978. "The Dilemma of Secondary Comprehensive School Reforms in Western Europe." *Comparative Education Review* 22, no 3: 434–451.

Levin, Henry M. 1980. "Educational Production Theory and Teacher Inputs." In Charles Bidwell and Douglas Windham, eds., *The Analysis of Educational Productivity: Issues in Macroanalysis* 2. Cambridge, MA: Ballinger.

Levin, Henry M. 1995. "Raising Educational Productivity." In Martin Carnoy, ed., *International Encyclopedia of Economics of Education.* Oxford, UK: Elsevier Science.

Lindzey, Gardner, ed. 1954. *Handbook of Social Psychology.* 2 vols. London: Addison-Wesley/Pearson.

Loveless, Tom. 2013. "PISA's China Problem." Washington, DC: Brookings Institution, Brown Center Chalkboard, October 9. https://www.brookings.edu/research/pisas -china-problem/.

Loyalka, Prashant. Forthcoming. "The Perceived Strengths and Shortcomings of Randomized Experiments: Reflections from REAP's Experiences in China." In R. Goror, S. Sellar, and Gita Steiner-Khamsi, eds., *World Yearbook of Education 2019: Comparative Methodology in an Era of Big Data and Global Networks.* New York: Routledge.

Loyalka, Prashant, Xiaoting Huang, Linxiu Zhang, Jianguo Wei, Hongmei Yi, Yingquan Song, Yaojiang Shi, and James Chu. 2015. "The Impact of Vocational Schooling on Human Capital Development in Developing Countries: Evidence from China." *World Bank Economic Review* 30, no. 1: 143–170.

Loyalka, Prashant, Chengfang Liu, Yingquan Song, Hongmei Yi, Xiaoting Huang, Jianguo Wei, Linxiu Zhang, Yaojiang Shi, James Chu, and Scott Rozelle. 2013. "Can Information and Counseling Help Students from Poor Rural Areas Go To High School? Evidence from China." *Journal of Comparative Economics* 41, no. 4: 1012–1025.

Loyalka, Prashant, Lydia Liu, Guirong Li, Elena Kardanova, Igor Chirikov, Shangfeng Hu, Ningning Yu, Liping Ma, et al. 2018. "Skill Levels and Gains in Undergraduate STEM Programs Across the US, China, India, and Russia." Mimeo. Stanford University.

Loyalka, Prashant, Anna Popova, Guirong Li, and Henry Shi. 2018. "Unpacking Teacher Professional Development." Mimeo. Stanford University.

Loyalka, Prashant, Sean Sylvia, Chenfang Liu, James Chu, and Yaojiang Shi. Forthcoming. "Pay by Design: Teacher Performance Pay Design and the Distribution of Student Achievement." *Journal of Labor Economics.*

Lucas, Samuel R. 2001. "Effectively Maintained Inequality: Education Transitions, Track Mobility, and Social Background Effects." *American Journal of Sociology* 106: 1642–1690.

McEwan, Patrick. 2015. "Improving Learning in Primary Schools of Developing Countries: A Meta-Analysis of Randomized Experiments." *Review of Educational Research* 85, no. 3: 353–394.

McEwan, Patrick, and Martin Carnoy. 2000. "The Effectiveness and Efficiency of Private Schools in Chile's Voucher System." *Educational Evaluation and Policy Analysis* 22, no. 3: 213–239.

McLeod, Jane D., and Kathryn J. Lively. 2006. "Social Structure and Personality." In *Handbook of Social Psychology*, 77–102. New York: Springer.

Medrich, Elliot, and Jeanne Griffith. 1992. *International Mathematics and Science Assessment: What Have We Learned?* Washington, DC: National Center for Educational Statistics, Office of Educational Research and Improvement.

Memmi, Albert. 1965. *The Colonizer and the Colonized*. Boston: Beacon Press.

Meyer, John, John Boli, and George Thomas. 1987. "Ontology and Rationalization in the Western Cultural Account." In George Thomas, John W. Meyer, Francisco O. Ramirez, and John Boli, eds., *Institutional Structure: Constituting State, Society, and the Individual*, 11–38. Newbury Park, CA: Sage Publications.

Meyer, John W., and Michael T. Hannan, eds. 1979. *National Development and the World System*. Chicago: University Chicago Press.

Meyer, John W., Francisco O. Ramirez, Richard Rubinson, and John Boli-Bennett. 1977. "The World Educational Revolution, 1950–1970." *Sociology of Education* 50, no. 4: 242–258.

Meyer, John W., Francisco O. Ramirez, and Yasemin Soysal. 1992. "World Expansion of Mass Education, 1870–1980." *Sociology of Education* 65, no. 2: 128–149.

Meyer, John W., and Brian Rowan. 1977. "Institutionalized Organizations: Formal Structure as Myth and Ceremony." *American Journal of Sociology* 83, no. 2: 340–363.

Miliband, Ralph. 1969. *The State in Capitalist Society*. London: Weidenfeld.

Miliband, Ralph. 1973. "Poulantzas and the Capitalist State." *New Left Review* 82: 83.

Morrow, Robert A., and Carlos A. Torres. 2000. "The State, Globalization, and Educational Policy." In Nicholas C. Burbules and Carlos A. Torres, eds., *Globalization and Education: Critical Perspectives*, 27–56. London: Routledge University Press.

Morsy, Leila, Tatiana Khavenson, and Martin Carnoy. 2017. "How International Tests Fail to Inform Policy: The Unsolved Mystery of Australia's Steady Decline in PISA Scores." *International Journal of Education and Development* 60: 60–79.

Mundy, Karen. 1998. "Educational Multilateralism and World (Dis)order." *Comparative Education Review* 42, no. 4: 448–478.

Mundy, Karen. 2010. "Education for All and the Global Governors." In Deborah D. Avant, Martha Finnemore, and Susan K. Sell, eds., *Who Governs the Globe?* Cambridge: Cambridge University Press.

Mundy, Karen. 2016. "Leaning In" on Education for All: Presidential Address." *Comparative Education Review* 60, no. 1: 1–26.

Mundy, Karen, and Lynn Murphy. 2001. "Transnational Advocacy, Global Civil Society? Emerging Evidence from the Field of Education." *Comparative Education Review* 45, no. 1: 85–126.

Mundy, Karen, and Anthony Verger. 2015. "The World Bank and the Global Governance of Education in a Changing World Order." *International Journal of Educational Development* 40: 9–18.

Muralidharan, Kharthik, and Venkatesh Sundararaman. 2011. "Teacher Performance Pay: Experimental Evidence from India." *Journal of Political Economy* 119, no. 1: 39–77.

Muralidharan, Kharthik, and Venkatesh Sundararaman. 2015. "The Aggregate Effect of School Choice: Evidence from a Two-Stage Experiment in India." *Quarterly Journal of Economics* 130, no. 3: 1011–1066.

Murnane, Richard J., and Frank Levy. 1996. *Teaching the New Basic Skills: Principles for Educating Children to Thrive in a Changing Economy.* New York: Free Press.

Murnane, Richard J., and John B. Willett. 2010. *Methods Matter: Improving Causal Inference in Educational and Social Science Research.* Oxford: Oxford University Press.

Murnane, Richard J., John B. Willett, and Frank Levy. 1995. "The Growing Importance of Cognitive Skills in Wage Determination." *Review of Economics and Statistics* 77, no. 2: 251–266.

National Center for Educational Statistics (NCES). 2013. *The Nation's Report Card: U.S. States in a Global Context: Results from the 2011 NAEP-TIMSS Linking Study.* Washington, DC: NCES.

Neave, Guy, ed. 2006. *Knowledge, Power and Dissent: Critical Perspectives on Higher Education and Research in Knowledge Society.* Paris: UNESCO.

Nguyen, T. 2008. "Information, Role Models and Perceived Returns to Education: Experimental Evidence from Madagascar." Unpublished manuscript.

Noah, Harold. 1973. "Defining Comparative Education: Conceptions." In Reginald Edwards, Brian Holmes, and John H. Van Der Graaff, eds., *Relevant Methods in Comparative Education,* 109–118. *International Studies in Education 33.* Hamburg, Germany: UNESCO Institute of Education.

Noah, Harold, and Max Eckstein. 1969. *Toward a Science of Comparative Education.* New York: Macmillan.

Noonan, R. 1973. "Comparative Education Methodology of the International Association for the Evaluation of Educational Achievement (IEA)." In Reginald Edwards, Brian Holmes, and John H. Van Der Graaff, eds., *Relevant Methods in Comparative Education: A Report of the Meeting of International Experts,* 199–207. *International Studies in Education 33.* Hamburg, Germany: UNESCO Institute of Education.

Offe, Claus. 1972. *Strukturprobleme des kapitalistischen Staates.* Frankfurt: Suhrkamp.

Offe, Claus. 1973. "The Capitalist State and the Problem of Policy Formation." In Leon Lindberg, Robert Alford, Colin Crouch, and Claus Offe, eds., *Stress and Competition in Modern Capitalism.* Lexington, MA: DC Heath.

Oishi, Shigehiro, Selin Kesebir, and Benjamin H. Snyder. 2009. "Sociology: A Lost Connection in Social Psychology." *Personality and Social Psychology Review* 13, no. 4: 334–353.

Organization for Economic Cooperation and Development. 2011. *Lesson from PISA for the United States: Strong Performers and Successful Reformers in Education.* Paris: OECD.

Organization for Economic Cooperation and Development. 2016. *PISA 2015 Results: What Students Know and Can Do: Student Performance in Mathematics, Reading and Science.* Vol. 1. Paris: OECD.

Parkes, J., ed. 2015. *Gender Violence in Poverty Contexts: The Educational Challenge.* London: Routledge.

Parry, Taryn Rounds. 1996. "Will Pursuit of Higher Quality Sacrifice Equal Opportunity in Education? An Analysis of the Education Voucher System in Santiago." *Social Science Quarterly* 77, no. 4: 821–841.

Parsons, Talcott, and Edward Shils. *Toward a General Theory of Action*. Cambridge, MA: Harvard University Press, 1951.

Phillips, David. 2006. "Investigating Policy Attraction in Education. *Oxford Review of Education*, 32, no. 5: 551–559.

Phillips, David, and Kimberly Ochs. 2003. "Processes of Policy Borrowing in Education: Some Explanatory and Analytical Devices." *Comparative Education* 39, no. 4: 451–461.

Phillips, David, and Michele Schweisfurth. 2007. *Comparative and International Education: An Introduction to Theory, Method, and Practice*. London: Bloomsbury Academic.

Postlethwaite, Neville. 1967. *School Organization and Student Achievement: A Study Based on Achievement in Mathematics in Twelve Countries*. Stockholm: Almqvist & Wiksell.

Poulantzas, Nicos. 1976. "The Capitalist State: A Reply to Miliband and Laclau." *New Left Review* 95: 63.

Poulantzas, Nicos. 1978. *State, Power, Socialism*. London: New Left Books.

Psacharopoulos, George. 1973. *Returns to Education*. San Francisco, CA: Jossey Bass.

Psacharopoulos, George. 1981. "Returns to Education: An Updated International Comparison." *Comparative Education Review* 17, no. 3: 321–341.

Psacharopoulos, George. 1985. "Returns to Education: A Further International Update and Implication." *Journal of Human Resources* 20, no. 4: 583–604.

Psacharopoulos, George, and Keith Hinchliffe. 1970. "Rates of Return to Investment in Education and the Impact on Growth and Development: An International Comparison." Mimeo. London School of Economics, Higher Education Research Unit.

Psacharopoulos, George, and Harry Patrinos. 2004. "Returns to Investment in Education: A Further Update." *Education Economics* 12, no. 2: 111–134.

Raftery, Adrian E., and Michael Hout. 1993. "Maximally Maintained Inequality: Expansion, Reform, and Opportunity in Irish Education." *Sociology of Education* 66, no. 1: 41–62.

Ramirez, Francisco O. 2012. "The World Society Perspective: Concepts, Assumptions, and Strategies." *Comparative Education* 48, no. 4: 423–439.

Ramirez, Francisco O. 2016. "Education, Gender, and Development." In Alan Sadovnik and Ryan Coughlan, eds., *Leaders in the Sociology of Education: Intellectual Self-Portraits*, 171–184. Rotterdam, The Netherlands: Sense Publishers.

Ramirez, Francisco O., and John Boli-Bennett. 1987. "The Political Construction of Mass Schooling: European Origins and Worldwide Institutionalization." *Sociology of Education* 60: 2–17.

Ramirez, Francisco O., and Christine Min Wotipka. 2001. "Slowly but Surely? The Global Expansion of Women's Participation in Science and Engineering Fields of Study, 1972–92." *Sociology of Education* 74, no. 3: 231–251.

Ramirez, Francisco O., Yasemine Soysal, and Susan Shanahan. 1997. "The Changing Logic of Political Citizenship: Cross-National Acquisition of Women's Suffrage Rights, 1890 to 1990." *American Sociological Review* 62: 735–745.

Raskin, Marcus. 1971. *Being and Doing*. New York: Random House.

Ravitch, Diane. 2013. *Reign of Error: The Hoax of the Privatization Movement and the Danger to America's Public Schools*. New York: Vintage.

Ripley, Amanda. 2013. *The Smartest Kids in the World*. New York: Simon and Shuster.

Rivkin, Steven G., and Jeffrey C. Schiman. 2015. "Instruction Time, Classroom Quality, and Academic Achievement." *Economic Journal* 125: F425–F448.

Rosa, Leonardo, Eric Bettinger, Martin Carnoy, and Pedro Dantas. 2018. "Time to Teach? The Impact of Increased Instructional Time on Student Outcomes: Evidence from Brazil." Mimeo. Graduate School of Education, Stanford University.

Rose, Pauline, Liesbet Steer, Katie Smith, and Asma Zubairi. 2013. *Financing for Global Education: Opportunities for Multilateral Action*. Washington, DC: Center for Universal Education at Brookings.

Rosenbaum, Paul R., and Donald B. Rubin. 1983. "The Central Role of the Propensity Score in Observational Studies for Causal Effects." *Biometrika* 70, no. 1: 41–55.

Rubin, Donald B. 1974. "Estimating Causal Effects of Treatments in Randomized and Nonrandomized Studies." *Journal of Educational Psychology* 66, no. 5: 688–701.

Rumberger, Russell W., and Martin Carnoy. 1980. "Segmentation in the U.S. Labour Market: Its Effects on the Mobility and Earnings of Whites and Blacks." *Cambridge Journal of Economics* 4, no. 2: 117–132.

Russell, S. Garnett. 2016. "Global Gender Discourses in Education: Evidence from Post-Genocide Rwanda." *Comparative Education* 52, no. 4: 492–515.

Sawyer, S. W. 2015. "Foucault and the State." *Tocqueville Review* 36, no. 1: 134–164.

Schmidt, William H., Curtis C. McKnight, Richard Houang, HsingChi Wang, David Wiley, Leland S. Cogan, and Richard G. Wolfe. 2001. *Why Schools Matter: A Cross-National Comparison of Curriculum and Learning*. San Francisco, CA: Jossey-Bass.

Schmidt, William H., Curtis C. McKnight, and Senta A. Raizen. 1997. *A Splintered Vision: An Investigation of U.S. Science and Mathematics Education*. Dordrecht, The Netherlands: Kluwer.

Schneider, Barbara, Martin Carnoy, Jeremy Kilpatrick, William Schmidt, and Richard Shavelson. 2007. *Estimating Causal Effects Using Experimental and Observational Designs: A Think Tank White Paper*. Washington, DC: American Educational Research Association.

Schnittker, Jason. 2013. "Social Structure and Personality." In *Handbook of Social Psychology*, 89–115. Amsterdam: Springer.

Schoenfeld, Alan H. 2006. "What Doesn't Work: The Challenge and Failure of the What Works Clearinghouse to Conduct Meaningful Reviews of Studies of Mathematics Curricula." *Educational Researcher* 35, no. 2: 13–21.

Schultz, Theodore W. 1961. "Investment in Man." *American Economic Review* 51, no. 1: 1–17.

Schultz, Theodore W. 1963. *The Economic Value of Education*. New York: Columbia University Press.

Schwartz, Daniel L., Jessica M. Tsang, and Kristen P. Blair, K. 2016. *The ABCs of How We Learn*. New York: Norton.

Schwille, John. 2017. *Internationalizing a School of Education: Integration and Infusion in Practice*. East Lansing: Michigan State University Press.

Sennett, Richard, and Jonathan Cobb. 1972. *The Hidden Injuries of Class*. New York: Cambridge University Press.

Shah, Payal. 2014. "Spaces to Speak: Photovoice and the Reimagination of Girls' Education in India." *Comparative Education Review* 59, no. 1: 50–74.

Shirazi, Roozbeh. 2015. "'These Boys are Wild': Constructions and Contests of Masculinities at Two Jordanian High Schools." *Gender and Education* 28, no. 1: 89–107.

Silova, Iveta. 2004. "Adopting the Language of the New Allies." In Gita Steiner-Khamsi, ed., *The Global Politics of Educational Borrowing*, 75–87. New York: Teachers College Press.

Skocpol, Theda. 1982. "Bringing the State Back In." *Items* 36, nos. 1–2: 1–8.

Smith, David H. 1994. "Determinants of Voluntary Association Participation and Volunteering: A Literature Review." *Nonprofit and Voluntary Sector Quarterly* 23, no. 3: 243–264.

Smith, David H. 2012. "Alex Inkeles: Biographical Memoir." *Proceedings of the American Philosophical Society* 156: 238–244.

Smith, David H., and Alex Inkeles. 1966. "The OM Scale: A Comparative Socio-Psychological Measure of Individual Modernity." *Social Psychology Quarterly* 29, no. 4: 353–377.

Smith, David H., and Alex Inkeles. 1975. "Individual Modernizing Experiences and Psycho-Social Modernity Scores: Validation of the OM Scales in Six Developing Countries." *International Journal of Comparative Sociology* 16, nos. 3–4: 155–173.

Smith, David H., Robert A. Stebbins, and Jurgen Grotz, eds. 2016. *Palgrave Handbook of Volunteering, Civic Participation, and Nonprofit Associations*. 2 vols. Basingstoke, UK: Palgrave Macmillan.

Springer, Matthew G., Dale Ballou, Laura Hamilton, Vi-Nhuan Le, J. R. Lockwood, Daniel F. McCaffrey, Matthew Pepper, and Brian M. Stecher. 2011. "Teacher Pay for Performance: Experimental Evidence from the Project on Incentives in Teaching (POINT)." *Society for Research on Educational Effectiveness*.

Stallones, Jared. 2002. *Paul Robert Hanna: A Life of Expanding Communities*. Stanford, CA: Hoover Institution Press.

Stanat, Petra, Dominique Rauch, and Michael Segeritz. 2010. "Schülerinnen und Schüler mit Migrationshintergrund." In Eckhard Klieme, Cordula Artelt, Johannes Hartig, Nina Jude, Olaf Köller, Manfred Prenzel, Wolfgang Schneider und Petra Stanat, eds., *PISA 2009. Bilanz nach einem Jahrzehnt*, 200–230. Münster, Germany: Waxmann.

Steiner-Khamsi, Gita. 2006. "The Economics of Policy Borrowing and Lending: A Study of Late Adopters." *Oxford Review of Education* 32, no. 5: 665–678.

Stromquist, Nelly P. 1995. "Romancing the State: Gender and Power in Education." *Comparative Education Review* 39, no. 4: 423–454.

Stromquist, Nelly P. 2016. *Feminist Organizations and Social Transformation in Latin America*. London: Routledge.

Stromquist Nelly, and Karen Monkman, eds. 2000. *Globalization and Education*. Lanham, MD: Rowman and Littlefield.

Suárez, David. 2007. "Education Professionals and the Construction of Human Rights Education. *Comparative Education Review* 51, no. 1: 48–70.

Tarlau, Rebecca. 2017. "State Theory, Grassroots Agency, and Global Policy Transfer: The Life and Death of Colombia's *Escuela Nueva* in Brazil (1997–2012)." *Comparative Education Review* 61, no. 4: 675–700.

Tarlau, Rebecca. 2018. *Occupying Schools, Occupying Land: How the Landless Workers Movement Transformed Brazilian Education*. Oxford: Oxford University Press.

Tax, Sol. 1953. *Penny Capitalism: A Guatemalan Indian Economy*. Washington, DC: Smithsonian Institution, Institute of Social Anthropology.

Teachers College, Columbia University. N.d. http://www.tc.columbia.edu/international-and -transcultural-studies/international-and-comparative-education/people/emeritus-faculty/.

Thornton, Arland. 2005. *Reading History Sideways: The Fallacy and Enduring Impact of the Developmental Paradigm on Family Life*. Chicago: University of Chicago Press.

Thornton, Arland, Shawn F. Dorius, and Jeffrey Swindle. 2015. "Developmental Idealism." *Sociology of Development* 1, no. 2: 69–112.

Unterhalter, Elaine. 2007. *Gender, Schooling and Global Social Justice*. London: Routledge.

Unterhalter, Elaine. 2009. "What Is Equity in Education? Reflections from the Capability Approach." *Studies in Philosophy & Education* 28, no. 5: 415–424.

Unterhalter, Elaine. 2012. "Poverty, Education Gender and Millennium Development Goals: Reflections on Boundaries and Intersectionalities." *Theory and Research in Education* 10, no. 3: 253–274.

Unterhalter, Elaine. 2014. "Thinking About Gender in Comparative Education." *Comparative Education* 50, no. 1: 112–126.

US Congress. 2002. Education Sciences Reform Act of 2002. H.R. 3801. https://www2.ed.gov/policy/rschstat/leg/PL107-279.pdf.

Wallerstein, Immanuel M. 1973. "The Rise and Future Demise of the World Capitalist System: Concepts for Comparative Analysis." *Comparative Studies in Society and History* 16: 387–415.

Wallerstein, Immanuel M. 1974. *The Modern World-System: Capitalist Agriculture and the Origins of the European World-Economy in The Sixteen Century*. New York: Academic Press.

Watts, Ronald. 1992. "The Federal Context for Higher Education." In Douglas Brown, Pierre Cazalis, and Gilles Jasmin, eds., *Higher Education in Federal Systems: Proceedings of an International Colloquium Held at Queen's University, May 1991*, 3–26. Ottawa: Renouf Publishing.

Weiler, Hans N. 1966. "Koloniale Erziehung und afrikanische Umwelt; zur erziehungspolitischen Diskussion in der britischen Kolonialverwaltung seit 1920." Inaugural PhD diss., Universität Freiburg.

Weiler, Hans N. 1972. "Political Socialization and the Political System: Consensual and Conflictual Linkage Concepts." In Michael W. Kirst, ed., *State, School, and Politics*. Lexington, MA: Heath.

Weiler, Hans N. 1973. "Memo." Mimeo. School of Education, Stanford University.

Weiler, Hans N. 1983. "Legalization, Expertise, and Participation: Strategies of Compensatory Legitimation in Educational Policy." *Comparative Education Review* 27, no. 2: 259–277.

Weiler, Hans N. 1984. "The Political Dilemmas of Foreign Study." *Comparative Education Review* 28, no. 2: 168–179.

Weiler, Hans N. 1985. "Politics of Educational Reform." In Richard L. Merritt and Anna J. Merritt, eds., *Innovation in the Public Sector*, 167–212. Beverly Hills, CA: Sage.

Weiler, Hans N. 1989. "Education and Power: The Politics of Educational Decentralization in Comparative Perspective." *Educational Policy* 3, no. 1: 31–43.

Weiler, Hans N. 1991. "Some Notes on a New World Bank Initiative to Build Educational Research Capacity in Developing Countries." *NORRAG News* 10: 19–23.

Weiler, Hans N. 1993. "Control Versus Legitimation: The Politics of Ambivalence." In Jane Hannaway and Martin Carnoy, eds., *Decentralization and School Improvement*, 55–83. San Francisco: Jossey-Bass.

Weiler, Hans N. 1994. "The Failure of Reform and the Macro-Politics of Education: Notes on a Theoretical Challenge." In Val Rust, ed., *Educational Reform in International Perspective*, 43–54. Greenwich, CT: JAI Press.

Weiler, Hans N. 2005. "Ambivalence and the Politics of Knowledge: The Struggle for Change in German Higher Education." *Higher Education* 49, nos. 1–2: 177–195.

Weiler, Hans N. 2006. "Challenging the Orthodoxies of Knowledge: Epistemological, Structural and Political Implications for Higher Education." In Guy Neave, ed., *Knowledge, Power and Dissent: Critical Perspectives on Higher Education and Research in Knowledge Society,* 61–87. Paris: UNESCO Publishing.

Weiler, Hans N. 2011. "Knowledge and Power: The New Politics of Higher Education." *Journal of Educational Planning and Administration* 25, no 3: 205–221.

Willis, Paul. 1977. *Learning to Labor.* New York: Columbia University Press.

Wolfe, Alan. 1977. *The Limits of Legitimacy: Political Contradictions of Contemporary Capitalism.* New York: Free Press.

Wotipka, Christine Min, and Francisco O. Ramirez. 2008. "World Society and Human Rights: An Event History Analysis of the Ratification of the Convention on the Elimination of All Forms of Discrimination Against Women." In Beth A. Simmons, Frank Dobbin, and Geoffrey Garrett, eds., *The Global Diffusion of Markets and Democracy,* 303–343. New York: Cambridge University Press.

World Bank. 1997. *World Development Report: The State in a Changing World.* New York: Oxford University Press.

Zakharov, Andrey, Gaelebale Tsheko, and Martin Carnoy. 2016. "Do 'Better' Teachers and Classroom Resources Improve Student Achievement? A Causal Comparative Approach in Kenya, South Africa, and Swaziland." *International Journal of Education and Development* 50: 108–124.

Zins, Joseph E., Roger Weissberg, Margaret Wang, and Herbert Walberg, eds. 2004. *Building Academic Success on Social and Emotional Learning: What Does the Research Say?* New York: Teachers College Press.

Index

World Bank, 40–42, 51, 56, 68, 132;
international education, 161, 168,
174–75; nation-state and, 165; as
producer of research, 16, 182; reciprocal legitimation and, 135–36
world culture theory, 24, 176–77. *See
also* world society theory
world economy, 25, 41, 101, 105, 162–64,
223; expansion of, 171–73. *See also*
globalization
world educational revolution, 109–10
"World Education Revolution,
1950–1970" (Meyer and Ramirez), 111,
122
world environment, 107–8

world society theory, 24, 40, 74, 95,
107–22, 218; convergence impact,
117–18; expansion of education and,
109–15; global ideology, 107–8, 111;
loose coupling, 120; modernity studies
and, 86; nation-state, 108–13; new
directions, 221–23; other ideological
phenomena and, 115–18; reflecting on,
118–21; stratification system, 110–11;
women's rights/gender issues, 116–19
world systems theory, 95, 107, 110, 177
World War II, 12, 91

Yale University, 43
Young Lives project, 195